"The stories of everyday people changing the nation through service come to life in this book. Shirley Sagawa has been at the center of service policy for two decades, and if we follow the blueprint she offers, together we can solve the pressing problems of our day."

—*Alan Khazei, founder, Be the Change, Inc.,*
and co-founder, City Year

"Leaders agree: with the many challenges facing America, we are at a critical moment when real change is needed. Service can play a central role in that transformation, and this book spells out how everyone can participate."

—*Lisa Paulsen, president and chief executive officer,*
Entertainment Industry Foundation

"Shirley Sagawa has written an invaluable how-to book for accomplishing nothing less than the transformation of our nation. Shirley was present at the creation of the America's Promise Alliance in 1997 and, more significantly, guided its recent 're-invention.' If we are effective today, it is because we benefited from the lessons she brings to life in this book."

—*Marguerite Kondracke, president and CEO,*
America's Promise Alliance

"Through this important book, Sagawa offers a compelling case for the idea that citizen service is a critical strategy for solving the pressing problems of our time."

—*AnnMaura Connolly, steering committee member,*
Voices for National Service

"This book, written by one of the country's most influential advocates for service, shows how we can improve the quality of life in America's communities through policies that encourage a lifetime of service."

—*Stephen Goldsmith, chairman, Corporation for National*
and Community Service, and author of
The Power of Social Innovation

"Shirley Sagawa is the godmother of national service and volunteerism. In this book, she takes her ideas to the next level and outlines a new approach to national problem solving—one that asks each of us to help reshape America."

—*Jeanne Shaheen, U.S. Senator from New Hampshire*

"No one has a better sweep of the ways and means Americans can use their power to change the world than Shirley Sagawa. This book highlights some of the most innovative and successful programs of our time and should be read by any policymaker or active citizen who is looking for effective strategies to solve our most critical social problems."

—*Harris Wofford, former U.S. Senator from Pennsylvania, author of* Of Kennedys and Kings, *and former CEO of the Corporation for National and Community Service*

"Gone are the days of volunteers just stuffing fundraising envelopes. Sagawa vibrantly showcases our new opportunity to leverage civic energy to make a lasting impact. Policy makers, community leaders, and volunteers: this is your road map."

—*Karen Baker, Secretary of Service and Volunteering for the State of California*

SHIRLEY SAGAWA

The

AMERICAN WAY

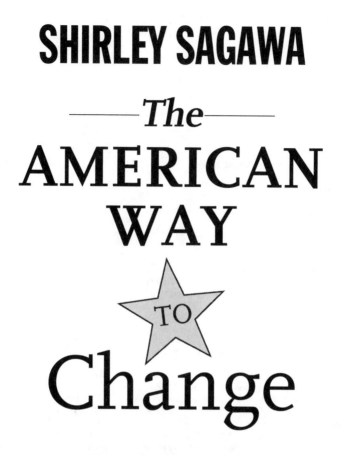

TO

Change

HOW NATIONAL SERVICE & VOLUNTEERS ARE TRANSFORMING AMERICA

Foreword by Michelle Nunn

Prologue by John Podesta

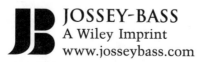

JOSSEY-BASS
A Wiley Imprint
www.josseybass.com

Published by Jossey-Bass
A Wiley Imprint
989 Market Street, San Francisco, CA 94103-1741—www.josseybass.com

Jossey-Bass books and products are available through most bookstores. To contact Jossey-Bass directly call our Customer Care Department within the U.S. at 800-956-7739, outside the U.S. at 317-572-3986, or fax 317-572-4002.

Jossey-Bass also publishes its books in a variety of electronic formats. Some content that appears in print may not be available in electronic books.

Library of Congress Cataloging-in-Publication Data
Sagawa, Shirley.
   The American way to change: how national service and volunteers are transforming America / Shirley Sagawa.
     p. cm.
  Includes bibliographical references and index.
  ISBN 978-0-470-56557-5 (hardback)
  1. Voluntarism-United States. 2. Volunteers-United States. I. Title.
  HN90.V64S24 2010
  361.3'70973-dc22
                2010003891
Printed in the United States of America
FIRST EDITION
HB Printing 10 9 8 7 6 5 4 3 2 1

Contents

This book is dedicated to the memory of Senator Edward M. Kennedy and Eli J. Segal, who shaped our future through their service.

Foreword

America's vitality is rooted in the volunteer spirit. From the country's founding through every significant chapter of its history, the imagination and energy of our citizens have written our narrative of change. From Ben Franklin to Martin Luther King Jr., volunteer leaders have shaped our nation. Volunteers built institutions such as the Sierra Club, United Way, Red Cross, and the Salvation Army and shifted the nation's moral compass through the civil rights movement, the women's movement, the environmental movement, and every campaign for change that has transformed our nation and often the world.

Today we need this spirit more than ever. At this time of possibility and peril we must awaken the true power, potential, and will of the American people to imagine and then forge the change we need. This book, *The American Way to Change*, is a roadmap to guide policymakers and citizens on how to seize this moment.

Shirley Sagawa is singularly equipped to show us how to rebuild the nation through service. Shirley stands as the most thoughtful, well-versed student of the policy and legislative history of our national service agenda. As the author of the original national service legislation and a policy adviser to every administration over the past twenty years, she uniquely is both author and actor on the public stage. Most important, Shirley is an intellectual and a passionate change agent—combining research, data, storytelling, and analytical insight with a passion to equip our nation to solve its greatest problems.

While volunteering may be seen as something nice to do, it is not always understood as central to our history and our future. And yet, the enduring words of our nation's greatest leaders were often centered on a call to what is best in all of us—from Lincoln's invocation of the "better angels of our nature" to Roosevelt's declaration that "this generation of Americans has a rendezvous with destiny" to President Kennedy's mandate to "ask not what your country can do for you, but what you can do for your country." Indeed, the activation of our volunteers and citizen leaders is truly at the core of our nation's story and a defining hallmark of presidential leadership.

In 1989, President George H. W. Bush invoked a Thousand Points of Light, which became not only a lasting metaphor in the public's mind but a touchstone for a presidential commitment to lift up volunteer service. With the passage of the National and Community Service Act of 1990, the president and Congress created a platform to power the "twin engines" of national service and community volunteerism. Over the next twenty years, each president extended this legacy of service. President Clinton gave life to the long-held dream of a national service program that would bring together young people across differences of race and socioeconomics to tackle the toughest problems in our communities and, in the process, to transform themselves. President George W. Bush embraced the call to service and extended both AmeriCorps and a broad mantle of service that included Citizens Corps and Volunteers for Prosperity to engage our nation's human capital in the wake of 9/11, natural disasters, and the needs of the developing world.

It is notable that in two decades characterized by polarization and political defamation, the call to service has been a unifying rallying cry. U.S. presidents have joined together over the importance of citizen action—from the 1997 America's Promise Summit to the pairing of former Presidents George H. W. Bush and Bill Clinton in the wakes of Hurricane Katrina and the tsunami in Indonesia. Over this time, we have seen remarkable progress. We have twenty-three million more volunteers serving annually today than we did when President Bush called for us to turn to the only resource "that always grows in times of need—the goodness and the courage of the American people." We have gone from an idea about the power of young people joining hands to solve our nation's problems to a corps of more than a half million, who have worked in thousands of programs across the country with measurable impact in lifting up test scores and graduation rates, conserving our resources, and restoring economic stability to families. Through this service, we are creating life-long habits of engagement, exposing a new generation of citizen leaders to the serious challenges of their day, and imbuing a sense of the patriotism that draws individuals into something larger than self.

We now stand at a pivotal moment. We have, in President and Mrs. Obama, leaders who are rooted deeply in service through their values and careers. Mrs. Obama ran an AmeriCorps program, Public

Allies (one of the pilot initiatives that President Bush's legislation supported). President Obama, a community organizer, has a profound understanding of the import of activism to create change. In the first hundred days of his administration, with long-time service champions Senators Kennedy and Hatch, the landmark Edward M. Kennedy Serve America Act was passed to grow national service exponentially, spark social innovation, and greatly expand volunteer engagement. While President George H. W. Bush helped create a culture of service in which "definition of a successful life must include service," President and Mrs. Obama are embracing a vision of service as "central to our national priorities."

In the words of President Obama, our history is the "story of patriots who set forth the ideals that animate our democracy, and all those who fought and died for those ideals. It's the story of women who reached for the ballot, and people who stood up, and sat in, and marched for justice. It's the story of firefighters and police officers who rushed to those burning towers, and ordinary people who rushed to the aid of a flooded American city. That's always been the story of this nation—the story of those who stepped forward in our darkest hours to serve it."

Those who rose to answer the defining questions of their time—colony or country? free or half free? separate but equal or truly equal?—weren't in it for the money. They were volunteers. Their service wasn't "extra." It was the work that changed this country. The courage, the patriotism, and the compassion that drove them to act are the same qualities we need today as we seek to answer the questions of our own time. Will this continue to be a land of opportunity where all things are still possible for all people? Or will it be a place where those born without advantages of wealth, health, and good luck have the deck stacked against them? Will we engage with the world to confront our shared threats? Or will we hope against hope to defer them to the next administration, the next generation?

In *The American Way to Change*, Shirley Sagawa outlines a plan to engage our citizens in answering the call to continue to remake our nation and our world.

MICHELLE NUNN
CEO, Points of Light Institute
Co-founder, HandsOn Network

Prologue

The Center for American Progress (CAP) is in the business of generating and lifting up solutions to America's biggest challenges. We like to think of CAP as idealistic enough to believe change is possible and practical enough to make it happen.

Service fits squarely into that vision. In this spirit, in 2007 we decided to add national service as a focus area for CAP and turned to Shirley Sagawa to join CAP as a fellow. As a legislative aide for Senator Edward Kennedy, Shirley negotiated landmark legislation—signed by President George H. W. Bush—to create the Commission on National and Community Service. She helped to draft the legislation that created the Corporation for National and Community Service during the Clinton administration and then went on to help lead the startup of AmeriCorps. She joined our team to develop a new agenda for the next stage of federal policy for national service.

I knew from experience early in my career at the ACTION agency that volunteers can play a crucial role in helping low-income people find ways out of poverty. Today a rich array of effective service programs are proving that volunteers, AmeriCorps members, and VISTA members should be part of comprehensive strategies to improve health, education, and the environment, as well as economic opportunity.

The National Service agenda that Shirley wrote for CAP had a significant influence on the Edward M. Kennedy Serve America Act, one of the first pieces of legislation signed by President Barack Obama after his election. That legislation has the potential to inspire a new era of service in America. This book takes the next step by spelling out how.

It could not come at a more critical time, as America struggles to emerge from the Great Recession stronger than ever, with Americans who are healthier, better educated, and well-prepared for the jobs of the future. It's important to remember that during the Great

Depression, President Franklin D. Roosevelt created the Civilian Conservation Corps to direct the efforts of destitute young men toward building the great national parks and conserving our natural resources. And that during the Cold War, President John F. Kennedy created the Peace Corps to build goodwill with emerging nations, countering the image of the "Ugly American." President Lyndon Johnson followed through on President Kennedy's desire to create a domestic Peace Corps, launching VISTA as part of the War on Poverty, and President George W. Bush created the Freedom Corps to mobilize Americans in the wake of the 9/11 tragedy.

So when Bill Clinton called AmeriCorps "the American way to change America," he was right. He proposed the AmeriCorps program and took it from a pledge in a campaign speech to a national program with 60,000 members. President Obama followed that tradition, signing the Serve America Act, the first step toward making good on his pledge to expand AmeriCorps to 250,000 members.

This book makes the case that we should not pursue that expansion for its own sake but rather as an effective strategy to solve the problems that plague our nation. Volunteering and national service should be part of any plan to make America a land of boundless opportunity where people can better themselves, their children, their families, and their communities through education, hard work, and the freedom to climb the ladder of economic mobility. This book deserves consideration from every policymaker looking for new solutions—and every American who wants to be a part of the answer.

JOHN PODESTA
CEO, Center for American Progress

Preface

The last time I spoke to Ted Kennedy, he was grinning ear-to-ear in the ornate Senate lobby after the passage of the Serve America Act on March 27, 2009. Senator Orrin Hatch, a conservative senator from Utah, had graciously asked the Senate to name the legislation for its lead sponsor, the senior senator from Massachusetts. Despite his amazing forty-six-year legislative record, few programs had been named for Senator Kennedy, and it seemed he could not stop smiling. Leaning on a cane and with his wife Vicky by his side, he thanked a small group of us who had worked on the bill, then posed for photo after photo. It was a joyful moment that I will always treasure. He died just a few months later.

I was interning for Senator Kennedy in college in 1981 when I first encountered the question that is the central focus of this book: Can volunteers solve important problems facing our country? Senator Kennedy led the Democrats on the Labor Committee, which was controlled by Republicans. It was the beginning of the Reagan Revolution. Social program after social program was on the chopping block. To replace government efforts, the president called for increased volunteering. The Kennedy staff, crammed in a small office in a crumbling Senate annex building, spent much of its time fighting program cuts and working to reinvent government programs along lines that would be more appealing to conservatives—for example, public employment programs for poor people had been characterized as wasteful make-work; public-private partnerships took their place. Student financial aid grants shifted toward loans. Targeted, narrowly defined programs became flexible "block grants" that could be spent at the direction of state officials.

I spent much of my six months as an intern carrying typewritten papers back and forth in the muggy Washington heat, from the annex to the Senate Russell Building, where Senator Kennedy's main office was located. I copied documents, drafted letters, and even wrote a few statements that were published in the Congressional Record under Senator Kennedy's name. My substantive contribution was limited. But I learned a great deal—both about how a bill becomes a law and how to think about public policy in an era of scarce resources. And I gained a career goal—to become a policymaker who would make things better, particularly for poor children whose life chances were dimmed by their economic circumstances.

I had come to the Kennedy staff as a Republican, albeit a moderate, western New York–style one, not a hardcore conservative. I left as a Democrat, convinced that there was an important government role in solving critical social problems and that volunteers could not replace public programs. But a question stayed with me after that internship. Even if volunteers could not replace public programs, couldn't they make an important contribution?

I have to admit that I had never really thought much about volunteers. As a child growing up in a small canal town surrounded by farmland, I wasn't aware of formal volunteer programs. And yet, I realize that voluntary help was all around me. My father, who had come to the United States as a Japanese immigrant on a cargo ship with nothing but a trunk and a medical degree, sometimes treated farm workers and other people in our rural town without pay. My mother, a nurse, from a poor family herself, seemed always to be taking on hard cases, acting as a sort of informal mentor to drug addicts, depressed children, and lost souls. She ran the Sunday School, was active in Band Boosters, ran our 4-H Club, and nurtured sick animals that turned up in our yard.

My family benefited from volunteer help too. I spent time in a Girl Scout Brownie troop, and my brother was a Cub Scout and Little Leaguer—all volunteer-led activities. We went on field trips chaperoned by parents, and on longer school trips paid for through local fundraising efforts. When a sudden blizzard stranded my brother and sisters at school, a neighbor drove them home on a snow plow. People helped each other out.

These things that people do not because they are required to but because they choose to are essential to a strong community. These responsibilities start with the individual (we go to school, do our homework, get a job and pay our bills) and extend to the rest of one's family. We do our best to raise our kids, take care of aging relatives, tend to sick siblings, and reach out to family members in crisis. We do favors for friends, keep our lawns mowed, and take our turn at carpooling. We don't expect the government to do these things for us, and at some level, appreciate the obligation that we all have to one another.

And yet, what about those people who don't have friends or family to help meet their needs? What about challenges facing whole communities that can't be addressed without extra resources? What happens when everyone has a role to play, but some people don't do their part?

In the face of circumstances such as these, there may be an important role for government and volunteers, not to mention non-profit organizations and business institutions. It's not, however, an either-or situation. Government can't—and should not—replace the everyday efforts of people taking responsibility for themselves, their families, and their communities. And volunteers can't solve every problem.

In fact, every challenge facing our country exists in a complex ecosystem that requires multiple actors if we are to meet it. Roads out of poverty, for example, can't be built by government alone. Government may provide free public education; college aid; and funding for child care, job training, and safety nets. Businesses can offer good jobs with benefits, credit, transportation, or affordable housing. Nonprofits may run programs that offer a hand up. And volunteers can tutor, mentor, or teach skills to people, or help them find the help they need. All of these efforts are part of an informal cross-sector network that may work well or poorly, presenting opportunity to all or leaving vast parts of the population behind.

NATIONAL SERVICE POLICY

I returned to the Senate Labor Committee as a young lawyer, immediately after graduating from law school in 1987. At this time, the Democrats were in charge of the Congress, and Senator Kennedy was the chairman of the Committee. The following year, a Republican president, George H. W. Bush, was elected. He pushed volunteering as part of his "kinder, gentler" platform and created an office of national service in the White House, the first of its kind, led by his long-time friend Gregg Petersmeyer. However, a group of new-thinking Democrats, including then-Governor Bill Clinton and known as the Democratic Leadership Council (DLC), had their own proposal—to require young people to earn their student financial aid through several years of full-time national service.

The DLC proposal presented Senator Kennedy with a quandary. His brother John's call to service had become a memorable defining moment of his presidency. Senator Kennedy's brother-in-law, Sargent Shriver, sent a proposal from Notre Dame president Ted Hesbergh, a family friend, in support of a Peace Corps ROTC along with a note of support for the idea. Massachusetts, the state Senator Kennedy represented, was home to cutting-edge programs and outspoken advocates for service of all kinds—both City Year and YouthBuild, two national model programs with highly respected leaders, were based there, as were some of the country's best student service programs. On the other hand, it also was home to dozens of universities, and the higher education community was almost universally opposed to the DLC idea of requiring service in order to receive federal financial aid. The full-blown DLC plan had been estimated to cost the federal government at least $60 billion a year in 1980s dollars—an amount most people thought was too pricy for an untested public program.[1] In addition, the Democrats on the Education and Labor Committee in the House of Representatives were united in their opposition to the DLC plan.

Senator Sam Nunn's staff gamely pursued the DLC plan with the help of Senators Barbara Mikulski and John McCain, indicating their willingness to work with us to pilot the idea. Senator Kennedy asked me to see if I could put together legislation that would advance service but avoid the punitive aspects of the DLC plan. There were plenty of good ideas afloat. Over the past several decades, state and local youth corps had been created, modeled on the Depression-era Civilian Conservation Corps. I also heard from people who saw the power of service for college students. Others, such as Senator Kennedy's niece Kathleen Kennedy Townsend, were committed to the power of something called "service-learning" for students as young as kindergarteners.

Senator Kennedy hosted a dinner for a small group of national leaders to explore the parameters of possible legislation. From this dinner came a set of ideas to promote youth service that would become Kennedy's major focus.

I set up a series of meetings with key Senate staff to see if we couldn't compromise on a comprehensive bill. We settled on the creation of the bipartisan Commission on National and Community

Service that would make grants to test each of these program ideas and report back to Congress and the president with its findings. We then pursued the House Committee, hoping that it would agree to this greatly scaled back demonstration version of the DLC proposal. Gene Sofer, the lead drafter and negotiator for the House Committee, developed a plan that would provide support for youth service, but without any link to financial aid.

An ally came from a seemingly unlikely place. Senator Orrin Hatch, the ranking Republican on the Senate Labor Committee, was a conservative not prone to support new government programs. And yet, as a Mormon who had done several years of service through his church, Hatch appreciated the transformative role that service could play. He reached out to Senator Kennedy, indicating his willingness to work on a bill together, provided that it included limited new spending.

A THOUSAND POINTS OF LIGHT

All along, we had kept President Bush's national service director, Gregg Petersmeyer, informed about our progress. The president was advancing service in other ways, using the bully pulpit and power of the White House. President Bush had spoken of "a thousand points of light" in his 1988 acceptance speech at the Republican convention: "For we're a nation of community; of thousands and tens of thousands of ethnic, religious, social, business, labor union, neighborhood, regional and other organizations, all of them varied, voluntary and unique. This is America—a brilliant diversity spread like stars, like *a thousand points of light* in a broad and peaceful sky [emphasis added]."[2] This evocative line became the president's "brand" of service. Every day, he honored a volunteer with a Daily Point of Light Award. And a group of the president's friends and supporters worked to create the Points of Light Foundation.

Gregg Petersmeyer was sympathetic to the legislation we were developing, but he had few allies in the Bush White House. When he finally let us know, at the eleventh hour, that he could work on a bill with us we were elated. We worked out a compromise bill on the eve of floor action in the Senate that ensured we would have enough votes for final passage and to overcome a filibuster. But that didn't mean that dozens of senators wouldn't offer amendments—including provisions to condemn human repression in China and elections in Nicaragua.

After an exhausting floor fight that went on for two weeks, the legislation moved quickly through the House and was signed by the president in November 1990. Recently married and planning to start a family, I left the Senate staff shortly thereafter.

THE COMMISSION ON NATIONAL AND COMMUNITY SERVICE

The National and Community Service Act of 1990, while modest in scope and little noticed, turned out to be an important piece of legislation. It created the Commission on National and Community Service, as envisioned by the Democratic negotiators, and authorized funding for four new programs: student service-learning; youth service and conservation corps; a demonstration program to test tying education benefits to service; and the Points of Light Foundation. President Bush consulted with the bill's sponsors in making the Democratic appointments to the Commission, which would be uncompensated Senate-confirmed part-time positions. The president appointed me to the Commission at the suggestion of Senator Kennedy.

The members of President Bush's commission represented the full breadth of the service field, from Alan Khazei, the founder of City Year, to George Romney, the former Republican governor of Michigan and auto company chairman who had championed volunteer centers.[3] President Bush took a hands-off approach to the Commission, keeping it free from political pressure. Supported by a small but talented staff, led by Catherine Milton, commissioners worked hard, meeting for days at a time, debating selection criteria, reading grant proposals, and designing the evaluation of the programs. I vividly remember co-chairing a day-long hearing conducted by the Commission and televised on C-Span in December of 1992. Nine months' pregnant, I must have looked like an elephant on camera and could not sit comfortably. My first son, Jackson, was born just two days later.

AMERICORPS

The Commission shared its recommendations in its January 1993 report to Congress and the president, titled "What You Can Do for Your Country."[4] It could not have come at a more critical time for service. Arkansas governor Bill Clinton had been elected president in November 1992. His pledge to create a "domestic GI Bill" that would enable young people to pay their way through college with a year or two of national service had been wildly popular on the campaign trail.

In anticipation of the election, Melanne Verveer, Hillary Clinton's campaign chief of staff, convened a group to work on a plan to implement Clinton's pledge. Meeting in a borrowed law firm conference room, with the campaign issues director, Bruce Reed, calling in from the campaign bus, we sketched out an ambitious plan informed by the Commission's work.

After the election, Melanne asked me to join the Office of the First Lady as Hillary Clinton's representative on the Domestic Policy Council staff. President Clinton appointed his good friend business-man Eli Segal to head the White House Office of National Service with the responsibility to shape the legislation. We all agreed that national service ought to be a "first hundred days" priority. Dubbing themselves "The Little Engine That Could," Eli's team soon found that the rest of the White House was badly distracted by other pri-orities, from gays in the military to health care reform. The national service team asked for my help, which the first lady enthusiastically supported.

I worked with Jack Lew, a long-time staffer for Tip O'Neill, and the rest of Eli's staff to design the new legislation. It would keep the student programs authorized by the 1990 bill, as well as funding for the Points of Light Foundation. (When President Bush met with President-elect Clinton, it was reported that the only thing he asked was that the Points of Light initiative continue.) But it would dramatically grow the program that tied service to educational opportunity.

The final product was unveiled on the 101st day of the Clinton Administration. Like the Commission's demonstration program, AmeriCorps, as the new program would later be known, would build on state and local efforts, not be operated by the federal government. Anyone seventeen or older could serve and receive a living allowance, health care and child care benefits, and an education award if they served full time for a year.

While the new proposal was unveiled with great fanfare, it could not become law until both houses of Congress passed and agreed upon the details of the legislation. We had worked with both the House and Senate Labor Committees to develop the proposal, and sat at the drafting table in the Senate legislative counsel's office making sure every line made sense. Eli Segal's tireless efforts resulted in a handful of Republicans joining the bill. But many vocal opponents made it clear that they would not agree to any legislation that "paid volunteers." The resulting floor fight in the Senate took two weeks, with amendments designed to whittle back the programs and their benefits. The House faced a similar battle. Finally, a bill reached the president's desk in September 1993.

The signing ceremony on the South Lawn of the White House was a celebration with a popular grunge band, celebrities, the senators and representatives who had championed the bill, and more than a thousand giddy supporters under a giant tent. When President Clinton crossed the lawn with fifty corpsmembers from programs across the country, the band launched into Clinton's campaign theme song, "Don't Stop Thinking About Tomorrow." The crowd jumped to its feet and erupted in applause. Clinton acknowledged three young people who were volunteers, and recognized two veterans of the Roosevelt-era Civilian Conservation Corps. Noting that "if we challenge people to serve and we give them a chance to fulfill their abilities, more and more and more we will all understand that we must go forward together," Clinton signed the bill with pens that President Kennedy had used to enact the Peace Corps legislation and Franklin Roosevelt had used to create the CCC.

"The Little Engine That Could" had finally made it over the hill.[5]

THE CORPORATION FOR NATIONAL AND COMMUNITY SERVICE

Soon after the bill signing, Eli asked me to help him lead the creation of the Corporation for National and Community Service. I was sorry to leave the White House but pleased by the opportunity to help implement the new programs. The Senate confirmed my appointment to be the managing director of the Corporation in October of 1993.

In a very short period of just a few years, national service had gone from idea to reality. Its supporters typically had one of two reasons for their enthusiasm for the concept. Some, such as the DLC and People for the American Way, felt strongly that civic engagement was waning in America. Others believed in the power of serving to change the lives of the server—whether they are young students, high school dropouts, college students looking for a purpose, or older adults needing to remain active. That was the focus of some House Democrats, who even supported giving low-income people priority for AmeriCorps education awards.

However, few advocates thought its most important benefit was to solve problems facing the nation. Of course, everyone, from the president to a local program head, would give a nod to this goal. And in fact, volunteers would quickly know if their activities were "make work" or "making a difference." But service was largely absent when policymakers put forward strategies to improve education, health, or the environment. To change this we made the motto of the new program, "Getting Things Done."

These early classes of AmeriCorps members would teach us a lot about the opportunities and challenges presented by federal involvement in service. We learned that certain issues were a good fit for AmeriCorps, while others were a stretch. One particular strength of AmeriCorps members turned out to be managing volunteers. Senator Harris Wofford, who succeeded Eli Segal as CEO of the Corporation, made volunteer recruitment a priority for AmeriCorps. He underscored the importance of volunteering by organizing a convening that George Romney had called for years earlier, to bring all the living former presidents together to call the nation to service. In July of 1997, every living president (except Ronald Reagan, who was represented by his wife, Nancy) joined President Clinton in Philadelphia at The Presidents' Summit for America's Future. I had helped with early planning for the summit but attended as a spectator, having left the Corporation earlier that year to take care of my growing family—my second son, Matthew, had been born in 1995.

While AmeriCorps and the other Corporation programs did enjoy bipartisan support, their opponents in Congress made it impossible to extend, improve, and expand them. In 1999, I was again working for First Lady Hillary Clinton. To build support for the program, we decided to celebrate the fifth anniversary of AmeriCorps. At the huge White House event on October 20th, attended by over a thousand supporters including Coretta Scott King and General Colin Powell, I was again enormously pregnant. My third son, Thomas, was born just eight days later.

PRESIDENT GEORGE W. BUSH

When President Clinton left office, I was told he followed the tradition of his predecessor, asking George W. Bush to protect AmeriCorps as Bush's father had asked President Clinton to take care of the Points of Light Foundation. The new president did, always requesting funding for AmeriCorps in his budget and using political pressure when necessary to move Republicans in Congress. However, Bush's support was tested when, in 2003, a series of miscalculations and external factors created a crisis for the program—after a push to increase the number of AmeriCorps members, not enough money was left in the Trust Fund to pay AmeriCorps education awards. When the Corporation shifted money from program grants to cover the shortfall, the resulting reduced pool of funds required substantial cuts in AmeriCorps, in some cases the closing of entire sites.

The field rallied to save the program, organizing one hundred hours of testimony on Capitol Hill, obtaining support letters from 44 governors, 150 mayors, 250 business and philanthropic leaders, 190 college and university presidents, 701 citizens from as far away as Alaska, and 1,100 community-based organizations that work with AmeriCorps. Almost one hundred editorial boards wrote in favor of the program, and eventually the president weighed in and Congress appropriated a record amount of funds.[6]

This victory strengthened the resolve of AmeriCorps advocates to take the program to scale. Following President George W. Bush's reelection, it was clear that 2008 would offer the first open presidential election, in which no incumbent president or vice president was running, in forty years. I had spent the years since the Clinton Administration running a consulting business to help nonprofits, and had joined the Center for American Progress as a part-time visiting fellow working on national service issues. With a new president, it seemed possible that the national service laws might finally be successfully revisited, but bold plans were needed.

Across the field of national service programs, there were specific things that stood out. First, it seemed that service programs were making a substantial contribution in certain fields. At the top of the list was education. Why not focus new national service funds on expanding those organizations that were getting results in priority areas?

Second, national service provided an important source of human and financial capital for programs started by social entrepreneurs. AmeriCorps provided important support for innovative organizations—from Teach For America to Habitat for Humanity—that were ready to go to scale but did not fit neatly into other federal funding streams.

Third, it had become clear that national service can transform lives, particularly during periods of life transitions. For example, service offers particular benefits for young people leaving childhood for the teen years. These young people are at high risk for dropping out, not to mention for substance abuse and teen pregnancy. The creation of a rite of passage through a summer of service before high school could help young teens find purpose and connect their studies to positive real-life experiences.

Finally, there were clear opportunities to use federal support to grow other service strategies, not just AmeriCorps. For example, by 2007, more than five hundred thousand people had served in Ameri-Corps. These alumni had been sworn into AmeriCorps pledging to "get things done for America" and to "carry this commitment with me this year and beyond." They had been trained in organizing volunteers, in first aid, and in many other skills. Why not engage them in a reserve corps that would provide skills useful in times of crisis?

I laid out these and other ideas in a paper I wrote for the Center for American Progress in 2007.[7] It called for growth funds to expand highly effective national service programs meeting specific priority needs, expanding specific national service opportunities for Americans during key life transitions, and amplifying the long-term impact of national service by investing in AmeriCorps alumni. It also proposed a new role for the Corporation—to strengthen nonprofit organizations in ways beyond their volunteer capacity.

I was not alone in sensing that the time to revisit national service policy had come. Senator Kennedy, who had been recently diagnosed with brain cancer, directed his staff to work quickly on a bill that could move in the early days of the next administration. Senator Hatch, who had been Kennedy's partner on national service legislation decades earlier, independently decided to work on a bill, drawing on his own experience as a Mormon missionary engaged in service as a young man.

Nor was the value of national service lost on the presidential candidates running in 2008. Two AmeriCorps alumni set out to get each candidate on record in support of a simple goal: to increase AmeriCorps by one hundred thousand members.[8] Their startup organization, ServeNext, had a shoestring budget. And yet, armed with a video camera, they and their friends attended rallies across New Hampshire, asking candidates to pledge to grow AmeriCorps by one hundred thousand and recording their answers. Amazingly they managed to obtain commitments from every Democratic candidate and Republican Mike Huckabee.

One of the most enthusiastic candidates was Barack Obama. He pledged to make service "a cause of his presidency," and to expand AmeriCorps to 250,000 members. Republican John McCain, while declining to sign the pledge, had been a strong supporter of national service for more than two decades. He had sponsored legislation in the Senate to expand national service to 250,000 positions, and proposed his own Service to America Act.

Senator Kennedy, who had endorsed Barack Obama for president, sought to align the new legislation with the candidate's pledges, hoping for a quick win in the new administration. His talented young staffperson, Emma Vahdera, worked closely with Senator Hatch's staff; with Voices for National Service, an advocacy group for the service field led by AnnMaura Connolly; and with a newly formed coalition, ServiceNation, put together by Alan Khazei.[9]

A major piece of the ServiceNation agenda was to grow AmeriCorps from seventy-five thousand to one million Americans serving. And to make this a reality, the convenors led an effort to bring both major-party presidential candidates to New York for a summit on September 11, 2008, just two months before the election. With support from *Time* magazine, whose managing editor Rick Stengel had written a cover story on national service months earlier, ServiceNation succeeded in attracting both major-party candidates to the New York City event, along with five hundred leaders from all walks of life, from celebrities and elected officials to military brass and service program leaders. Senator Hatch joined the event to announce the introduction of the Kennedy-Hatch Serve America bill. All of us who worked on the bill were thrilled that both Senators Obama and McCain joined as original co-sponsors of the proposal.

PRESIDENT OBAMA

When President Obama was inaugurated four months later, he called the nation to service. He said, "What is required of us now is a new era of responsibility—a recognition, on the part of every American, that we have duties to ourselves, our nation and the world." President Obama's charge went well beyond AmeriCorps or even volunteering, encompassing whole careers and simple acts of personal responsibility. He signaled a new way to think about service as something that everyone should do throughout their lives.

As they had planned, the bill drafted by Senators Kennedy and Hatch was ready to go. And shortly after the Inauguration, President Obama asked Congress "to send me the bipartisan legislation that bears the name of Senator Orrin Hatch as well as an American who has never stopped asking what he can do for his country—Senator Edward Kennedy."[10] Committee Chairmen Kennedy and George Miller, in the House, worked hard to move the legislation quickly, even reaching a quiet agreement so the Senate bill could incorporate many of the House's priorities, thereby avoiding a need for a conference to work out differences.

The Edward M. Kennedy Serve America Act of 2009 moved national service to a new level. It authorized an increase in Ameri-Corps from seventy-five thousand slots to a quarter million over ten years. It created new corps focused on education, health, energy, economic opportunity, and veterans, with specific outcomes for each. In view of the impact service has on people making key life transitions, the bill targeted youths enroute to high school, retiring Baby Boomers, and returning veterans. Recognizing the link between service and social innovation, it created the Social Innovation Fund, which I had helped to develop with America Forward, a coalition of leading social entrepreneurs organized by the venture philanthropy organization New Profit. And it expanded the role of the Corporation from supporting service to building stronger nonprofits, with a new volunteer management fund and grants for training and technical assistance to help small and mid-size nonprofits increase their capacity.

After decades of incremental progress, the United States is at a critical juncture in the history of national service. Across America today, service programs are changing lives, tackling tough problems,

creating innovative solutions, and engaging citizens in their communities. With the Kennedy Serve America Act, the service movement
is suddenly poised to achieve significantly greater impact *if* we can
leverage the true potential of national service and volunteering and
manage this important resource effectively.

Acknowledgments

This book was inspired by the hundreds of programs I have seen that engage volunteers and national service participants to solve America's toughest problems. But their stories aren't well known, and stereotypes and misinformation about service abound. I thought that by writing this book people might see the power of service more clearly.

Putting this book together required the cooperation and assistance of dozens of people. First, I am in debt to my business partner, Deb Jospin, who helped to build the service movement as director of AmeriCorps and helped me make the manuscript as compelling as possible while we struggled to manage our regular workload.

Second, I am truly grateful to the Center for American Progress, especially John Podesta and Sarah Wartell, for allowing me to serve as a fellow and for encouraging this book. I am also deeply appreciative of the clients of sagawa/jospin who have taught me a great deal about what works, especially my friends Vanessa Kirsch and Kim Syman at New Profit.

Many people contributed to the creation of the book, including my agent, Jim Levine, and editor, Jesse Wiley. I want to thank the entire team at Jossey-Bass, including Mickey Butts, who offered wise edits; Nina Kreiden; Dani Scoville; Dave Horne; and Diane Turso. Tamara Chao and Nigel White provided research assistance. Thanks also to the ServiceNation team including Greg Propper and Elizabeth Wilner, who provided access to their database.

My family deserves thanks in countless ways—especially my mother, Patricia Sagawa; my late father, Hidetaka Sagawa; my husband, Greg Baer; and my sons, Jackson, Matthew, and Thomas Baer, who always help me put things in perspective.

Finally, I wish that I had room to acknowledge every person who has contributed to building the national service movement. In addition to the late Senator Edward M. Kennedy and the late

Eli Segal, I could write whole chapters about the contributions of people such as President Bill Clinton and Hillary Clinton, Gregg Petersmeyer, Senator Barbara Mikulski, Steve Goldsmith, Gene Sofer, Bill Basl, Wendy Spencer, Secretary Karen Baker, AnnMaura Connolly, Michael Brown, Alan Khazei, Michelle Nunn, John Bridgeland, Bruce Reed, John Gomperts, Jim Kielsmeier, Susan Stroud, Dorothy Stoneman, Sally Prouty, Senator Harris Wofford, Catherine Milton, Mal Coles, the other current and former staff of the Corporation for National and Community Service, and hundreds of other program directors, policymakers, advocates, and, of course, people who have served. They have made the case for service by their ideas and deeds, and I have been honored to be a part of their work. Of course, much of this book is my interpretation of history as I remember it. If there are errors and omissions, they are my own.

SHIRLEY SAGAWA
March 2010

About the Author

S hirley Sagawa is a visiting fellow with the Center for American Progress, where she is a leading expert on national service policy. She is also the co-founder of sagawa/jospin, a consulting firm that provides strategic counsel to nonprofits. She has been called "a founding mother" of the modern service movement, and in 2009 received the Lifetime of Service Award from AmeriCorps Alums.

Sagawa served as a presidential appointee in both the first Bush Administration and the Clinton Administration, and led the Obama transition for the Corporation for National and Community Service. As special assistant to President Clinton for domestic policy, Sagawa drafted the legislation that created AmeriCorps and the Corporation for National and Community Service. After Senate confirmation as the Corporation's first managing director, she helped lead the development of the new agency and its programs. She also served as deputy chief of staff to First Lady Hillary Clinton.

Sagawa was the founding executive director of the Learning First Alliance, a partnership of national education associations. She has served as the chief counsel for youth policy for the Senate Labor Committee and as senior counsel to the National Women's Law Center. She has also served on numerous nonprofit boards.

She is the coauthor of the recent book *The Charismatic Organization: Eight Ways to Grow a Nonprofit That Builds Buzz, Delights Donors, and Energizes Employees* (Jossey-Bass, 2008) as well as coauthor with Eli Segal of *Common Interest, Common Good: Creating Value Through Business and Social Sector Partnerships* (Harvard Business School Press, 2000).

Sagawa is a *cum laude* graduate of Harvard Law School, holds an MSc degree from the London School of Economics, and graduated *magna cum laude* from Smith College.

The
AMERICAN
WAY
Change

CHAPTER ONE

Introduction

W e're at a pivotal time in America. We face crises in nearly every corner. Whole communities that are stuck in poverty, and middle-class families that are slipping downward. Public schools that don't graduate half of the African American and Latino students who come through their doors. A majority of people of all ages who suffer from obesity and related health problems and millions of Americans without a place to go for regular health care. Conflict among different religious, ethnic, and other groups, and many Americans uneasy connecting with people unlike themselves. The largest cohort of older adults in history threatening to overwhelm systems of care and outlive their savings. Climate change threatening to wipe away whole cities around the world and make entire species extinct.

Many people look to government to solve these problems. But none of these can be solved by government alone. In fact, none can be solved without the committed efforts of the American people, taking action on their own or in concert with others.

Service is the American way to change America. Bill Clinton called it that when he proposed AmeriCorps, but service has always been part of America's defining character. From colonial days when neighbors banded together to fight fires or raise barns to the Victory Gardens and civil defense system of World War II to the swarms of volunteers who descended on New Orleans in the wake of Hurricane Katrina, Americans step up. In recent years, in the face of dire challenges, ordinary citizens seem ready to take action. Applications for AmeriCorps, which engages adults in substantial service in exchange for money for college, tripled in 2009, reaching an all-time high since the program was created. Legislation authorizing the largest expansion of national service since the Great Depression was signed in the first hundred days of the Obama Administration with strong bipartisan support. While numbers of volunteers have held steady over the decade, informal volunteering is on the rise, suggesting that

1

more people would serve if only they were asked.[1] The human capital we need to put to our biggest challenges is poised and ready.

What would they do? Consider the crisis in education. Qualified professionals in the classroom and leading the schools are absolutely critical to children's ability to succeed. But teachers will be quick to tell you that a child who is disruptive can ruin learning time for the whole class. That a student who misses school—due to illness, because of child care responsibilities, or because he doesn't see the point—won't be able to learn. Neither will students in schools where low achievement is the norm, where doing well in class violates unwritten cultural rules. Nor will students who need extra time or extra help that the teacher doesn't have time to give. Government can pay for buildings, books, principals, teachers, and counselors— but something more is needed to solve these complex problems. Volunteers can help by promoting a learning culture, acting as role models, offering one-on-one help, and expanding available services.

Or think about health. The public debate about health care is really about insurance reform—how we make sure that every person has insurance so they can pay for the medical help they need. But health is about a much broader range of things. It's about preventing diseases through good habits such as eating right and exercising and avoiding risky behaviors. About disease prevention and managing chronic conditions, and receiving support when challenges arise, whether they are the loss or illness of a loved one or an addiction you can't beat on your own. About informed parenting so children get off to a healthy start, and enabling older adults to live independently in their own homes as long as possible, connected to social networks. Volunteers can help with all of these things. True, they can't pay for health insurance for the uninsured, but they can let people know about public health insurance programs and help them sign up (in 2009, there were more than six million children who were eligible for health coverage under Medicaid or SCHIP [State Children's Health Insurance Program] but not enrolled). They can't run a hospital, but they can help patients navigate the health care system, translate for people struggling with English, offer a calming presence to children in emergency waiting rooms—or keep people out of the hospital altogether by helping them prevent medical problems.

Unfortunately, service is often left out of the public problem-solving toolbox. We debate teacher salaries or public subsidies for health insurance and spend billions, even trillions of taxpayer dollars to solve these pieces of the problem while we neglect those aspects of the solution that could be addressed inexpensively by leveraging the human capital of caring communities.

When policymakers think about service it is often for its own sake, or for ideological reasons—to link rights with responsibilities. The problem they are trying to solve is "We need more national service" not "How do we help struggling students succeed?" or "How do we make low-income communities healthier?"

But that need not be the case. It is time to get serious about solving the problems that are holding us back as a nation by making it possible for ordinary citizens to play a part. We now have the know-how and evidence to support large-scale efforts to use service to address our national priorities. This book spells out how. It identifies programs that are working against our biggest challenges, from getting every preschool child ready to learn to reducing our energy consumption as a nation.

It also explains how service supports innovation in the social sector, helping to identify and take to scale new solutions. We need innovation in the social sector just as we need it in business or science. Because of innovation, we don't buy the same cars we did in the 1960s, or treat cancer the same way. In those worlds of business and science there are systems that finance research and development, test new products and services, and scale those that work.

In the social sector, similar efforts are poorly resourced and disjointed. Nonetheless, people who care about innovation in how we solve public problems can find a ready tool in service. Volunteers often provide the human capital necessary to start an organization, especially when financial backing is hard to come by. For example, in the nation's earliest days, fire departments and public libraries began with volunteers, at the inspiration of one of America's first social entrepreneurs, Ben Franklin. Many of the country's best known nonprofits, from Goodwill to the American Cancer Society, began as volunteer efforts.

Once an innovation is tested and proves successful, society is served by additional investment—both human and financial—to expand the program or organization. Volunteer support often proves critical to this expansion, as it has been for many organizations that make such service central to their delivery systems. AmeriCorps continued this tradition, providing human and financial capital necessary to take today's startup organizations and proven programs alike to the next level.

We also know that engaging Americans in service will pay added dividends by changing the lives of those who serve. While we address our national priorities through service, we can also use service to help everyday Americans connect with one another and find purpose in their lives. Service is particularly meaningful for individuals undergoing critical life transitions.

For example, early adolescence is a developmentally important period when youths make choices that either propel them forward or put them at significant risk. Service experiences help them see themselves as valued contributors and connect learning to a positive future—another way that service supports school success.

Similarly, service makes a difference for youths who have dropped out of school. By putting these disconnected youths on a pathway to employment and engaged citizenship, service helps them find a road out of poverty—another of America's great challenges.

Young adults graduating from college may not seem like a group worth investing in—they already have the degree they need to achieve the American Dream. But without a clear career direction and access to entry opportunities, these young people may turn away from fields where their talents are most needed. National service has produced leaders for the nonprofit sector, along with frontline troops and mid-level managers. It steers people into health, teaching, youth work, and green jobs—all careers that will give their lives a sense of purpose as they help the nation with its problems.

People facing extreme challenges, such as the loss of a job or the death of a loved one, often find new meaning through service. In this way, service improves the nation's mental health while it brings important new human resources to the community.

Those who are leaving the workforce at the ends of their careers often suffer from health problems resulting from social isolation and lack of purpose. Service can fill that void and actually improve the physical and mental health—and longevity—of older adults. Service ought to be a conscious way we shape the lives of Americans of all backgrounds, from youth through adulthood.

Finally, a thriving democracy demands that citizens become engaged in a variety of ways, from voting and running for office to awareness of issues and participation in community groups. For many supporters, revitalizing our democracy and bridging divides that undermine civic trust are major reasons for public investment in service, especially when few other tools serve these ends. These outcomes deserve to be pursued with greater intention.

ABOUT THIS BOOK

This book is intended to guide those who will write the next chapter on service—the policymakers, program directors, nonprofit leaders, and, of course, the volunteers themselves.

I began this book intending to tell the story of AmeriCorps and the difference it has made for the people who serve and the people they help. I realized that it is impossible to limit the book in this way, because of the interconnectedness of AmeriCorps national service and other forms of organized service. This book does not attempt to be a comprehensive analysis of every kind of helpful voluntary action or public service. It doesn't tell the story of faith-based volunteering, or everyday acts of kindness, or the responsibilities of family members to one another. It doesn't spell out the vital role that advocacy by volunteer activists has played in changing America for the better. Nor does it discuss the vital contributions of government and nonprofit workers, or those who serve in the military. All of these forms of service are noble and essential, but too vast to cover in this book.

Instead, it focuses on specific ways that organized service can transform America. In this book, *service* refers broadly to both *volunteering* and *national service*.

I define *volunteering* as service by people who help others of their own free will and typically without any remuneration. Sometimes low-income volunteers do receive modest stipends, substantially below market-based wages, to offset the costs of volunteering. Many people would not consider such individuals to be volunteers, and might call them something else. But rather than confusing people with too many terms, I've included modestly stipended volunteers in my definition. I also see little point in distinguishing volunteering from community service. Sometimes community service is what people are sentenced to do after misdemeanors. That's not what I'm writing about, although there is nothing wrong with it. But given the potential for confusion, I've avoided that term.

National service is a related term. National service programs enable people to help others of their own free will but (1) are federally connected; (2) may provide living allowances, educational or other benefits, and other supports that enable and entice people of all backgrounds to serve; and (3) require substantial ongoing service over a long period, often over a year or more. AmeriCorps is an example of a national service program. It provides its full-time members with a living allowance (usually at the poverty level), health and child care benefits, and, if they complete their term of service, usually a year, an education award, known as the Segal AmeriCorps educational award, worth the same amount as a Pell Grant. Some people are confused about why these benefits are appropriate and ridicule the idea of "paid volunteers." I've tried to avoid referring to AmeriCorps members as volunteers (even though the term has long been used for Peace Corps volunteers who receive living allowances and even for the all-volunteer army who are of course paid salaries and benefits). It may be useful to think about why programs provide these supports. Sometimes benefits are offered as an *incentive* to encourage people to step forward to serve, often at a sacrifice in terms of what they could be making elsewhere. Sometimes the Segal AmeriCorps Education Award services this purpose—70 percent of AmeriCorps members report that the education award was quite or very relevant in motivating them to join.[2] Other benefits may be *enablers*—supports that make it possible for people who are not financially comfortable to serve. The AmeriCorps living allowance and other benefits play this role for most full-time members, but so do transportation reimbursements paid to traditional volunteers. Finally, still other benefits may be *rewards* that honor the efforts of a committed volunteer; for example, a gift certificate or scholarship often serves this purpose. When one thinks about the various benefits in these ways, they are easier to understand. And as the rest of this book attempts to illustrate, there are situations when full-time service is far more beneficial than occasional volunteering.

Finally, although there are many stereotypes about volunteers— the average volunteer is a middle-aged college-educated woman with kids at home while the average AmeriCorps member is a young woman with some college experience[3]—there is really no typical volunteer or national service participant. Here are two examples of volunteers.

I met my first Foster Grandparent on the first site visit I took as a young Kennedy staffer. With the newly assigned responsibility of overseeing the ACTION agency—one of the predecessor agencies for the Corporation for National and Community Service—I joined then-ACTION director Jane Kenny and Massachusetts State Director Mal Coles to see a Foster Grandparent in action.

I held my breath as we entered the intensive care prenatal unit of a Boston hospital. In the late 1980s, "crack babies"—the premature newborns born to drug-addicted mothers—were a serious concern. In the ward were a half dozen such babies. The size of kittens, these babies were wired up in their plastic incubators, with tubes and sensors all over their tiny bodies. They would spend their first months in this hospital, abandoned by their mothers and unfit for adoption. Perhaps they would never leave this ward alive.

No government or charitable funds would pay for doctors or nurses to hold these babies. Public funds would pay for their incubators, exams, and wiring. Public funds would pay for doctors to diagnose and treat their multiple medical problems, and for nurses to monitor them and administer medicines and nutrition. But there was no money for nurses to spend a half day, or even an hour just holding them.

The Foster Grandparent assigned to this ward did hold them. This elderly, low-income African American woman was probably in her late seventies, or even early eighties. She would not be a prime candidate for a regular job, and might well have spent her days watching soap operas instead of trekking to this tragic place. She received $2.20 an hour for her time, to offset her expenses. My friends from law school would not have dug around the seats of their cars to recover that amount. But she held those babies, for hours at a time, in a rocking chair that seemed oddly out of place in the room of beeping monitors and fluorescent lights.

This elderly woman in no way resembled the marketing executives I met two decades later, as part of a focus group of service leaders for AmeriCorps Alums, the alumni association for the AmeriCorps program. This group was led by volunteers from the Taproot Foundation, a nonprofit that matches pro bono marketing, HR, IT, and strategy management consultants with nonprofit clients. The young marketing professionals Seemin Qadiri and Khalid Smith worked for top firms. Using their professional skills, the volunteers led us through a guided discussion, featuring a detailed PowerPoint presentation aimed at refining the organization's plans for the next five years. I was impressed by both their sophisticated approach to the challenge and their commitment to the success of this valuable organization.

The frail Foster Grandparent and savvy marketing professionals seemingly have little in common. But they represent the full diversity of volunteers who are available to help solve America's greatest challenges.

This book points to four ways in which service has had an impact, opportunities in which even greater results could be obtained with greater investment of human and financial resources.

First, it looks at how serving changes the lives of those performing the service. It then examines the impact of service on civil society and the way that citizens engage in their communities. Next, it looks at the impact on specific challenges facing the nation and how service can address them—child development, education, health, poverty, aging, energy conservation, environmental protection, and disaster response. It examines the role that service has played in social innovation. Finally, it offers a new blueprint for future action to maximize the potential of service to point the way forward for America.

While service is sometimes justified as an inexpensive way to get things done in an age of limited resources, I am convinced that there are far better reasons to make service a strategy to solve America's problems, big and small. There are challenges government can't meet, help that money can't buy. Service is not nice—it's necessary. Having spent the past two decades helping to build solutions to some of America's biggest problems, I believe that we will not solve them until every agency incorporates service into its toolbox and every American makes service a part of everyday life. Together, we can solve the seemingly intractable problems holding back this country from achieving its full potential. This book offers a rationale and a roadmap to reach that endpoint.

Changing Lives: Impacts on Those Who Serve

As Steve Waldman pointed out in his now classic book *The Bill*, describing the passage of the original AmeriCorps legislation, national service is like a Swiss Army knife, able to accomplish many goals with the same tool.[1] In Part One, I examine the impact of service on those who serve, first looking at how service helps people through important life transitions and then examining the role that it can play in instilling civic values.

Many of the most effective advocates for service place a high priority on these outcomes. They see the power of service to turn around the lives of young people who have dropped out of school or to help an elderly adult stay youthful. They see service as a strategy to motivate struggling students, or to help wounded veterans regain their health helping others.

They may care about the way that service puts people on a path to civic engagement in all its forms. They want rights to be tied to responsibilities, are concerned about democratic participation, or hope to build strong communities out of the diversity that is our nation. They care about social capital, and worry that weak ties among neighbors herald the decline of a strong America.

They're right—service does address these challenges, which are very real.

Service works in a simple way. It exposes volunteers to the plights and predicaments of real people or places. Volunteers are not passive observers—they are part of the solution, people with a purpose. And that's very potent, whether the volunteer is a Tween or a Boomer, starting a new career or ending one. This ability to make a difference may point to a future vocation or a continued commitment to a cause. And it may trigger a desire to do more—to engage others, take action, pursue a new policy, or push for political change.

Part One examines the many ways that service changes the lives of those who serve. It is a powerful tool—not just in the difference it makes for others, but for those who take the time to find their purpose. In serving others, people find themselves and their way in the world.

CHAPTER TWO

Powering Life Transitions

A rthur Jacuinde was a high school dropout with no work experience, on juvenile parole, and living in a group home. Institutionalized at seventeen for assault with a deadly weapon with a gang enhancement, Arthur realized that he needed to change. "Other inmates—gang members—shared their stories with me. They talked about how hard they worked to get out . . . but would be locked up again almost immediately if they were involved in or linked to a fight once released," he recalls. "I didn't want to go through that cycle. I knew things needed to be different for me."

After his release, Arthur joined the Fresno Local Conservation Corps, seeking a fresh start. There he worked alongside other young people, some of whom also had been involved with the justice system, to learn job skills related to clean energy and conservation. He participated in solar panel installations and materials reuse and recycling at construction sites.

Through his service, Arthur found a new path that he hopes will one day lead to a career as a firefighter. As he finishes his term with the Corps, he waits for a spot at the Fire Academy at Fresno City College. "I realize now that nothing is impossible," says Arthur. "Even though I cannot change my past, I am in total control of my future."[1]

When Doris Thomas retired from Case Western Reserve, she "felt sort of empty." So after reading a newspaper ad for Experience Corps looking for school tutors, she called right away. As a graduate of Cleveland Public Schools, she had received a top-quality education. But she had watched the schools decline over the years. "I spent most of my life helping the richest and brightest students in the city at Case Western," she explains. "In retirement, I wanted to give back to those in need."

Doris has tutored with Experience Corps for more than five years, working with elementary-level students who begin the year one or two grades behind in reading. Under the direction of their teachers, Doris provides each of six students a half hour of one-on-one attention several times a week, giving them a chance to improve their skills by practicing phonics and reading together. She's proud that at the end of the year, her third-graders can read at the fourth-grade level.

When Doris came down with leukemia, she kept up her tutoring, missing only a few weeks during treatment. "It takes my mind off of myself and off of my health problems," she explains. "Just to see their shining little eyes when they get the point makes me feel great." She has signed up for a sixth year with the program.[2]

While in some ways Doris Thomas and Arthur Jacuinde could not be more different, they have something in common: they found life purpose through service. And that sense of purpose has helped them in profound ways. For Arthur Jacuinde, it has given him a reason to try hard to achieve. And for Doris Thomas, it has given her something to take her mind off her troubles, and a reason and opportunity to stay active in her retirement years.

Over the past several decades, support for service has come as much from those who believe that it can change the lives of those who serve as from those concerned with strengthening civic engagement and solving community problems. For certain groups, service can indeed be transformative, particularly people undergoing critical life transitions—young teens in search of a reason to achieve; out-of-school youths, like Arthur Jacuinde, needing a path to further education and careers; college graduates wanting to make a difference and explore the world; adults who have experienced a life crisis looking for hope; and retiring adults, like Doris Thomas, seeking new challenges.

In each of these cases, serving others offers powerful promise for people looking for new or renewed purpose. Studies and simple observation demonstrate that service experiences may provide other important benefits to those who serve. It may help them learn academic subjects or new job skills. It may teach teamwork, leadership, or communication skills. It may set them on a path to college, or help them get into the college of their choice. It may help them get a job or choose a career. It may improve their health or help them make new friends. And by helping them find a purpose, it can make them happier.

Purpose is an important theme of this chapter. While the importance of life purpose has been studied by researchers over the decades, it has recently received greater attention in the fields of child and youth development. I had the opportunity to speak on a panel at the Hudson Institute with William Damon, who had just released his book *The Path to Purpose,* which spoke to the importance of helping children find their calling in life. Damon, an expert on adolescent development, set out to understand why some young people thrive while others are rudderless, at serious risk of never fulfilling their potential. To answer this question, he and his team surveyed over twelve hundred young people between the ages of twelve and twenty-six, and interviewed in depth about a quarter of those surveyed. They asked them what they care about, what they hope to accomplish, what support they receive from friends and family, and what life choices they have made so far. He discovered that about one in five youths has a strong sense of purpose, and one in four has none at all. The large majority in the middle did what was expected of them, tried things, showed up. They were "dreamers" or "dabblers." But they had no passion behind their efforts. And he found that purpose correlated with success, and the lack of purpose resulted in drifting and disengagement.[3]

Damon defines *purpose* as "a stable and generalized intention to accomplish something that is at the same time meaningful to the self and consequential for the world beyond the self."[4] He makes a strong case for purpose as central to raising children who will go on to deeply satisfying and productive lives. He supports his findings with research from psychology, which shows that a sense of purpose is key to health and happiness as well as a major factor in resiliency, the ability to overcome severe trauma and adversity.[5]

As I read Damon's book in preparation for the panel, it seemed clear that much of the power of service is unlocking that sense of purpose. Damon himself confirmed it at the event, noting that "service is useful in building not only purpose, but also skills and networking capabilities and all kinds of real-world abilities that end up serving the individual."[6] And while his insights stem from child development, it also seems obvious that this need for purpose exists throughout life, and that service can help individuals find it at any age, whether they are students starting out or seniors looking to start again.

This chapter focuses on five critical life transitions when finding purpose through service can be life changing. I don't mean to suggest that service by other people of other ages and stages can't benefit the server—anyone can improve their own lives by serving others. But for some people, particularly at key life crossroads, finding purpose through service can be transformative.

TRANSITION TO THE TEEN YEARS

Parker was a kid you didn't usually notice. He didn't cause trouble in class, and earned mostly B's with the occasional C. He didn't join clubs or play on a school sports team or win awards. He occasionally developed an interest in something—Civil War history or magic tricks—but never stuck with these hobbies for long. His parents couldn't fault him for his behavior but worried about his lack of commitment to schoolwork—homework was always a struggle. He would start high school next year, and they hoped that something would "light a fire under him soon."[7]

Parker is typical of Bill Damon's "dabblers," a young person who has difficulty finding a motivating life purpose. There are many ways that Parker might find that purpose—through religion, sports, exposure to an appealing career, or the desire to overcome a challenge. However, without purpose, Parker could just as easily succumb to the perils of early adolescence and make choices that will significantly limit his future possibilities.

Too many young people lose their way at this age. Their brains are growing and changing, responding to the various stimuli around them. How they spend their time during this period may set them on a course of positive development or one of unhealthy behavior.[8] In fact, the majority of dropouts leave school in ninth grade, after several years of missed classes, acting out, or failed courses.[9] One in eight teens has sex before age fifteen, 40 percent of eighth graders have tried alcohol, and one in five has used illegal drugs.[10] Others may not face these catastrophic challenges but drift along like Parker, without motivation. Unfortunately, instead of promoting positive development, youth-focused investments tend to emphasize problems, not potential. We spend money to tell teens to stay away from drugs, to keep youth offenders off the streets, to discourage teen pregnancy.

Yet research—and common sense—tells us that giving young people something to say "yes" to is an essential part of teaching them to say "no."

That's why when the National Campaign to Prevent Teen Pregnancy looked at research to identify effective pregnancy prevention programs, it included two service-learning programs on its list.[11] And why when the National Dropout Prevention Center identified fifteen research-based strategies effective in dropout prevention, service-learning was on that list too.[12] And why when America's Promise sought to identify the key ingredients for positive youth development, it found that "the opportunity to give back" was one of five "promises"—the developmental resources that young people need for success in life.[13] When young people find a purpose, they conform their behavior to achieve their goals.

Bill Damon's purpose study found that when two conditions apply, there is every likelihood that the child will thrive: (1) forward movement toward a fulfilling purpose and (2) a structure of social support consistent with that effort.[14] Service can help with both: exposing young people to needs and their own ability to make a difference and providing the support and validation that can be found in service programs, whether they are based in schools, community groups, faith-based organizations, or family.

Mary Barahona found that experience through her school. Today she is a poised young adult, comfortable making speeches to roomfuls of experts. But just a few years earlier, she was a nervous middle schooler, recently transplanted from the Bronx to suburban Orlando. She remembers her culture shock. "There were cows along the highway!" Although she was a good student, she felt very alone. "I was a newbie," she recalls. "I was very shy."

In ninth grade, Barahona signed up for a service-learning class, knowing she needed seventy-five hours of service to win a scholarship. "I was going to get my seventy-five hours and I'm out of here," she says. But the class opened her eyes to "a world I never knew existed," says Barahona. "I was surprised to learn that slavery still exists today, even though I had studied slavery in history class." She wanted to do something about it. She took another service-learning class the following year, and then another. "It gave me a meaning and a purpose," she says. "Service changed my life for sure." As a high school senior, Barahona is planning a campaign at her school to raise awareness of the dropout crisis.[15]

Service-learning links educational objectives with community service activities. It can take many forms and occur in any setting:

- In a Chicago Public Schools Environmental Science course, students learned about biodiversity by reading about a variety of threats, including invasive species. Students visited a local forest preserve to study plant and animal life, including invasive species, spending part of the day clearing a prairie area of invasive buckthorn. The class decided to return to continue this work because they learned that native plants only flourish if invasive plants are contained. After the trip, the teacher guided students to consider various strategies to contain and control the introduction of invasive species.[16]

- Concerned about the number of students in her school who were reading below grade level, a Minnesota principal implemented a multigrade peer-tutoring program. Teachers trained every fourth-grader to be a tutor to a student in the primary grades whom teachers had identified as needing extra help with vocabulary development or reading fluency. Even those who struggled with reading were able to tutor younger students successfully, and in the process they strengthened their own reading skills and developed the confidence they needed to succeed in school.[17]

- Even kindergarteners can learn through service. To learn the letter Q, the teacher read students books that provided historical and cultural background on the origins of quilts and talked with them about how quilts relate to family traditions. They discussed the emotional and physical comfort a quilt can provide, and went on to create a quilt to comfort a baby living in a nearby shelter. The students used their imaginations and artistry to create quilt squares. The process culminated when the baby and mother visited the classroom and the children proudly presented their gift.[18]

- The Rural School and Community Trust developed a partnership with the National Oceanic and Atmospheric Administration for a pilot program that would provide academic benefits to students, learning opportunities for educators, and new connections between students and their communities. Students in two high schools in coastal Maine documented and preserved the rich knowledge and experiences of local fishermen for future generations, while promoting an unusual collaboration between fishermen and scientists on the health of the waters. A success, the project continued into a second year, with teachers aligning the project with local assessments and state standards. It was subsequently replicated in other waterfront communities.[19]

- To improve their language skills, students studying Spanish at East Tennessee State University spent twenty-five hours serving the community, translating materials for the Volunteer Income Tax Assistance program at a local veterans organization, preparing Spanish-language brochures for migrant workers, teaching elementary school students Spanish, and translating newspaper articles into Spanish.[20]

A growing body of research confirms that service-learning projects like these can help increase academic achievement, motivation, and important skills, as well as connection to community. Studies have found that service-learning leads to more engaged students and improves attendance, which leads to better educational outcomes including diploma attainment. These programs are linked with decreased disciplinary referrals and risk behaviors, and contribute to the development of young people's moral and civic identity. Several studies have also linked service-learning courses to better standardized test scores.[21]

Unfortunately, as schools increasingly focus on preparing for high-stakes tests and face constraints of both time and budgets, service-learning in schools may be declining. In 1999, service-learning was found in half of all secondary schools, and one-third of all K–12 public schools. By 2008, those numbers had declined to one-third and one-fourth, respectively.[22] Furthermore, schools in low-income areas are less likely than other schools to offer students either community service or service-learning opportunities.[23]

Making use of out-of-school time, such as summer vacation, may hold particular promise for engaging students in high-quality service experiences. And because of the critical nature of the middle school years, I am convinced a focus on students undergoing this important transitional period may be as beneficial developmentally as it is practical. Working families are often hard-pressed to pay for supervision for young teenagers during the summer, but government funding for child care programs focuses on younger age groups.

When Montgomery College designed a program to help struggling students finish high school and get a head start on college, it incorporated service-learning into the curriculum, initially because Montgomery County, Maryland, requires that students perform seventy-five hours of service-learning in order to graduate. But for Zita Nagy, the service-learning experience organized by the program gave her the motivation she needed to achieve in school. Before the program, she skipped school a lot, initially in order to work to help her family but later because school was "not a place where I felt motivated. I didn't see what the point was." A service-learning trip to the Red Wiggler Community Farm exposed her to a solar home, organic farming, and "community-supported agriculture" that provides produce to local food banks. As she planted seeds and harvested crops she "saw that by doing something little, I could make a big difference," she recalls. "I realized all the work that it takes to feed all the people on the planet." She was hooked. Additional service, including an "alternative spring break" trip to Philadelphia and the chance to help out in the program's office, convinced her that she wanted a career with a nonprofit. As she became more confident and purposeful, she began to choose more challenging classes, including math, which had always been hard for her. "In high school I tried to get as far away as possible from math. Now thinking about pre-calculus doesn't scare me." And she has not only completed enough service-learning hours to graduate, but is working toward a "Meritorious Certification" for exceeding 260 hours of service.

Source: Interview with Zita Nagy, July 31, 2009; Interview with Yvonne Hu-Cotto, July 28, 2009.

Summer school is often only for those who are struggling, not those who want to expand their horizons. Federal law prohibits young teens from working, and older teens have the highest unemployment rate of any age group. As a result, most young people making the difficult transition from middle to high school have no organized activities during periods when they are out of school, and many are left unsupervised, at risk of engaging in potentially harmful activities.

In many cultures, the transition from childhood into the teen years is marked by a rite of passage in which the young person engages deeply in learning and self-reflection, and takes on new "adult" responsibilities. For example, Jewish children at age thirteen are bar or bat mitzvahed; many Latina girls celebrate their fifteenth birthday with a Quinceañera; and in Africa, the young Masai men and women come of age at fifteen, taking on new responsibilities in their communities. These rites of passage are a central way in which groups of people pass on their values, culture, and history from generation to generation.

In this spirit, the National Indian Youth Leadership Project's Walking in Beauty supports young native girls in the transition from adolescence to womanhood. Based on a traditional Navajo ceremony, the program builds girls' resiliency and life skills, and includes both experiential learning and service. Girls experience cultural teachings from Native Elders; assist with preparations for ceremonies; learn the geology, biology, tribal, and pioneer history of the Grand Canyon while hiking a challenging trail into the gorge; and serve at the Navajo Tribal Zoo. According to NIYLP, Walking in Beauty "signifies the teachings of the traditional knowledge of a young adult: one who demonstrates a sense of mental, emotional, physical and spiritual balance is thought to be 'in well being,' and is thus prepared to embrace the transition into maturity. Walking in Beauty reflects the positive attitude and behaviors necessary for young women to successfully navigate this unique stage of life."[24]

While some young Americans experience such rites as part of their religious or cultural traditions, most do not. In our relatively young country, the establishment of a "Summer of Service" rite for young Americans of all backgrounds could help them find a sense of purpose at a pivotal age.

Imagine what such a rite might look like. At age thirteen, when young teens are leaving middle school for high school, they might spend four weeks of their summer engaged in an intensive service-learning project, working in teams led by older youths, young adults, or even community "elders." This service would be an expectation but not a requirement, and community groups might offer options that would appeal to a wide range of interests.

I was pleased that a "Summer of Service" demonstration program was included in the Edward M. Kennedy Serve America Act. While small, this program could be scaled up in the future to serve the needs of communities and young people across the United States. Developing a national system to enable all young people to participate in service as a rite of passage would be possible if the system were built on the existing infrastructure of service and youth programs. It could be integrated into summer camps, community-based youth organizations, youth corps, AmeriCorps programs, or schools interested in service-learning.

Over time, a summer of service before high school could become a rite of passage—enabling young people to enter their teenage years with a positive experience that reinforces their connections to the community, enlivens their education, and strengthens their personal and civic values. At the same time, communities across America might find an important new resource in their own backyards—young people who are ready to serve, if only they are asked.

TRANSITION TO PRODUCTIVE ADULTHOOD

I left high school when I was a sophomore. I was having a lot of trouble around that time. I see now that I was making a lot of wrong decisions, but I didn't see that at the time. My girlfriend got pregnant, and I dropped out. I started selling drugs and going on the streets—really going down the wrong path. Then I heard about YouthBuild. I needed my GED, and construction is something I'm very interested in, so I decided to join.... Before YouthBuild, I didn't know what I wanted to do with my life. I had no goals, no plans—I had nothing. If it was past next weekend when I was partying and in the street, I had no plans.

Now it's completely different, and YouthBuild did that for me. Now I actually have goals. When I finish the program, I want to do an apprenticeship and go to school full time at night and take courses on architecture or graphic design.... Now I go home so excited, I can't wait to tell my girlfriend and my mom what I did today. They're so happy for me, and I'm happy for me and proud of myself. This is what I was looking for, and this is what I needed.... I was so caught up in the streets and with all these people that claimed to be my friends, that I didn't really know what I was capable of and I didn't want to see it. Now that I'm away from all that, I actually see myself in the future and see what I'm capable of and what I can do with my life.

Manny Negron
YouthBuild student[25]

Before he joined YouthBuild, Manny Negron was typical of another group of young people in need of help making important life transitions: disconnected young adults who are neither in school nor employed. Many, like Negron, dropped out of high school or graduated without the skills for either college or a job. Some have had trouble with the law, are teen parents, or are substance abusers. And many without a pathway out will end up on public assistance, in jail, or addicted to drugs.

YouthBuild began in East Harlem in 1978, when founder Dorothy Stoneman asked a group of teenagers what they would do to improve the community if they had adult support. "We'd rebuild the houses. We'd take empty buildings back from the drug dealers and eliminate crime," they told her. Together, they and Stoneman renovated a tenement, and YouthBuild was born.

YouthBuild combines service building and renovating low-income housing with employment, education, mentoring, counseling, life skills, and leadership development to change the lives of sixteen- to twenty-four-year-old youths. YouthBuild students are low-income young adults facing multiple challenges:

- One out of three is a youthful offender.
- One in four is a parent.
- One in four is on public assistance.
- Nine out of ten lack a GED or high school diploma.
- They read on average at the seventh-grade level.
- Approximately one in ten has been in the foster care system.[26]

Their needs are complex. Most YouthBuild students have fared poorly in school and other programs that fail to provide a respectful, supportive climate for learning. Most are ineligible for the military, and many are ineligible for programs that exclude ex-offenders, require participants to live apart from their children, don't provide living expenses, or require a GED or diploma.

During the nine- to twenty-four-month full-time YouthBuild program, participants spend half of their time learning construction trade skills by building or rehabilitating housing for low-income people; increasingly, YouthBuild programs are practicing green construction and preparing their students for green jobs. The other half of their time is spent in a highly supportive YouthBuild classroom earning a high school diploma or equivalency degree. Students typically alternate a week in the classroom with a week on the construction site. YouthBuild is the only national program that puts equal emphasis on education and service-oriented employment training. Students also earn a modest living allowance to help support themselves and their families, and the opportunity for a Segal AmeriCorps Education Award to help pay for postsecondary education. Personal counseling, job and college placement, and training in life skills and financial management are provided, as are leadership development skills and opportunities. The students are a part of a community of caring adults and youths committed to each other's success and improving the conditions in their neighborhoods. Upon graduation, they become members of a supportive alumni network for a lifetime. YouthBuild USA continues to work with graduates who have shown leadership potential to create a pipeline into civic leadership in local communities and a voice in public policy for young adults who grew up poor.

It works. More than half of YouthBuild students who complete a program cycle receive their GED or diploma, and 76 percent are placed in jobs or go on to higher education. They earn an average wage of $8.60 per hour on exit. Fifteen percent enroll in community or four-year colleges. Years later, YouthBuild alumni stay on track. According to a Brandeis University study of eight hundred YouthBuild completers, within seven years after graduation 75 percent were either in postsecondary education or in jobs with an average wage of $10 per hour. Eighty-five percent were involved in community activities.[27]

YouthBuild is an example of a youth corps, broadly defined as a program that combines education, job skills training, and service to advance the development and life chances of teenagers and young adults. Typical youth corps organize members in teams or crews, guided by adult leaders or experienced corpsmembers. They may pay a modest living allowance and often enable youths to earn a GED or high school diploma. The most common service projects are in the field of conservation, but urban building and human service projects are also typical. Because of their service, many corpsmembers are eligible to earn a Segal AmeriCorps Education Award.

One group that seems particularly to benefit from the youth corps experience are youths who have been involved in the criminal justice system. The recidivism rate for YouthBuild graduates who were formerly convicted of felonies ranges from 5 to 22 percent in various studies, compared to a national rate of 67 percent rearrested and 51 percent reincarcerated within three years. A study of YouthBuild's re-entry program showed that every dollar spent on a court-involved YouthBuild student produced a value to society of at least $10.90, and up to $43.80. A study of court-involved or incarcerated youths who participated in the Civic Justice Corps, a program sponsored by the Corps Network at fourteen youth corps, found that this group's first-year outcomes included a recidivism rate of just 9 percent and a rate of 96 percent of retention in jobs or college placements.[28]

Such results are not surprising. Many young people turn to crime because they see no other alternative or have no goals. Service in youth corps helps youths see the importance of education—according to a longitudinal study of AmeriCorps, two-thirds reported this outcome; the numbers were even higher for African American, Latino, and disadvantaged participants.[29] By helping young people see a better future, youth corps can help them turn their lives around.

Youth corps are the modern-day incarnation of a program that once engaged millions of young men, in some cases saving them and their entire families from desperation during the Great Depression. Fulfilling a campaign promise from the 1932 election, President Franklin Delano Roosevelt created the Civilian Conservation Corps (CCC) by executive order as an emergency response to widespread unemployment. In March 1933, nearly fourteen million Americans were unemployed. Long "bread lines" fed the hungry, and two million young men drifted across the land in a futile search for jobs.[30]

The CCC had a second purpose—to conserve the nation's natural resources. Data from the period showed that although forests had once covered eight hundred million acres of land, only one hundred million acres remained forested in 1933. One-sixth of the fertile soil in the United States had been destroyed, and a third of it was in danger of destruction.

President Roosevelt had yet a third objective for the CCC: to advance the "moral and spiritual" well-being of the young men. "We can take a vast army of the unemployed out into healthful surroundings. We can eliminate to some extent at least the threat that enforced idleness brings to spiritual and moral stabilities."[31]

Ultimately three million young men served in the CCC, most at residential camps in the wilderness hundreds of miles from home. The average enrollee, according to promotional materials of the day, was twenty years old, underweight, unmarried, out of work for at least nine months, and from a family of six children with an unemployed father. A typical day began at six A.M., with work ending at four P.M., followed by dinner and, for some of the men, an evening of classes on a wide range of topics, including reading and writing, social courtesy, first aid, citizenship, and mechanics. They earned a $30 a month stipend, and most sent $25 of this home to their families.[32]

The CCC did not end the Depression—World War II did. But it sustained millions of families during this difficult time, and built many of America's treasured parks and monuments. From 1933 through 1942, the corps planted 2.5 billion trees, replanted 814,000 acres of grazing land, restocked 972 million fish, protected 154 million square yards of river banks and 40 million acres of farmland from erosion, built 125,000 miles of road and 13,100 of trails, strung 89,000 miles of telephone line, created 52,000 acres of campgrounds, built 800 state parks, and renovated nearly 4,000 historic buildings.[33]

To this day, former CCC members recall their experience with reverence. "The CCC was the starting point of my life and career," wrote Frank J. Kuhn Jr., who served in Flagstaff, Arizona.[34] "The CCC was a wonderful thing. You learned the value of money, and it helped you to become a man. You learned to do hard work and earn your keep," wrote Leonard Anglin.[35] In fact, one of my late friend Eli Segal's favorite stories to tell in the early days of AmeriCorps was of Mr. Ryan, an elderly man whom he met in a Philadelphia neighborhood while promoting the new national service program. As Eli told it, Mr. Ryan listened thoughtfully as Eli talked about the new program that would change lives as it changed neighborhoods for the better. Mr. Ryan then opened his wallet and pulled out a tattered identification card from his days in the CCC. He had carried it with him for more than half a century.

The CCC inspired the creation of modern-day youth corps, beginning with the Student Conservation Association in 1957 and followed by the California Conservation Corps in 1973 and a series of short-lived federal programs in the 1970s and 1980s. A 1997 Abt Associates–Brandeis University random assignment study confirmed the value of youth service and conservation corps for young people. According to the study, corps generate a positive return on investment; it documents that

- Significant employment and earnings gains accrue to young people who join a corps.
- Positive outcomes are particularly striking for African American men.
- Arrest rates drop by one third among all corpsmembers.
- Out-of-wedlock pregnancy rates drop among female corpsmembers.[36]

In 2009, twenty-six thousand young people served in 136 youth corps, from Alaska to Florida, supported by a diverse range of federal, state, and local public funds, along with private sector support.[37] However, this number is dramatically less than the number of those who served in the original CCC and far below the need for such opportunities.

Each year, one million young people leave school without graduating, including 50 percent of young people of color and those growing up in low-income communities. The low-income youths who have already dropped out of school without jobs not only face dim prospects for productive adulthood and a high likelihood of committing crimes or experiencing persistent unemployment, they are also likely to become young parents of children who will repeat the cycle. An estimated 1.4 to 5.2 million low-income youths ages sixteen to twenty-four are out of work and out of school, not currently incarcerated but nonetheless facing a desperate future. YouthBuild programs alone turn away fourteen thousand young people each year due to lack of funding. Furthermore, more than 1,800 community organizations submitted full applications to the federal government to run YouthBuild programs between 1996 and 2006 but three-quarters were turned down due to lack of funding. Other programs don't fill the gap.[38]

Many of these young people could benefit from the chance to build their skills while they find a life purpose, whether it is a career helping others or the chance to give their family a better life. As Jahi Davis put it, "Once I was part of YouthBuild, I could see what could be accomplished, and with the help of YouthBuild, I cut out all the negativity and replaced it with positive thoughts and objectives." Before the program he felt he was a victim of stereotypes, believing "no one would give me an opportunity as long as they knew I was from the ghetto." Through YouthBuild, Davis discovered he loved working with children and wanted to help people. He went on to get a bachelor's degree from Temple University and a master's degree from the University of Phoenix and become a consultant to youth programs.[39]

TRANSITION FROM COLLEGE TO CAREER

I'm a son of two refugees from Vietnam. After high school, I went to Pepperdine University and got a double major in economics and political science. Upon graduation, I decided to take a gap year before going back to get my M.S. in Accountancy and pursuing my dream of going into business. That was until I found City Year Los Angeles.

I currently serve as a Whole School Whole Child corps member at a school where 98 percent of the students are of Latino descent and over 90 percent of the students qualify for free or reduced lunch. In addition, 40 percent of these students are English language learners. More personally, my work there has revealed to me, in an intimate way, the challenges that students must face day in and day out. There is educational disparity that exists and it has been made very real to me.

The question is: how do we eliminate this disparity? I truly believe City Year is the answer. I've been working with these two 6th graders, Julissa and Virginia, for about 3 months.... When I was first introduced to them by Mr. C their teacher, he shared with me their scores on their most periodic assessment test. They weren't very good. Virginia received far below basic, the lowest marks one can receive. Julissa didn't do much better, scoring below basic. Because they were so far behind, we had to work twice as hard to catch them up. Mr. C allowed me to pull these girls out of class and take them to the library where I would mirror his lesson plan for the day and spend our extra time reviewing old concepts they were unfamiliar with. Over the past 3 months, their eagerness to learn has skyrocketed in conjunction with their quiz scores, because the personal attention I gave them helped them develop a solid foundation to build upon. Just this previous week, they took another periodic assessment and the results surprised both the girls and me. Virginia went from far below basic to proficient. That's a reason to celebrate and affirms my belief that City Year does work!

You know, after serving for about 6 months, I realize the extreme challenges that face our educational system. And I've decided to become a teacher. Growing up, I never considered a career path in education. However, City Year changed all that. My manager and mentor told me earlier this month, "Now that you have seen this disparity with your very own eyes, you will never forget. Now that you know, you have no right to fail." And you know what? I will not fail.

Kevin Diep
City Year Los Angeles[40]

Kevin Diep is typical of many AmeriCorps members who signed up expecting to spend a "gap year" before beginning their real career but discovered their real passion.

Most AmeriCorps members, like Kevin, are in their early to mid-twenties—a time when career choices loom large but meaningful jobs may be hard to come by. It's an age when many young adults struggle to find jobs that fit their goals, and unemployment rates are high (the highest for any group except teens).[41] Interest in a career typically begins in adolescence, and by the time young people reach their twenties, they should be trying out different options in search of the one that best fits their preferences and interests. However, many young adults are uncertain of their career interests, even after completing an undergraduate course of study. Still others are saddled with debt and constrained in their choices. And some have settled on careers that they think will please their families or offer them financial security, but may not provide them lasting satisfaction.

Some young adults join AmeriCorps to see a different side of America, or to give back before starting graduate school or a career. About half of the people who join AmeriCorps do so for job-related reasons—to gain new skills. These members report almost universally (99 percent) that their goal was met, and most alumni (91 percent) report that they have used the skills they learned since completing their term of service.[42] These skills include problem solving, listening to others, leading a team, negotiating, and managing time—the kinds of twenty-first-century skills rated highly by employers in almost every field.[43]

Corporate leaders point to volunteering as an effective strategy for even seasoned managers to develop new capabilities. "Learning occurs in a low-risk setting," according to Harvard Business School professor James Austin, whose study of the volunteer involvement of U.S. executives includes surveys of nearly ten thousand Harvard Business School graduates and of 316 CEOs of Fortune 500 companies.[44] A survey of professional women put leadership skills and communication skills at the top of the list of skills they developed through volunteering.[45] A Deloitte survey found that 86 percent of employed Americans said volunteering can have a positive impact on their careers. Nearly four out of five respondents (78 percent) see volunteering as an opportunity to develop business skills including decision making, problem solving, and negotiating.[46]

Over the past fifteen years, AmeriCorps has proven an effective means to channel those who serve into important jobs that experience shortages of workers—teaching, health care, youth work, nonprofit management, and other public service careers.

In 1999, the Corporation for National and Community Service set out to understand the impact of AmeriCorps on those who serve in it. To do so, it commissioned Abt Associates, a well-respected independent firm, to track the life experiences and attitudes of two groups of people: two thousand individuals who served in AmeriCorps in 2000–2001 and a similar number of individuals who applied to AmeriCorps but ultimately did not serve. In this way, the researchers could control for the likely possibility that those who are attracted to AmeriCorps already share certain characteristics that would make comparison to the general population, for example, unfairly skewed.

The researchers tracked the study participants for eight years after they completed their service. What they found makes a strong case for the power of service to change the lives of those who serve. AmeriCorps alumni were more engaged in their communities and felt more empowered and likely to take action to improve their communities. They were more likely to go into public service careers than the comparison group. And ultimately, they were more satisfied with their lives than their counterparts.[47]

Over the next decade, as the Baby Boomers retire, experts predict even more serious shortages in helping fields. The nonprofit sector will lose more than 50 percent of its current leadership, requiring 640,000 new leaders. The federal government needs to hire more than 270,000 workers for "mission-critical" jobs over the next three years, according to the results of a government-wide survey. At least 23 percent of the public health workforce, nearly 110,000 workers, will be eligible to retire during the next presidential term. And by 2020, we will need an additional 250,000 public health workers.[48] Today's young adults can fill those positions. While ensuring that America has the helping workforce it needs, an investment in full-time service can help young people find the opportunities that will make their calling their career.

TRANSITION FROM CAREER TO RETIREMENT

"This is part of my dream in life: to do something for so many who are affected by this terrible disease," says Gladys Schmidt Roy, an RSVP volunteer. She became interested in helping patients with memory loss after caring for her husband, Hank, who had a family history of Alzheimer's. In the years since Hank's death, Gladys, eighty-five, has been visiting several nursing homes a week, bringing friendship and homemade cookies to the residents. During her visits, Gladys noticed that patients' memories could be jogged to recall things from the past. One woman would hardly say a word during Gladys's visits, until the day Gladys reminisced about going downtown on the streetcar each spring to buy an Easter bonnet at a popular store. The woman suddenly came to life, and talked excitedly about how she used to enjoy doing the same thing.

Gladys found research that backed up her observation: exposure to things that are personally meaningful can draw the person out of the patient. Then she developed a plan to put together memory books using historical photos of local landmarks. Despite a setback caused by a serious fall, Gladys finished selecting the fifty photos to go in each book, and is excited about putting the books together. "I'm slower, I'm older, but I'm not dead yet," she says. "I'm going to keep it up."[49]

The value of service for older adults has long been understood. In fact, long before Ethel Percy Andrus founded AARP in 1958, she wrote that older adults "have a responsibility to remain active in retirement, . . . to cooperate with responsible . . . agencies concerned with programs and activities that will make our nation strong." She founded AARP with the motto "To Serve, Not to Be Served" and argued that "we learn the inner secret of happiness when we learn to direct our inner drives, our interest and our attention to something outside ourselves." The first U.S. Commissioner on Aging, William

Bechill, honored her vision, noting "Dr. Andrus was one of the first to realize that our nation was neither seriously facing the question of meaningful use of the retirement years nor concerned enough with a place of respect and purpose for older people in the world around us."[50]

Research has borne out Andrus's notion that service is central to healthy aging. A study of Experience Corps, profiled in Chapter Four, found that compared with a control group, the older volunteers in the tutoring program had better overall health, including strength, cognitive ability, and physical activity levels. They also watched less television and had a bigger social network than the seniors in the control group.[51]

Numerous studies confirm that individuals who volunteer are happier and healthier than those who don't. Volunteers have improved mental health, including less depression than those who don't serve others. While younger volunteers also receive health benefits from volunteering, volunteers age sixty and older benefit more greatly. Studies also suggest that the "volunteering threshold" to receive significant health benefits is forty to a hundred hours per year or volunteering with two or more organizations.[52]

Studies point to the likely reasons for this link: the personal sense of purpose and accomplishment and stronger social networks that are built through service buffer stress and reduce disease risk.[53] So for people like Gladys Schmidt Roy and Doris Thomas, service becomes not just a nice thing to do but central to their long-term health. Work can also play this role, as expert Marc Freedman points out in *Encore: Finding Work That Matters in the Second Half of Life*. But even when it comes to work, "helping people" is a "very important" factor in work plans.[54] The list of the top ten most popular post-retirement occupations includes teaching, nursing, and child care—fields with chronic shortages that could well benefit from the growing population of older workers. In their late work years, people "want work that is personally fulfilling, work that makes a difference in the world," according to Freedman.[55] To offer them role models, Freedman invented the "Purpose Prize," which offers $100,000 each year to five social innovators who started their new projects after the age of fifty.

The National Council on Aging's "RespectAbility" project seeks to achieve similar ends—to promote efforts by local organizations to develop entrepreneurial approaches to attract and support adults fifty-five and older to fill important leadership roles. Its first round of award winners included a dozen creative approaches to this challenge.[56]

The time is right for ideas like these. In 2006, the first of nearly seventy-six million boomers turned sixty. Every day another eight thousand people join them, a demographic trend that will accelerate through the 2020s. By 2030, nearly one in four Americans will be over sixty. They can expect to live another twenty to twenty-five years, far longer than the life expectancies of Americans in the 1930s, when Social Security was created. We could think of older adults as a drain on society, a group requiring support. But it's better to turn that thinking on its head, close the "purpose gap," and benefit from the important resource experienced adults represent. And in so doing, we will improve the mental and physical health of a population that has much to give.

TRANSITION FROM CRISIS TO COPING

Ken Thompson's mother died in the bombing of the Oklahoma City federal building. She was the last person identified in the rubble, more than six weeks after the event. According to Michele Turk's history of the Red Cross, *Blood, Sweat and Tears,* Thompson made two promises to himself: "To make my mom proud of me every day, and to give back to the people who helped us." To fulfill those promises, he helped to form the National Memorial Institute for the Prevention of Terrorism, including an outreach committee of family members who would be able to help others if another attack occurred. A few years later, when the twin towers of the World Trade Center fell, Thompson led a delegation from Oklahoma City to New York to volunteer with the Red Cross, returning twenty-five times in the three years after 9/11. "We weren't there trying to fix anyone. . . . What we really wanted them to know was that they would make it through this some day, but each of them had to find their own path." When he was honored for his efforts in 2005 by the President's Council on Service and Civic Participation, Thompson noted, "I have a huge desire to give back and it's incredibly healing to do so."[57]

Ken Thompson's compulsion to deal with his grief by helping others is a story that is part of the history of many helping efforts today. Mothers Against Drunk Driving; the Adam Walsh Child Resource Center (which later merged with the National Center for

Missing and Exploited Children); My Good Deed, founded to make 9/11 a national day of service; and dozens of other organizations were all created in the wake of personal tragedies by family members wanting something good to come of the loss of loved ones. Bold efforts like these, or more modest volunteer service during the recovery process after a death, divorce, or other adverse circumstance, are understood to be an effective way for people to deal with their grief.

In *The Healing Power of Doing Good*, author Allan Luks documented this phenomenon. Luks opens with the story of Randee Russell, who as a senior in college saw her boyfriend die in a car wreck. She spent the first year after his death in denial, imagining that it was all an elaborate joke. Then for the next twenty years she would spend long periods preoccupied with death. "For months at a time and longer she would think that she had fully recovered, until some trigger, perhaps the sight of a highway accident, would bring it all up again, and again her days would be interrupted by split-second fantasies of her own destruction, her nights haunted by dreams that Michael was still alive."[58] And then, at age thirty-nine, Russell decided to volunteer for Hospice of Los Angeles. Her experience helping an elderly woman with terminal lung cancer through her final months pushed aside her terrible fantasies. "By helping another person face death she helped herself most of all," writes Luks.[59]

Why does this work? Luks, examining the results of a national survey, explains that most people experience a "helper's high" after serving, followed by a sense of calmness. This in turn causes people to feel, and in fact, become healthier. Luks concludes that "[r]egular helping of others can diminish the effects of disabling chronic pain and lessen the symptoms of physical distress. And it can ease the tension of able-bodied people who are overworked and living in stressful times."[60] Research by Suzanne Kobasa, a psychologist at the Graduate School of the City University of New York, confirms the link between handling stress and a commitment to a larger mission. Kobasa studied executives at Illinois Bell during the stressful three-and-a-half years when it broke off from AT&T and found that executives who combined the following attitudes were the least likely to become ill: (1) they felt control over their own fate, (2) they viewed the tasks they faced as a challenge, and (3) *they felt a strong sense of commitment to some overriding purpose.*[61] Other studies similarly suggest a strong link between volunteering and the recovery of people who experience mental illness.[62]

When officials at the Angola state prison in Louisiana recognized that the large number of "lifers"—three out of four inmates at the facility—would in many cases one day need hospice care, they recruited volunteers from among the prison population to help meet inmates' end-of-life needs. According to a *USA Today* profile of the program, inmates are taught basic hospice practices and how to counsel a dying inmate. An added bonus: not only are dying prisoners able to receive care, the inmate volunteers experience their own transformation, learning compassion and redefining their lives. Noted one volunteer serving a life sentence for two murders, "This program has brought me to my own existence, my own humanity.... When I was young I didn't care about nothing. This gives me something to care about."

Source: R. Jervis, "Inmates Help in Prison Hospices," *USA Today,* November 30, 2009, 3A.

The Mission Continues recognizes the importance of continued service by a group of Americans who have already sacrificed greatly for the good of others: wounded veterans. One would hardly think these individuals should be asked to give more. But The Mission Continues disagrees, understanding the value of service to help these men and women rebuild their lives.

Consider the story of Army Staff Sergeant Sonia Meneses, whose truck was hit with an explosive device and whose convoy was attacked on additional occasions during her two deployments to Iraq. While Meneses did not seem to sustain significant wounds, during her second deployment she was medically evacuated after losing consciousness several times. Eventually, she was diagnosed with Ménière's Disease—an abnormality of the inner ear that causes dizziness, vertigo, tinnitus, hearing loss, and pain—and was medically retired from the Army with complete hearing loss in one ear and 60 percent hearing loss in the other.

At home, Meneses endured periodic spells of extreme dizziness, loss of consciousness, and seizure-like symptoms. For two years, her lifestyle was extremely limited, and she rarely left the house. In June 2008, Meneses decided that she would no longer allow her disabilities to hold her back. She applied for a fellowship through The Mission Continues, a nonprofit project that enables disabled veterans to continue serving others through volunteer and civic engagement.

Meneses was awarded a fellowship with Big Brothers Big Sisters of Clarksville, Tennessee. At BBBS she volunteered forty hours each week, helping with administrative tasks and working with children, including a "little sister" of her own, taking time off only for surgery to correct her balance difficulties. Less than a week after the surgery she was back at BBBS volunteering ten to twelve hours per day. Since completing her fellowship, Meneses continues to volunteer for BBBS on a less intense schedule. Her civilian service helped her triumph over her disease, and she pledges to remain a "big sister" as long as she is needed.[63]

While it may seem counterintuitive, even unfair, to think that people who have sacrificed so much for their country ought to do more, the case of Meneses and countless people like her suggest the opposite: that an important part of the healing process is finding renewed purpose through service to others. The Edward M. Kennedy Serve America Act makes veterans a target community for AmeriCorps-style positions, a policy that may help many more people who are suffering as a result of their military service to rebuild their lives.

POTENTIAL FOR TRANSFORMATION

There are many ways that volunteer service benefits those who serve. Service can

- Reinforce academic learning and motivate students to increase their effort.
- Build skills such as teamwork and leadership or specific competencies such as carpentry or horticulture that are useful in the job market and other aspects of life.
- Offer opportunities to make friends and develop other social ties.
- Expose people to career options, enabling them to make better choices and professional connections.
- Improve physical and mental health.

Underlying many of these benefits is the opportunity to develop a sense of purpose and means to achieve it. Having a purpose is as important for youths making choices about their futures as it is for people rebuilding their lives after a crisis or older adults finding a way to make their retirement years meaningful. Service is not the only path to purpose, but it is a well-walked one that can help Americans of all ages and backgrounds transform their own lives for the better.

CHAPTER THREE

Strengthening Civic Engagement

C ynthia Gentry thought a new playground would be a fitting way to memorialize her next-door neighbors—a mom and her two young children who were killed in an automobile accident. After consulting the grief-stricken father, she teamed with other friends and neighbors who wanted some good to come of the tragedy. But where to begin? Gentry knew that the playground that the young family had once frequented was in terrible shape, with moldy plastic equipment and mud-covered ground, and thought that fixing up the space would be an appropriate tribute. Gentry searched the Web, found the KaBOOM! online playground planner, and used the Do-It-Yourself tools to help organize the project. Gentry led hundreds of community members who raised funds, solicited donated materials and worked together to build a new place to play. Seven months later, the emotional grand opening of the park, which featured a fire truck, playground equipment for both younger and older children, gardens, and a memorial sculpture, drew more than five hundred community members.

As a result of this experience, Gentry "fell in love with the power of community." She kept in close touch with KaBOOM! and became a strong advocate for play. She became one of the most active "Playmakers" in the KaBOOM! National Campaign for Play; helped teach others playground-building skills; enlisted the support of Atlanta Mayor Shirley Franklin in programming for play; and rallied her city to become an official Playful City USA community, creating a new advocacy group, the Atlanta Taskforce on Play. When budget cuts were proposed for Parks and Recreation Department funding, she led the charge to restore the funds. In her role as playground champion, Gentry works tirelessly to bring play to Atlanta's children.[1]

————

The path that Cynthia Gentry took, from volunteer to civic activist, is well-traveled.

Our democracy depends on robust civic participation. Volunteer service is one form. So are engagement in the political process—from voting to volunteering in a campaign or running for office—and participating in community or civic organizations. Pursuing a public service career is often counted, and so is policy advocacy—sharing views, persuading others, and even lobbying a policymaker. All of these kinds of actions make up a civically engaged community, and numerous studies document that civic engagement points to heightened social capital, which in turn leads to higher educational achievement, better-performing government institutions, faster economic growth, and less crime and violence.[2] Many advocates have supported federal investment in service because they believe that people who serve will ultimately become civically involved in other ways, even if they do not engage in these activities as part of their service.

These advocates are right, to a degree. The civic outcomes of volunteer and national service take many forms (Table 3.1). Some volunteers, such as Cynthia Gentry, go on to become advocates in the public arena. Many are the PTA moms who move from volunteer to PTA president and eventually to school board candidate. It's easy to find former members of VISTA (Volunteers in Service to America)—and increasingly, AmeriCorps alumni—among today's nonprofit leaders and community activists. Some have run for office. Still others are reformers, tackling challenges through a wide variety of strategies including starting their own innovative nonprofits or inventing new methods to solve problems. When addressing a group

Type	Examples
Democratic participation	Voting, volunteering for political candidates, or advocating for policy change
Public service careers	Working in a government or nonprofit job
Community engagement	Participating in a neighborhood group or staying abreast of issues that affect the community
Personal responsibility	Doing the right thing
Continued service	Long-term volunteering
Forging diverse ties	Learning to connect with people of different backgrounds

Table 3.1.   Examples of the Civic Outcomes of Service.

of nonprofit leaders, I have often asked AmeriCorps, VISTA, and Peace Corps alumni to raise their hands, and end up seeing half of the room waving enthusiastically.

Other civic outcomes are more subtle but no less important to our democracy. Studies have tied service to voting, or to activities such as attending public meetings or writing letters to the editor. Some kinds of service are linked to open-mindedness, and respecting people of different racial, religious, or ethnic backgrounds. And those who serve are more likely to continue to volunteer throughout their lives, demonstrating an ongoing commitment to the betterment of their community.

Engaged citizens are essential to the transformation equation. The supply of both organized and informal volunteers depends on people stepping forward in a spirit of personal responsibility and community commitment. Public awareness of community problems and assets will lead to better problem-solving organizations and more-informed public agendas. Stronger citizen participation can create the leaders we need to create the change we need and the voters to support it.

SERVICE AND CIVIC ENGAGEMENT

Service can help bring about a transformation of the civic fabric of our country, and prominent supporters of national service consider this linkage to be the most important reason for public support of service programs. The desire to strengthen citizenship has been a driving force behind federal service policy for over fifty years. If Franklin Roosevelt's CCC of the 1930s was a jobs program with a secondary focus on conservation and education, John Kennedy's call to "[a]sk not what your country can do for you, ask what you can do for your country" spoke to citizen responsibility first and foremost.

When, nearly three decades after President Kennedy created the Peace Corps, the Democratic Leadership Council (DLC) issued a ground-breaking national service proposal, it called it "a novel blueprint for reviving the American tradition of civic obligation and activism."[3] The proposal argued that "a strong ethic of civic obligation—of equal sacrifice for the common good—is integral to the success and survival of a free society." The DLC went on to suggest that a broad-scale program of national service would "profoundly alter the character of our society" by breaking down social barriers and bringing Americans of different backgrounds into closer and more frequent contact with each other" and "build social solidarity and counteract forces in our pluralistic culture that engender anomie and alienation."[4]

Toward this end, the DLC's 1988 proposal featured a comprehensive plan that would extend G.I. Bill benefits to include civilian as well as military service to the nation. In return for one or two years of service at subsistence wages in either the military or civilian service, young enlistees would earn vouchers worth substantial federal aid for college, vocational or job training, or housing. Under the proposal, national service vouchers would replace existing grants and loans as the primary source of federal aid to students.

People for the American Way, another organization that actively promoted service legislation in the late 1980s, was also moved by a concern for civic activism. Alarmed by declining voter participation among young adults, it had assembled the Advisory Commission on Democracy's Next Generation, co-chaired by Hillary Clinton, then a law firm partner, and commissioned a study by Peter Hart and Associates. This 1989 study confirmed the skeptical cynicism many young people had toward the values that underpin democracy in America. For example, when a focus group of non-voters aged eighteen to twenty-four were asked to name some qualities that made this country special, "the young people sat in silence until one young man offered, 'Cable TV.' Asked how to encourage more young people to vote, one young woman replied, 'Pay them.'" Among the initiatives proposed by People for the American Way to respond to this perceived crisis was a range of voter registration reforms and programs, along with community service in schools. The study concluded that "[t]hose who have participated in community service activities gain a strengthened sense of investment in civic life" and recommended that all students "participate in a service project as a requirement for high school graduation."[5]

These ideas laid the groundwork for the National and Community Service Act of 1990, the first purpose of which was to "renew the ethic of civic responsibility in the United States."

Running for president a few years later, the DLC's former chair, Governor Bill Clinton, made national service a prominent part of his campaign. While his stump speeches tended to emphasize educational opportunity—the chance to earn money for college in exchange for a year or two of full-time service—his post-election speeches spoke to civic values. When he signed the legislation that created the AmeriCorps program and the Corporation for National and Community Service, he underscored the legislation's potential "to rebuild the American community" by helping "to strengthen the cords that bind us together as a people."[6]

In their campaigns, President Obama and Senator John McCain also focused on civic obligation in their respective calls for expanded national service. McCain's earlier writings on service, including a *Washington Monthly* article written shortly after the 9/11 tragedy, argued that conservatives should support national service because it strengthens civil society, "the rich web of neighborhood, nonprofit, and faith-based groups outside of government that provide services to those in need." He spoke to the opportunity to increase "patriotic service to the nation" by expanding AmeriCorps, noting that those who have served in the program "have begun to glimpse the glory of serving the cause of freedom. They have come to know the obligations and rewards of active citizenship."[7]

Candidate Obama similarly invoked these themes. "Loving your country shouldn't just mean watching fireworks on the 4th of July. Loving your country must mean accepting your responsibility to do your part to change it," he told the students at the University of Colorado. When President Obama signed the Serve America Act, he spoke to its ability to "harness this patriotism" of Americans who want to do their part.[8]

Today's push for universal service comes largely from this place ... the idea that the rights of citizenship ought to be accompanied by responsibilities, such as a required year or two of full-time service.

For example, ServiceNation describes its vision as "an America where citizens unite to take responsibility for strengthening communities and building a better future, and where service is a core ideal of citizenship." The American Jewish Committee, calling for "universally available" national service for eighteen- to twenty-five-year-olds, stressed that "a national commitment to voluntary service would link the rights and privileges of being American with a clear sense of responsibility."[9] And the editors of *Time* magazine, advocating for universal national service, lamented that "the two central acts of democratic citizenship are voting and paying taxes" and suggested that "the way to get citizens involved in civic life, the way to create a common culture that will make a virtue of our diversity, the way to give us that more capacious sense of 'we'—finally the way to keep the Republic—is universal national service."[10]

Rahm Emanuel, the former congressman who went on to serve as President Obama's chief of staff, and his coauthor Bruce Reed, formerly President Clinton's domestic policy adviser, similarly pointed to civic outcomes when they called for universal citizen service in their book *The Plan*. Recalling President Kennedy's call to the nation, Emanuel and Reed suggested that "[w]hile the rights of citizenship are explicit in our Constitution, the implicit responsibilities are every bit as crucial." They suggest that all Americans between the ages of eighteen and twenty-five be required to go serve their country by going through three months of basic training, civil defense preparation, and community service. Among the benefits they expect to see from this charge is the opportunity to bring "people of vastly different backgrounds together to serve side by side and find common ground with a common purpose."[11]

HOW SERVICE HELPS

The powerful advocates described in the previous section have high expectations for the ability of service to strengthen American democracy. But their visions won't be realized without better alignment of intended outcomes and program designs. Not every service experience, even those that are full time, results in more robust participation in democratic processes. Certain types of service experiences in fact do lead to greater civic participation and unity in our diverse nation. But these outcomes take many forms and do not result with consistency from every service experience. It seems clear that while in some cases civic outcomes flow organically from a service experience, those programs that seek to achieve specific results are more likely to achieve them than are those that are less intentional.

For example, as discussed in other chapters, service often leads participants to pursue public service jobs or become social entrepreneurs. Both of these career paths are natural extensions of a strong commitment to improve the community. Although the AmeriCorps longitudinal study found that AmeriCorps members are more likely than a comparison group to pursue public service careers, Public Allies, a full-time AmeriCorps program whose main purpose is to develop diverse young leaders, has found that more than 80 percent of its alumni go on to work in the nonprofit and public sectors—a percentage far exceeding that of the average AmeriCorps program.[12]

Similarly, service helps to build an ethic of personal responsibility or good character, values that underlie strong communities. When experts researched strategies for "character education," they found that service-learning resulted in such outcomes as altruism, caring, respect, and the ability to tell right from wrong.[13] Other studies have come to similar conclusions, finding that service-learning helps students develop ethics, such as a willingness to stand up for what is right and a sense of responsibility for others.[14] These programs typically involve students in planning their service activities and reflecting on their experiences—the core components of a high-quality service-learning program—and may be used as a strategy that is part of a larger curriculum aimed at promoting personal responsibility.[15]

Connection to community and continued volunteering are also considered civic outcomes of service programs. For example, college students who volunteer are more likely to serve in the future than those who do not. The AmeriCorps longitudinal study found that alumni were more connected to their communities and had a greater understanding of local problems than a comparison group. They also were likely to continue to serve after their terms of service ended, with nearly three-fourths volunteering. In addition, those individuals who had not volunteered before AmeriCorps were more civically engaged than those who expressed interest in AmeriCorps but ultimately did not serve, with a twenty-five percent difference in their rates of volunteering.[16]

Another civic rationale for national service is its ability to connect individuals from diverse backgrounds with one another. This long-standing rationale for national service, articulated by many of the early advocates, has been coming into greater focus as the country becomes increasingly diverse, with white Americans expected to become a minority in America by 2050.[17] Recent research by Robert Putnam, well-known for his work on the decline of civic engagement described in *Bowling Alone*,[18] suggests that the more diverse a community is, the less people care about and engage with that community, breeding distrust and disengagement. He calls it "hunkering down" and suggests that such a withdrawal from community means less confidence in government, lower voter turnout, less volunteering, less happiness, fewer friends, and more time spent watching television. Few institutions today bridge diverse communities, and Americans are increasingly segregated where they live, study, worship, and play. Putnam suggests that national service that intentionally connects individuals from different backgrounds could be an antidote to these pathologies.[19]

City Year has been one of the most successful national service organizations to take on this challenge by creating truly diverse teams of corpsmembers. Each team of eight is internally diverse; a single team might include a high school dropout from the inner city, a student taking a "gap year" on her way to the Ivy League, an immigrant or refugee youth, and a recent college graduate uncertain of his future career. While recruiting a diverse corps takes time and resources, City Year points to this aspect of its program as critical to its goal of "uniting young people of all backgrounds." In fact, more

Joe Staszak-Rodriguez and Joe Andolina are two City Year alumni who could not have been more different. Joe S. grew up in a Puerto Rican neighborhood in North Philadelphia. A convicted crack dealer, he learned about City Year when he was under house arrest and pursued it as a way to cut short his sentence. Joe A. grew up in New Jersey and graduated from Princeton University. He looked to City Year as a do-good stop on his way to law school. When they found themselves on the same City Year team, serving in a Philadelphia elementary school in Joe S.'s neighborhood, they viewed each other with suspicion. But by serving side by side for a year, they came to appreciate each other.

Joe A. recalls Joe S.'s ability to "fit in with any group, to listen, and somehow emerge as a leader." Joe S. thought Joe A.'s leadership empowered him to think he could do anything; as he reflected on his fellow corps members' reasons for joining City Year, he said, "That's where I think my spark came in; I realized that I hadn't been living up to my full potential.... That's when I realized I actually wanted to do another year of service."

than 90 percent of alumni reported that their City Year experience contributed to their ability to work as part of a team and with people from diverse backgrounds.[20]

Project SHINE offers another model for bridging social divides and advancing civic outcomes. Through Project SHINE, students at San Francisco State University, the City College of San Francisco, and other higher education institutions across the country help older immigrants learn English and prepare for the citizenship exam, using a model developed by the Intergenerational Center at Temple University. Most students participate through a course such as anthropology, foreign language, political science, or sociology, and spend at least twenty hours tutoring during a semester. With support from Learn and Serve America and other funders, Project SHINE has engaged more than nine thousand students in service to almost forty thousand immigrants. Civic outcomes, however, are not limited to the older learners—the college students demonstrated significant increases in civic skills and knowledge of U.S. immigration compared with a group of similar students who did not participate. They also

Joe S. and Joe A. discovered they had much in common. Joe A. recalls that "before City Year, I thought that diversity was only about appearance. But being on a City Year team forces you to make decisions and build consensus only after taking into account the viewpoints of people who only months before, you thought you had nothing in common with. Through City Year, you realize, however, that you have more in common with people than you think." Joe S. agrees. "City Year put Joe and me in a unique position to learn from each other. We were from total opposite walks of life, you know, but we were put into service together." He credits the program with his new outlook, to build and not destroy: "City Year for me was a reciprocal change; while I was out there trying to help change things, City Year helped change my life."

Today Joe S. attends college and works for City Year as a recruitment manager and Joe A. is an attorney with a Philadelphia law firm. They remain good friends.

Source: Bradley Center for Philanthropy and Civic Renewal, Hudson Institution, Transcript, *Preventing Failure to Launch: Is Service a Path to Purpose?* Washington, DC, May 15, 2008; email from George Deveney to Shirley Sagawa, May 15, 2009, supplying quotations.

report increased appreciation for people of a different culture and age, whom they would likely not have met without the program.[21]

POLITICAL ACTIVISM

A long-standing hope—and concern—regarding national service has been whether it leads to increased political activity—from voting to political organizing. We had been pushed hard to allow AmeriCorps members to engage in advocacy, as part of their service, in order to address the root causes of problems. If it is more effective to end homelessness by lobbying the mayor for more programs, why shouldn't AmeriCorps members play this role rather than dish out soup in a shelter? We were sympathetic. However, Congress would not have allowed this—the idea that federal dollars would support protests, union organizing (or union busting), partisan political activity, or lobbying would have quickly killed the program. We expressly prohibited these activities in the regulations governing the program and believe this has been a major reason for AmeriCorps's bipartisan support and long-term success.

Conservative critics have often claimed that AmeriCorps members are being trained to be Democratic operatives and frequently point to an AmeriCorps grant made to the ACORN Housing Corporation in 1994; that grant, however, was quickly discontinued after the inspector general reported that the organization could not guarantee its AmeriCorps members would not be involved with ACORN, which engages in advocacy activities and other practices that cannot be supported with AmeriCorps funds.[22]

Ironically, political activity may be the weakest civic outcome associated with national service and volunteering, according to studies showing little direct connection between the two. In the case of AmeriCorps, some people speculate that a reason for this disconnect is a ban on AmeriCorps members' engaging in voter registration, partisan political activity, or advocacy on behalf of legislation. Another possibility is that AmeriCorps members have an intense experience that exposes them to dire problems which they then address largely through direct service. They believe in the efficacy of their efforts, and possibly see volunteering—helping individuals one-on-one—as a preferred alternative to political solutions.

However, this disconnect also occurs outside of AmeriCorps, with volunteers who are not restricted in their political activity.

Observing that volunteering is near an all-time high while confidence in democracy and government are near an all-time low, Richard Stengel of *Time* argued that "People, especially young people, think the government and the public sphere are broken, but they feel they can personally make a difference through community service. After 9/11, Americans were hungry to be asked to do something, to make some kind of sacrifice, and what they mostly remember is being asked to go shopping. The reason private volunteerism is so high is precisely that confidence in our public institutions is so low. People see volunteering not as a form of public service but as an antidote for it."[23] Cynthia Gibson, writing for the Case Foundation, concurred, arguing that as Americans feel more isolated and distrustful of public institutions, they turn to activities such as volunteering and charitable giving "that may be less an impetus for deeper civic engagement than attempts to assuage the inchoate yet palpable sense among increasing numbers of Americans that things are spiraling out of control."[24]

These two forms of civic engagement—volunteering and political activism—need not be cast as alternatives. In fact, there is evidence that well-designed service programs can promote civic participation in all its forms, including political action. For example, young people who discuss their volunteer experiences with others are twice as likely as others to volunteer regularly. And, they are also 16 percentage points more likely to try to influence someone's vote.[25] The AmeriCorps longitudinal study found that by a wide margin, AmeriCorps members have greater confidence in their ability to work with local government to address community problems than the comparison group.[26]

The Adopt-An-Alleyway Youth Empowerment Project is an example of a program that connects service to participation in the democratic process. In 1991, the Chinatown Community Development Center (CDC) created the program as part of its strategy to improve San Francisco's Chinatown. The CDC envisioned the youth program as a creative means of using Chinatown's forty-one alleyways, many of which serve as pedestrian paths, recreational space, and front streets for businesses, as a training ground for future community activism. While the youths did clean up the alleys, ridding them of graffiti and trash, they also developed and led tours of neighborhoods, after conducting historical research and interviews with elderly residents.[27]

Early surveys of youth participants were promising, suggesting that the program built leadership skills, public speaking ability, and self-confidence, while "breaking down stereotypes and giving students a stronger sense of identity and commitment to the community." The experience "got me interested in Asian American studies," wrote one student participant. "I had no idea that racism was such an issue and the impact it had in communities." "I am still going to be in business; however, I plan to use a portion of my money to help my community," wrote another. "Perhaps I'll even run for political office in the future."[28] Years later, the program is still going strong, and the teens are taking proactive roles on policy issues of importance to the neighborhood. For example, when a proposition to expand public transportation was proposed, the teens set up a booth at a street fair at which they collected more than five thousand signatures in support of the initiative, which they hoped would connect Chinatown with Visitacion Valley, which also had a large Chinese population. Although the students were too young to vote themselves, they were able to play a part in the successful effort. They have gone on to become active participants in the planning for the Central Subway, weighing in on issues that concern them, including the design of the new station and how it would affect light in a local schoolyard.[29]

As this example illustrates, policymakers and program leaders would do well to target youths if they seek to encourage long-term political engagement. Studies uniformly show that adults who participated in service projects as youths are more likely to vote and to join community organizations than are adults who were nonparticipants during high school. Service opportunities should start at a young age, before high school. Disadvantaged youths and immigrant groups who have less access to service opportunities should receive special focus. However, programs for students have received far less investment than programs for adults even though they are likely to pay a far higher return on investment. As funding for service grows, programs for school-aged youths ought to receive an increasing share of the pie.

POTENTIAL FOR TRANSFORMATION

Service offers a powerful first step onto the path to other forms of civic engagement, which can be accelerated with thoughtful enhancements. The path to civic activism typically begins with exposure to public problems.[30] Service serves the purpose of making real otherwise abstract problems—such as poverty or school inequality—that can motivate action. Incorporating opportunities for individuals and groups to reflect on their service experiences can enable them to see beyond immediate problems to think about their root causes. Without such introspection and analysis, a volunteer might easily believe the solution to hunger is to collect canned goods and serve free meals to the homeless, rather than thinking about what causes poverty and what broader solutions might bring about change, including those rooted in public policy.

A second step on the path is for a person to develop the capabilities he or she needs to make a difference. Volunteers typically will develop knowledge of ways to use service to address problems but also could learn other skills such as community organizing, which is often used in service, or advocacy, which can be supported by teaching public speaking, writing letters to the editor, and other tactics used to influence people.

Finally, effective civic participants need civic connections—they need to know others who can serve as role models and colleagues to support their efforts. An important role that any service program can play is to increase the social capital of its participants by introducing them to a wide range of role models and building ties among participants and others in the community.

In short, there is every reason to think that civic engagement outcomes can be achieved through service *if* programming is incorporated that builds civic skills beyond volunteering as well as connections to civic role models. Service need not be a fork in the road, leading away from political engagement. With thoughtful program design, it may be a path that leads to deeper engagement in our democracy.

However, service is not the only way to increase civic engagement; in fact many factors contribute to people's decisions to act. An inspiring youthful African American presidential candidate brought out young and African American voters in unprecedented numbers. Hurricane Katrina set the entire nation into action, collecting used clothing, raising money, and organizing van pools to New Orleans. The attacks of September 11, 2001, inspired millions of people to volunteer or join the military. World War II and Vietnam defined two generations and spurred civic activism—albeit in very different forms.

America is in a different place than it was two decades ago when the push for national service began in earnest. The last presidential election broke records for turnout, in high contrast to the low levels of the 1980s. Volunteering rates continue to creep upward, after peaks following the major disasters of the last decade. New technology tools make it easier to organize others for civic action, and to educate oneself about local issues and opportunities.

On the other hand, growing distrust of institutions and social isolation pose significant risks to our democracy. Lack of civic discourse leaves citizens vulnerable to negative campaigns, and partisan polarization leaves policy progress stalled. And while volunteering has increased, large populations of low-income and less educated Americans serve at much lower rates than their more advantaged counterparts.

Service in its many forms remains an important strategy to engage Americans to solve our problems—no matter what challenges the future may hold. It will have far greater impact, however, if programs define carefully the kind of engagement they seek and incorporate elements that will support this outcome. Organized service programs of all sorts can incorporate civic skill-building along with direct service to increase the resulting citizen engagement outcomes. By combining service with other strategies we can indeed address the civic challenges facing the United States and bring about the robust engagement that can transform our democracy.

PART TWO

Tackling Tough Problems: Impacts on Others

When we started AmeriCorps, we chose the motto "Getting Things Done" to make sure everyone—members, program directors, and the public—understood that the goal of making a difference for others was the primary purpose of the program. In fact, if the experience of serving was to have an impact on the server, it had to achieve something meaningful—the volunteers could tell if they were doing "make work" or "making a difference."

Too often when people think about how to solve important public problems, volunteers are not part of the picture, or are an afterthought at best. Even worse, professionals in some fields actively discourage the involvement of volunteers. They worry that volunteers will take their jobs or undercut their compensation. They may think that volunteers can't make a real contribution, or that they will be more trouble than they're worth. That's why many volunteers are asked to play administrative or fundraising roles, or are left out altogether, rather than being part of the program delivery team.

Volunteers play important nonprogrammatic roles in organizations. Many nonprofits could not operate without volunteers to help in these ways:

- *Board service.* With rare exceptions, nonprofit board members are not compensated for their service. This governance role is critical to nonprofits, as is the role board members play in championing the organization to build its financial, political, human, and social capital. A strong board can lift up an organization; a weak one can stymie it.

- *Administrative tasks.* Administrative tasks requiring little skill are often assigned to volunteers, either those who are looking to

Type	Examples
Many pairs of hands	• Volunteers read to children to increase school readiness. • Volunteers plant trees to prevent erosion and diminish air and water pollution. • Volunteers clean up debris after a disaster.
Pro bono	• MBAs advise low-income entrepreneurs. • Mental health professionals provide free services to veterans. • Individuals with "handyman" skills repair homes of elderly residents.
Social capital building	• Professionals offer support networks for youths preparing for office jobs. • Service exchanges knit together a community by building relationships. • Neighbors meet at a block party organized by teens.
Extra caring	• Older adults mentor struggling students. • Volunteers provide companionship to elderly and disabled adults. • College students take extra time to help low-income clients find help.
Community knowledge	• Bilingual immigrants translate for others who don't speak English. • Obese adults learn healthy cooking from neighbors who know their culture. • Children spread the word about energy conservation at home.
Community ownership	• Students promote a college-going culture in their own schools. • Neighbors maintain a community-built playground. • Residents commit to help their neighbors with disaster planning.

Table P2.1.   Examples of How to Use Service to Create Impact.

drop in when they have time or those who are able to commit to a regular schedule.

- *Fundraising.* Many organizations rely on volunteers to help raise the funds they need to operate. Whether they are wealthy donors who can reach out to other people of means or ordinary folks putting on a bake sale, the many hours of labor and relationships that these volunteers have to offer are assets that organizations often depend on.

I have not addressed these roles in this book because they are well understood. However, that does not minimize their value to organizations. Even though these kinds of roles do not involve direct service to clients, volunteers who help in these ways make it possible for organizations to carry out their missions and their work should be celebrated.

However, organizations that want to maximize the value of volunteers must go beyond these traditional assignments. As I've looked at the best service programs, I see patterns among the kinds of programmatic activities that are especially suited to volunteers and national service participants. You will see these patterns in the chapters that follow, but it will be easier to spot them if I highlight them here. (See Table P2.1 for specific examples.)

- *Many pairs of hands:* When a large, unskilled labor force is needed

  The prototypical old-fashioned volunteer activity—stuffing envelopes for a mass mailing—is an administrative manifestation of this way of using volunteer help. However, these same hands can help plant trees, paint a wall, or read to a child. Training and tools can make these volunteers even more effective—yielding, for example, a formidable army of tutors, conservationists, homebuilders, resource navigators, tax preparers, or emergency responders.

- *Pro bono:* When skills are needed but not supported by the market

  Sometimes skilled help is needed, but an organization, or the individual who needs it, cannot afford it. The classic example, of course, is the pro bono attorney who provides free help to nonprofits or represents low-income clients directly. This kind of help is not limited to the legal profession—other people with special skills can provide assistance as volunteers.

- *Social capital building:* When developing relationships outside an individual's network benefits an individual or community

  There are situations in which a population's lack of access to people with connections, knowledge, or other assets limits opportunities. Service programs that build this kind of "bridging social capital"—that is, relationships with people outside one's immediate circle—address this problem. Whether such volunteers provide access to jobs or information about how to apply to college, or, conversely, educate influential people outside the community about a community's needs, these bridges can offer important benefits.

- *Extra caring:* When the spirit of altruism and compassion favors volunteers as providers

  There are some contexts in which the extra caring that can be offered by a volunteer who does not need to rush on to another client is particularly valuable; in fact, for some recipients of service, the fact that the person delivering the service is doing so not because they are paid but because they want to be there may be particularly meaningful.

- *Community knowledge:* When knowledge of the community and credibility with specific populations enhance the service delivery

  When an organization hopes to educate or influence a certain population, it can be invaluable to have a person who is part of that community deliver the message. That is the thinking behind many fundraising efforts in which people ask their friends to buy a table or a ticket. But it is also the principle behind many programmatic efforts, from translating and outreach to community education.

- *Community ownership:* When community pride in a volunteer-created entity helps sustain it

  It is often the case that people value what they have created—that the park cleaned up by community volunteers stays clean, while the park maintained by government-funded employees faces litter and vandalism. This principle can apply to programs as well as physical properties and structures.

Type	Examples
Leadership	• AmeriCorps members staff the Citizen Schools after-school programs and engage community volunteers to lead students in hands-on "apprenticeships." • AmeriCorps members with Habitat for Humanity affiliates recruit and supervise volunteers, making increased production possible. • A single VISTA member can run a Time Bank that engages hundreds of community members in service to one another.
Consistency	• Jumpstart AmeriCorps members, although part-time, work one-on-one with the same Head Start students through the whole year, building strong relationships. • LIFT AmeriCorps members enable sites to remain operational year round, even when the college student volunteers are in exams or on break. • Rebuilding the Gulf region after Katrina requires a sustained, long-term commitment that short-term volunteer visitors cannot make.
Talent	• Teach For America recruits top college students to teach in low-income schools and retains a high percentage in education-related careers. • Community HealthCorps members typically remain in health careers. • Youth corps train disadvantaged youths for in-demand "green jobs."

Table P2.2. **Examples of Special Roles for National Service.**

In addition to these kinds of direct service, AmeriCorps members and other providers of long-term or full-time service are well-suited to offer leadership or consistent service provision. (See Table P2.2 for specific examples.)

- *Leadership:* When short-term volunteers must be recruited and led on projects

    AmeriCorps members often are responsible for recruiting and supervising community volunteers.

- *Consistency:* When daily participation over a period of months or a year is advantageous

    AmeriCorps members and similar service programs that offer minimal living allowances provide substantial service that organizations can count on when sustained and consistent participation is important.

- *Talent:* When maintaining a pool of entry-level staff with potential to become professionals in the field is important

AmeriCorps service exposes individuals to career opportunities in a deep way, sometimes attracting them to a vocation they might never have considered.

In the chapters that follow, you will see many examples of ways that organizations have deployed volunteers and national service participants to make a difference. An infinite number of other possibilities exist. I've chosen to focus on eight important national priorities: early childhood development, elementary and secondary education, health, aging, poverty, disaster, conserving energy, and protecting the environment. National service has been particularly effective in addressing these problems, but that doesn't mean service cannot be deployed against other challenges.

CHAPTER FOUR

Advancing Education

EARLY CHILDHOOD DEVELOPMENT

At the Bank Street Head Start Center on the Lower East Side of Manhattan, ten preschoolers rush into the room to greet the Jumpstart mentors assigned to the Center, ten college students wearing bright red t-shirts and welcoming smiles. The young children "sign in," carefully printing their names on a dry-erase board, then choose books to read with their Jumpstart partners. Some sit on laps, others on the floor side by side or in tiny chairs. When they finish their books, the children sit in a circle with their partners and sing a song together.

At the end of the song, the young students can choose an activity—on this particular Monday, almost all of the students choose to have their mentors trace their bodies on large sheets of paper, then work together to paint the shapes in wild colors while their partners talk about what happens when you mix paint colors together and help the preschoolers name the parts of the body. They will have this special time again on Wednesday afternoon. On other days, the preschoolers will see their college mentors in their regular classrooms, as their teachers carry out projects for which extra pairs of hands make a big difference.

The preschoolers selected for this special program are drawn from a pool recommended by the Head Start Center as neither at the top nor the bottom of the class, but likely to benefit from extra attention. From this group, ten are selected randomly. The college students at this particular center are work-study students from CUNY schools across New York City. While they are not education majors, they do receive extensive training, learning techniques to teach prereading skills and incorporate learning into fun, child-centered activities.

Stephen Antonelli, director of the Head Start Center, sees Jumpstart as one of his center's most important partnerships. The college students are "highly motivated and interested in children," he notes. The children have a long day—from 8:30 A.M. to 5:30 P.M. The afternoon change of atmosphere offered by Jumpstart, together with the consistency of seeing the same mentor throughout the year, helps ease their anxiety and spurs their development. "It's the only time in their day that they get an adult's undivided attention," notes Myung Lee, Jumpstart's Mid-Atlantic executive director.

And it makes a difference. In 2008, Jumpstart children improved their school readiness skills by 29 percent, bypassing their peers who did not benefit from the program. In 2009, fifteen thousand children received Jumpstart services in twenty states and the District of Columbia. Data showing ways to serve more children with the same number of college student mentors will allow for even greater future growth.[1]

How Service Helps

There is overwhelming academic consensus that from birth to age five is a critical period for cognitive development. Reading to children during this period builds key skills for literacy. For some children who lack early literacy stimulation, educational failure starts before they even begin school. In fact, the best predictor of whether a tenth-grader will read on grade level is actually whether the child knew his or her alphabet at the age of five. Although experts recognized the importance of preschool learning over a half century ago, young children living in poverty are still more than twice as likely as other children to be unable to recognize the letters of the alphabet, count to twenty or higher, write their name, or read or pretend to read—all skills they will need to enter kindergarten ready to learn.[2] Parents play a critical role in early learning, but not every parent knows what to do. Even when preschool programs are available, they may not be able to give children the individual attention they need.

Like Jumpstart, which helps thousands of low-income preschoolers enter kindergarten with the preliteracy skills they will need to succeed in school, service programs can improve early childhood development and increase school readiness in or out of a classroom by working directly with children or preparing parents to advance their children's development. Such programs achieve this through the actions described in the following sections.

SUPPORTING PROFESSIONALS IN THE CLASSROOM. Head Start, the nation's largest federal investment in early childhood education, has long encouraged the participation of volunteers, particularly parents, in the classroom. In fact, over thirty pages of policies guide Head Start volunteer programs.[3] Jumpstart, discussed earlier, is one of the most effective volunteer programs operating in Head Start and other early childhood centers. Founder Aaron Lieberman, the son of a director of a regional Head Start training center, came up with a way to take volunteers in Head Start centers to an even higher level. The summer before his senior year at Yale, he worked as a counselor at a camp for preschoolers with special needs and saw the difference that one-on-one attention made. When he returned to Yale, he set out to create a way for children to have that support throughout the year.

Aaron educated himself about early childhood development. He taught for a year as a lead preschool teacher at South End Head Start in Boston, and received his child development associate degree from the Council on Early Childhood Recognition. He founded Jumpstart in 1993. A partnership with the High/Scope Educational Research Foundation—the organization that created the famed Perry Preschool—helped to design top-quality research-based training for the college students, and support from AmeriCorps provided the college students with education awards.[4]

This training is critical to the effectiveness of Jumpstart volunteers. Research has consistently linked the preparation of the child care workforce to better outcomes for children. Jumpstart's sixty hours of training and coaching exceed both the minimum number of hours for professional child care staff required by most states and that recommended by the National Association for Child Care Resource and Referral Agencies.[5] Unfortunately, early childhood staff in this country are largely untrained, a fact that led some leaders in the field to be wary of AmeriCorps, fearing that it would compromise their efforts to professionalize the early childhood workforce—that the college student national service participants might have more education and training than the regular classroom teachers.

The Child Care Services Association (CCSA) in North Carolina found a unique way for AmeriCorps to support efforts to improve the skills of early childhood staff. While the organization, through its TEACH program, offered scholarships for early childhood workers to obtain additional education, it recognized that most of its target recipients were between a rock and a hard place. To go for additional education, they needed to be out of the classroom sometimes for days at a time; however, most child care centers operate with razor-thin budgets, leaving no funding for substitute staff to take their places so that desired staff-to-child ratios can be maintained. To solve this conundrum, CCSA set out to train AmeriCorps members to be the substitute staff. The model worked, and has enabled dozens of early childhood teachers each year to work toward their degrees.[6]

EDUCATING PARENTS. One of the most important ways to develop children's school readiness is for parents to talk and read to them from the youngest ages. However, childrearing practices are highly influenced by culture and the education levels of parents, and too often, poor educational performance is passed down across generations.[7]

Reach Out and Read is one large-scale strategy to encourage parents, particularly low-income parents, to read to their children. Sixteen percent of parents of children age three and younger do not read at all with their children, and these percentages are even higher among low-income families. Reach Out and Read was born out of the idea that doctor visits are the only time that parents of young children receive guidance on childrearing. The organization enlists doctors to provide developmentally appropriate books to at-risk children along with a "prescription" for parents to read to their children. Volunteers in the waiting rooms model techniques by reading to children before their appointments. Through these simple efforts, the odds of parents reading to their children three or more days a week increase tenfold for families in the program. By 2009, Reach Out and Read was reaching one-quarter of all low-income babies and preschoolers, with more than twelve thousand doctors and nurses participating.[8]

HIPPY—Home Instruction for Parents of Preschool Youngsters—offers a more intensive model for influencing parent behavior using AmeriCorps members among its teams of home visitors. Based on a program launched in Israel in the late 1960s, HIPPY operates in seven countries to increase school readiness and encourage parent involvement in their children's education. In the United States, HIPPY became one of the first AmeriCorps sponsors, as its leaders saw a good fit between AmeriCorps's goals and HIPPY's need for an affordable source of home visitors. Drawing largely from parents in the community to recruit members, HIPPY provides extensive training to its AmeriCorps members in child development. The members meet biweekly in parents' homes to instruct them in using the HIPPY educational materials. Their unique knowledge of their own communities allows them to develop trusting relationships with the families. Supervised by a professional coordinator, a model HIPPY site serves up to 180 children with one coordinator and twelve to eighteen part-time home visitors, making it a cost-effective way to promote school readiness.[9]

OTHER SERVICE-FOCUSED STRATEGIES. While the well-thought-out models just discussed address core challenges in the field of early childhood development, volunteers help in many other ways. Reading to preschoolers is a common and easily organized activity that requires minimal training but pays big dividends. Similarly, book drives that place reading material in the homes of low-income families also advance the literacy potential of young children. These common volunteer activities make a difference for young children facing significant disadvantages compared with their counterparts whose families are better able to advance their school readiness from an early age.

ELEMENTARY AND SECONDARY EDUCATION

In 1989, City Year founders Alan Khazei and Michael Brown set out to demonstrate that diverse teams of eighteen- to twenty-four-year-olds could serve side by side, putting their energy and idealism to work in communities. They hoped that policymakers would take notice, and that one day the most commonly asked question of a young person would be, "Where are you going to do your service year?"

The City Year pilot program succeeded in attracting funding from the Commission on National and Community Service and later became one of the models for AmeriCorps. With a mix of public and private support, City Year grew to nearly a thousand corpsmembers in the United States.

In its early years, teams served all around town at nonprofit organizations that expressed a desire and need for teams of young people. After fifteen years, it had become clear that the program's greatest impact was in urban schools, and the leaders of City Year embarked on a strategic planning process to understand how its corpsmembers could be most effective in the education space. Working with education experts and thought leaders, the organization discovered a number of common themes. The City Year culture combined with a team of role models working all day in schools helped students in even the most challenging environments improve academically, develop positive attitudes, build a strong work ethic, and get along with one another. Appreciating that corpsmembers were valued assets in schools, City Year put its organizational focus on education and the development of City Year's standardized Whole School Whole Child service model.

With the help of experts including Dr. Robert Balfanz, a national authority on the dropout problem, City Year explicitly connected its work to the "off-track" indicators that can predict which sixth graders will leave school without a diploma—those with poor attendance, unsatisfactory behavior, and course failure in math and English. City Year began to deploy its AmeriCorps members against these factors, focusing its efforts on students in grades three through nine. To create a welcoming environment, the corpsmembers greeted every student as they entered the school. They monitored attendance, calling parents when children were absent. They conducted intensive one-on-one and small-group literacy and math tutoring. They ate lunch with students, got to know them, and organized service-learning opportunities, running "Starfish Corps," a program for elementary students, and "Young Heroes," a Saturday program for middle schoolers. And after school they provided homework help and enriching after-school activities that reinforced what they learned during the school day. Because the corpsmembers were "near peers" they also served as role models.[10]

While many schools welcomed this resource, City Year was eager to demonstrate its value in the education reform arena. Washington, D.C., offered such a test. D.C. chancellor Michelle Rhee is not your ordinary school district leader. A committed school reformer, Rhee appeared on the cover of the *Time* magazine issue titled "How to Fix America's Schools" and was mentioned by both presidential candidates in the last election. But she had drawn the ire of teachers' unions and others who found her blunt style and reform plans disturbing and was widely regarded as an uncompromising figure who would never expend resources on programs that did not raise achievement levels.[11]

Initially, Chancellor Rhee focused on teachers and school leaders and looked for a commitment of resources from the private sector to finance reforms. She took a skeptical view of nonprofits that wanted to work in the schools. "I quite frankly did not think that City Year was going to play a large part in how I was going to transform the district," recalls Rhee.[12] But the program was already operating in the schools, and she decided to give it a try, hoping that a ten-member team could help change the culture and the expectations in the school.

Rhee agreed to put corpsmembers in charge of implementing a reading intervention that was managed in other schools by certified teachers. At the end of the year, the case was made. Not only had the City Year teams implemented the program with the most fidelity, their students had made the greatest gains.[13]

In fact, as Rhee visited City Year schools she found a common refrain: "The principal, the teachers, and the parents cannot say enough about the impact that the corpsmembers are having." While she is sparing with endorsements for school-focused nonprofits, she calls City Year "a program that I believe in." She decided to take City Year into thirty-three schools in Washington and to invest the money from her central office budget to make it happen.[14]

How Service Helps

Educational failure has been an intractable challenge for policy-makers for decades. Despite years of reform, racial and income gaps leave students of color and low-income students far behind their peers in educational achievement and attainment. These inequalities start with school readiness and continue through higher education. Affected students drop out of school at an alarming rate, leaving them three times more likely to be unemployed than college graduates and eight times more likely to be in jail or prison than high school graduates. Fifty percent of school dropouts nationwide are concentrated in just two thousand high schools—"dropout factories" where the typical freshman class shrinks by 40 percent or more by the time the students reach their senior year. These schools, and others characterized by low achievement rates, are likely to have less qualified teachers, fewer resources, and a culture that actually discourages achievement.[15] In many ways, the state of public education, which leaves so many children behind, is the greatest civil rights challenge of the new century.

City Year represents one way that service can transform American education: by deploying human resources against challenges not well addressed by traditional school systems. Education has been a sweet spot for AmeriCorps programs over its fifteen-year history, engaging more than half of AmeriCorps members. Schools have also been a popular place for traditional volunteers—including parents who want to be involved in their children's education, businesses that want to "adopt a school," and volunteers with nonprofit organizations that want to take their services "where the kids are." Schools are also the venue where students themselves can drive school progress through service.

Service supports education through the actions described in the following sections.

FILLING HARD-TO-FILL TEACHING POSITIONS. Experts agree that the most important determinant of school success is the quality of the classroom teacher. Sadly, it is often the children who struggle the most who have the teachers with the poorest preparation and skills.[16]

Twenty years ago, it was the rare Ivy League student who chose education as a career. Conventional wisdom was that it would be impossible to attract top students to teaching due to low pay and other factors. Wendy Kopp thought otherwise. As a student at Princeton, Kopp wrote her senior thesis proposing a program that would place talented graduates in low-income urban and rural classrooms. She had seen some of her classmates struggle to meet the academic demands of Princeton while others referred to it as a "cake walk," and as she learned more about educational inequity, she became convinced that it was one of our nation's greatest injustices. Even though she and her classmates were labeled the "Me Generation," she had a sense that there were thousands of talented, driven college students and recent grads who were searching for a way to make a real difference in the world and who would teach in low-income communities if only they were recruited to do so.[17]

By 2009, Teach For America was attracting more than thirty-five thousand applicants each year—including 11 percent of the graduating classes of the Ivy League—to fill four thousand positions. These new teachers are more diverse than teachers who were education majors—29 percent are teachers of color compared with just 14 percent of education majors. They serve in the highest-need classrooms in the country, where students begin the year on average at the 14th percentile against the national norm.[18]

Over the years, by studying and refining its systems for recruiting, training, and supporting its new teachers, Teach For America has achieved dramatic impacts in the classroom. According to Kopp, when the superintendent of Hartford, Connecticut, asked a group of high school seniors to name the teacher who made the most difference in their lives and then looked up the three teachers whose names came up the most, he discovered that they were all first-year Teach For America corpsmembers. In East San Jose, California, where the superintendent reconstituted a school and made first-year corpsmembers half of the faculty, the school increased its score on the California Academic Performance Index by 34 points, compared to the state's average increase of 6 points and the district's average of 3 points.

Rigorous research studies find similarly impressive results. One study found that North Carolina Teach For America corpsmembers were, on average, more effective than non–Teach For America teachers in all subject areas, especially in math and science. Another, utilizing random assignment to create a control group of students not taught by Teach For America teachers, found that students of corps-members made more progress in both reading and math in a year than would typically be expected, and attained significantly greater gains in math than students of other teachers in the study, even veteran and certified teachers. Yet another study found that nearly all principals rate Teach For America corpsmembers as effective as, if not more effective than, other beginning teachers, and rated them good or excellent at holding high expectations for students, planning purposefully to achieve these goals, and executing goal-oriented plans effectively to maximize student learning. Although early on the program was criticized for the low number of corpsmembers who stayed in the classroom after their term of service, today 60 percent stay after their two-year term ends, and more than a third stay for at least two additional years. Two-thirds of alumni remain in the education field, almost all working on behalf of low-income students.[19]

In addition to its impact in the classroom, Teach For America has had a dramatic impact on education reform. Some of the nation's top charter school networks were founded by alumni, and more than 300 school leaders, including Michelle Rhee, came from the program. In New York City alone 600 alumni are teaching and another 130 leading schools, including 30 percent of the city's charter schools. Another 70 serve in other key roles at the New York City Department of

Education and throughout city- and statewide charter management organizations.[20]

PROVIDING EXTRA SUPPORT FOR TEACHERS AND STUDENTS. Teachers, however, are only part of the solution. Strong teaching alone can't make children learn if they aren't motivated, need extra attention, or aren't there due to poor attendance. Children may not achieve their potential if another student's behavior problem disrupts the classroom, school culture discourages achievement, or students have no sense that they have a future that includes college or a serious career.

The traditional education model typically puts one teacher in a classroom of twenty to thirty-five students—far too low a ratio to allow for easy individualization of instruction. Volunteers and other national service participants support the work of professional teachers and offer one-on-one or small-group help to students who need it. For example, two thousand Experience Corps members, many of whom are part of AmeriCorps, work with twenty thousand students in 170 schools. They are age fifty-plus adults drawn from local communities, and one in five is a former educator. They work one-on-one with students, or in small groups, at the direction of teachers. And they get results—a rigorous study of more than eight hundred first-, second-, and third-grade students in urban schools found that students served by Experience Corps made 60 percent greater gains in sounding out new words and reading comprehension than similar students not served by the program. Another study found that third-graders working with Experience Corps members scored significantly higher on a state reading test than children in control group schools.[21]

In addition to providing individual attention, a major advantage of having extra help is the ability to keep order in the classroom. A single disruptive student may prevent the whole class from learning, but too often, a trip to the principal's office is the only option a teacher has to deal with the situation. A caring classroom volunteer or AmeriCorps member can take the time to talk to the disruptive student and discover the root of the problem, which may be missed meals, a violent household, or other situation that demands a sympathetic ear or outside intervention. A study of Experience Corps by Johns Hopkins Schools of Medicine and Public Health found that in schools with the program, referrals to the principal for classroom misbehavior decreased by half while referrals in control group schools remained about the same.[22]

Val Jackson, an Experience Corps tutor, knows that sometimes a sympathetic ear can make all the difference. An easily recognizable figure at Lucy Craft Laney Elementary School on the north side of Minneapolis, Jackson is a trim African American man with a quick smile, a British accent, and a button-down shirt and tie. The tie is a holdover, he says, from his thirty-three-year career as an electronics engineer. It's made an impression on several students he tutors—he's given several ties to young boys who wanted to wear one, too.

He recalls the day a teacher asked him to help resolve a disturbance among a few small boys while she kept the rest of the class on task. He eyed the group and decided to take aside the angriest little boy first. They sat down in the corner. Val hooked his arm around the back of the chair and said, "Marcus, you seem to be very upset today. Can you tell me what the problem is?"

Marcus said, "Those other boys are teasing me, and . . . and . . . and . . ." "And what?" Jackson said. Marcus's face started to scrunch up. "And, they don't know my grandma died this week." He burst into tears. Jackson could easily see that Marcus's grief was more important than anything else at this moment, and that he was the caring adult who had the time to help. He immediately took Marcus by the hand and implemented the "walk and talk" therapy he'd often used with other troubled students. They walked around the school, inside and out, talking all the while. They talked about Marcus's grandma, all the good memories he had, all the ways he can remember his grandma in the future.

Finally Jackson asked, "Do you think you're ready to go back to class now?"

"Yes, sir."

"Are you going to be able to do some work now?"

"Yes, sir. Thanks, Mr. Jackson."

And he did.

Source: Submitted by Jyni Koschak, Volunteers of America, Minnesota, to the ServiceNation database. Used with permission.

PROMOTING A LEARNING CULTURE AND SERVING AS POSITIVE ROLE MODELS. School culture has a dramatic and often underreported impact on school success. A school in which students do not value academic achievement—or worse, disparage it—will struggle to produce successful graduates. So will a school riddled with misbehavior or, even worse, violence. Placing young high school and college graduates in the schools as City Year does to serve as "near peer" positive role models, promote conflict resolution, and encourage positive behavior can make the difference between a school that works and one that doesn't.

That's why Harlem Children's Zone founder Geoffrey Canada began his effort to improve public schools by creating an Ameri-Corps program, the Harlem Peacemakers, that placed members in classrooms to help keep order and serve as positive role models. The effort was so successful that Harlem Children's Zone incorporated the Peacemakers into its acclaimed Promise Academy Charter School (see Chapter Eight).

Playworks (formerly Sports4Kids) has a similar impact. A single AmeriCorps member trained to organize play at recess, supported by a team of "junior coaches" (students in the school), not only increases the exercise level of virtually every student in the inner city schools where they serve but also improves the climate for learning. As Principal Willem Vroegh observes, the kids at George Peabody "learned ways to resolve their arguments with ro-sham-bo [rock paper scissors]," a practice that continues after recess. He has seen a change not just in playground behavior, but in the school culture in general. He's not alone—70 percent of principals with Playworks AmeriCorps members report that fights have decreased, and three out of four teachers report more cooperation among students and more focus in the classroom.[23]

PROMOTING PARENT INVOLVEMENT. Overwhelming evidence ties parent involvement to school success. Study after study documents that parent involvement in school programs and a strong relationship between school, family, and the larger community help students achieve.[24] However, parents who don't speak English or face other cultural barriers may feel uncomfortable making connections with teachers or attending school functions. Many depend on their children to translate for them—which is often problematic in a school context.

In a district where one in three students is considered an English language learner, San Francisco School Volunteers (SFSV) developed a unique program to remove barriers for parents who don't speak English to become involved in their children's education. To facilitate communication between school staff and parents in parent-teacher meetings and school events, SFSV provides bilingual volunteers with eighteen hours of interpretation training with the expectation that they will serve four hours each month at the request of teachers. As a result, teachers and families are able to work together to support the education of children from homes where English is not spoken.[25]

OFFERING ENRICHING PROGRAMMING DURING AND AFTER SCHOOL. Enriching activities are part of the educational experience of upper-income students whose families can foot the bill for everything from arts programming and writing classes to computer labs and leadership training. These kinds of opportunities help students put their learning in context and offer useful tools they can use to succeed both in and outside the classroom. But for other students, these learning activities may be out of reach because their families cannot provide them.

EducationWorks, which has been part of the AmeriCorps network since the beginning, works in dozens of low-income schools in Pennsylvania and New Jersey, serving twenty thousand students annually. In addition to providing classroom assistance, arranging service-learning projects, and running summer camps and after-school programs, the AmeriCorps members of EducationWorks enliven the school day through programs that aren't typically part of an urban education. They manage cross-age tutoring so older kids help younger kids, recruit and supervise adult volunteers in the schools, offer conflict resolution workshops, teach financial literacy, set up computer labs, and take students on unusual field trips. They also arrange enriching activities. For example, the AmeriCorps members took fifth- and sixth-graders to a local stable, where they groomed and rode horses—a first for all of them—as a strategy to help them practice teamwork and improve behavior. Another group learned healthy eating habits by picking apples at an orchard, and civic responsibility by taking apples to food pantries. And by making school more interesting, EducationWorks improves student attendance—students who had missed thirty-six to fifty-four days in the prior year improved their attendance by an average of twenty days, and those who had missed even more the previous year improved theirs by an average of twenty-six days—the equivalent of more than five weeks of school.[26]

Citizen Schools is another AmeriCorps program that brings enriching experiences to after-school hours by leveraging the time and talents of community volunteers. While AmeriCorps members help to staff the program, including providing rigorous academic support and leading learning trips in the community, they also make it possible for community volunteers to offer ten-week "apprenticeships" to teach the middle schoolers practical and fun skills that enliven their learning and help them make the connection between education and future career success. On any given week, at any of the forty-four schools with the program, a group of students might be making a movie, creating a directory of high schools in their area, designing an urban park, or learning to make sushi. Their efforts culminate in a "WOW!"—a product, performance, or presentation that enables the students to give back to the community. As a result of Citizen Schools programming and the "culture of achievement" it promotes, participating students do better in math and reading, have better attendance, and enroll in better high schools than their counterparts.[27]

IMPROVING THE PHYSICAL ENVIRONMENT IN WHICH CHILDREN LEARN. Studies link the physical condition of school facilities to reading levels and other indicators of student achievement. Poor school environments also can have a negative impact on staff and student health.[28] While public funding is needed for capital and maintenance needs, volunteer efforts to improve school facilities can also make a difference.

HandsOn Schools revitalizes educational environments by mobilizing resources to change schools into dynamic learning centers that foster student achievement and community engagement. For example, when the Buffalo Academy of Science Charter School moved to an old office building downtown, its founders could afford only the minimum necessary repairs such as a new boiler and converting offices into classrooms. But with the help of HandsOn Greater Buffalo, Home Depot, and Western New York AmeriCorps, in June of 2009 the school was transformed. "We laid out our dreams" to our partners, says school director Levent Kaya. A few months later, more than two hundred volunteers turned out—including the school's staff, students, and their families. Colorful murals, outdoor classrooms, a comfortable teachers' lounge, freshly painted hallways, and a school store emerged in a single afternoon—an inspiration to students and faculty alike.[29]

ENGAGING STUDENTS TO LEAD AND ASSIST THEIR PEERS. Peer and cross-age tutoring in which students help other students have been part of the informal education process since the beginning of time. They were a core feature of the "one-room schoolhouse" in America, when a single teacher had responsibility for children of all grade levels. Today it is well established through research that peer and cross-age tutoring benefit both the tutor and the student.[30]

One important role for student leaders is building a college-going culture. In a nation that prides itself on equal opportunity, students from the low-income quartile who get A's on standardized tests go to college at the same rate as their higher-income peers who get D's on the same tests.[31] College Summit works to build the capacity of schools in twelve states to increase college-going dramatically by providing students the supports they need to apply for college and financial aid. But to build a college-going culture, student leadership is key. College Summit high schools identify the most influential students from the rising senior class. These "Peer Leaders" participate in an intensive four-day boot camp where they are trained to build a college-going culture in their schools. Over the summer, more than a thousand adult volunteers serve as writing coaches and college counselors for over three thousand Peer Leaders who will work with twenty-five thousand students in their own schools the following fall. Back home, Peer Leaders help their teachers and principals to improve the academic performance of their fellow students through peer networks. The results of the program are dramatic: schools with the program increase college enrollment rates by an average of 16 percent over previous years.[32] Not only are the schools sending significantly more students to college, but the college persistence rate for these low-income students matches persistence rates for U.S. students from all income levels.

College Summit school principals point to Peer Leaders as central to the success of the program. At Decatur Central High School in Indianapolis, College Summit Peer Leaders were determined to lower the ninth-grade drop-out rate. Working alongside the principal and lead educators, the Peer Leaders created a student-driven drop-out reduction strategy before the school year began. Each Peer Leader then adopted several struggling ninth-graders to meet with regularly, and for whom they are called in to help address behavior and motivation issues. To reach all students, the Peer Leaders have built a website with informational and inspirational content for their classmates. School director Cathy Tooley reports, "In one year, there has been a complete culture shift in our school."

At Crossland High School in Prince George's County, Maryland, the Peer Leaders similarly committed to raising the school's college enrollment rate and supporting Principal Charles Thomas's reform strategy. The school has seen 90 percent of its seniors apply to four-year colleges, while enrollment in AP classes increased over 1,000 percent from 2004 to 2008. Thomas elaborated on the spillover effect of peer influence, noting that he "can set the academic agenda, but it's the students who set the social agenda. They are the ones who decide what's cool and what's not cool. They are the ones who decide what classes are cool to take and what classes are not." Notes Thomas, without the Peer Leaders "we would not have been able to change the culture of the school."[33]

POTENTIAL FOR TRANSFORMATION

Every child deserves a chance at school success, but too often, income determines outcome. Whether they attend a program like Head Start or depend on their families as teachers, low-income children can be positioned for success with the right help. Service can put extra help in every preschool classroom serving low-income children, and enable every family to employ effective simple ways to facilitate learning. Models such as Jumpstart, HIPPY, and Reach Out and Read operating at scale could have a transformational impact on the way America prepares young children for success in school.

Service can also lift up students once they get to elementary and secondary school. Teach For America, City Year, Experience Corps, College Summit, Communities in Schools, and other education innovators have used service as a powerful tool to change education outcomes for low-income students.

Despite their positive impact, however, none of these programs has achieved a scale equal to the need they seek to address. Imagine a talented trained teacher for every classroom, a team of AmeriCorps members for every struggling school, rich engagement of parents of all backgrounds, volunteers available to help in a myriad of ways, and peer tutors lifting up students at every age. These human resources are within our reach, should we choose to engage them.

CHAPTER FIVE

Improving Health and Well-Being

HEALTH

If you were an African American in the rural town of Mound Bayou in the Mississippi Delta in the 1950s and early 1960s, you probably lived in a tarpaper shack, with no running water, toilets, or showers. You might have washed in and drunk from a ditch. You likely had only four years of schooling, and no hope of getting ahead economically. You ate unhealthy starchy foods and had little access to fruits and vegetables even though you lived in one of the most agriculturally rich areas of the country. You rarely saw a doctor, and if you did, you entered through a back door, told him your symptoms, and got a diagnosis—without a physical examination. Chances are, you relied on a home health remedy when you got sick, and if you had a baby, you had it at home, in unsanitary conditions. Six out of one hundred babies died.

Mound Bayou was the site of the first community health center, piloted in 1965 as part of the War on Poverty. Located in a church parsonage, the center used the living room for the waiting room, the bedroom for exams, and the kitchen as a lab. Its founders, who included a young doctor from Tufts University, an African American pediatrician working in a rural area as a condition of his medical school scholarship, and local community leaders, understood that while the residents of Mound Bayou desperately needed access to a medical facility, they also needed much more. And so, in order to improve the health of those the clinic sought to serve, clinic staff and volunteers dug wells, installed sewage lines and outhouses, and offered services from transportation to education. Doctors performed exams and treated illnesses, but they also wrote prescriptions for healthy food and organized a cooperative vegetable farm to improve the diet of the community. In the center's first four years, infant mortality in the community dropped 40 percent.[1]

The early community health centers were controversial, sometimes facing the opposition of southern governors and established medical institutions. But they flourished nonetheless—expanding through dedicated federal funding to become the "family doctor" for fifteen million people. These individuals include uninsured families, homeless people, new immigrants, the urban poor, and residents of isolated rural communities. Today, community health centers are open to all, provide free care or charge on a sliding fee scale, and tailor their services to the community they serve. Like the center in Mound Bayou, community health centers often provide services that while not strictly "health care" nonetheless contribute to the overall health of the people they serve.

Volunteers and national service participants have assisted the development of community health centers since their earliest days. VISTA volunteers played an important part in many centers as did volunteers recruited from the community. Today, the National Association of Community Health Centers runs the largest health-focused AmeriCorps program, Community HealthCorps, which continues the tradition of connecting national service to community health centers. The AmeriCorps members, many of whom are recruited from local communities, aren't doctors or nurses, but they do what is necessary to improve health, not just provide health care. They help patients navigate the health care system, sign up for health insurance programs, and manage their chronic conditions such as asthma, obesity, diabetes, or depression. They also remind patients about appointments, help them with transportation, and lead support groups. Sometimes they connect patients to other services they need outside of the health care system. Corpsmembers have started exercise programs, coat drives for the homeless, and campaigns to clean up local parks. They also recruit neighborhood volunteers for projects and organize outreach efforts to make sure residents know about the services available. As an added bonus, more than 60 percent of corpsmembers go on to health careers. In San Francisco, for example, of 119 Community HealthCorps alumni surveyed, 15 were hired by health centers, 9 went on to other health-related positions, 45 went to medical school, 8 went to nursing school,

12 went to graduate programs in social work, and 6 returned for another year of service in the program.[2]

How Service Helps

As the founders of the community health center movement knew well, good health requires more than health care. Proper nutrition and exercise are important. So is a hazard-free environment, safe behavior, measures to prevent the spread of disease, and management of chronic conditions. Well-off families have access to these things— well-appointed playgrounds, fitness classes, farmers' markets, and organic groceries, not to mention hot running water and homes free from lead paint and toxic waste. They have family doctors, access to specialists, and insurance to pay for their visits. They don't have to choose between food and medicine.

Low-income people, however, often don't enjoy these benefits. Nearly fifty million Americans lacked health insurance in 2009. One in five had no "medical home"—a source of regular care. They may eat poorly, fail to exercise, and be exposed to all manner of disease and environmental hazards. When they have a health problem, it often gets worse when it could have been managed with simple steps. Dental and mental health care may be even more difficult to obtain.[3]

It's not a stretch to think that many of the health challenges facing communities of color stem from these inequities. Nearly half of the deaths and diseases in these communities are caused by an unhealthy lifestyle.

Roughly 13 percent of African Americans over age twenty suffer from diabetes—twice the rate of whites. African American women are more likely to be obese or overweight than any other group—80 percent are overweight and over 50 percent obese. Nearly half of American Indian and Alaska Native adults never engage in leisure-time physical activity.[4]

Lack of insurance also leads to a host of problems—health related and otherwise. Children in families without insurance are less likely to get preventive screenings. If they have health problems, they are diagnosed later, when their conditions are harder to treat. Their health problems may create developmental delays and put them at risk of school failure.[5] That's why America's Promise Alliance, a leading children's organization, made the health insurance strategy "All Kids Covered" one of its major initiatives to reduce the drop-out rate, recognizing the important link between health and education—if kids are sick, they don't go to school.[6]

While doctors and nurses, as well as health insurance, obviously are central to a system of health care, a system that promotes good health encompasses a wide range of activities that lay people can provide. In some cases, community credibility and knowledge are key assets; in others, trained volunteers can play an important part. Across the country, volunteers are improving the health of communities and, in some cases, even delivering the services underserved people need, through the actions described in the following sections.

STAFFING HEALTH CENTERS AND CLINICS. Volunteers may play important roles in many community health centers, but at the Rhode Island Free Clinic, they do it all—from patient care to data entry to Spanish interpreting. They treat patients, run health education workshops, and schedule appointments. A VISTA member manages the more than two hundred community volunteers who come from all walks of life—physicians, nurse practitioners, students, and other members of the community. In 2009, with only eight paid staff, the clinic provided four thousand patient visits, offering patients, who are selected by lottery, primary care services as well as diagnostic and laboratory services and a free pharmacy. For those who don't live nearby, the physicians in the clinic's network serve patients in their offices free of charge.[7]

Volunteers with Project HEALTH play a different role in health clinics. Founded in the Boston Medical Center Pediatrics Department in 1996, Project HEALTH works to break the link between poverty and poor health with volunteer-staffed family help desks. In these clinics, physicians can "prescribe" food or housing for their patients and their families, and Project HEALTH undergraduate volunteers then connect those families to local resources to meet these needs, enabling them to achieve the stability and opportunity that lead to better health for their children. Student volunteers continue to follow families until they obtain appropriate resources to meet each of their needs. Over three-quarters of family help-desk clients present with multiple needs. On average, each client receives assistance in accessing an average of three different community resources.

HELPING PEOPLE TO ACCESS HEALTH INSURANCE. Nine million children in America were uninsured in 2009. Half of them, however, were eligible for public insurance programs. While there are many reasons that families don't enroll in these programs, one common reason is lack of information—families don't realize they are eligible or they don't know how to sign up. Uninsured families are likely to rely on emergency rooms for their care—which passes on the cost of their care to all other health care consumers.

Texas has the highest rate of uninsured children in the United States. But the Children's Defense Fund-Texas is working to change that. Its strategies include enlisting school districts to ask about health insurance status on student forms, using PSAs and school automated-call phone systems to educate parents, and recruiting grocery stores to serve as outreach posts. Volunteers are central to the organization's efforts to reach uninsured families through community-based outreach events. "We want every family to receive the assistance they need where they live, work, and shop," notes Kelli King-Jackson, director of outreach for CDF-Texas. Having enough volunteers who are trained to help families with their paperwork gives families more opportunities to receive assistance in applying for the Children's Health Insurance Program (CHIP) or Children's Medicaid. Adult community members, college students, and even high schoolers all make good volunteers, according to King-Jackson. "The high school students are often themselves eligible for the children's insurance programs and can sign up their own families," says King-Jackson.[8]

Breast cancer survivor Andrea Ivory had been diligent about getting mammograms and credits early detection for her survival. But she realized that many women don't have access to recommended mammograms. She founded the Florida Breast Health Initiative to do something about it. The first three Saturdays of each month volunteers who include college students, senior citizens, and suburban moms in matching t-shirts swarm targeted neighborhoods to distribute educational materials and sign women up for free mammograms. On the last Saturday of the month a large mobile mammography van from a partner hospital provides the screenings. For her efforts, Ivory was nominated for a CNN Heroes award in 2009.

Source: "Army of Volunteers Saves Lives with Clipboards, High Spirits," CNN.com, http://www.cnn.com/2009/LIVING/04/23/andrea.ivory/index.html.

PROMOTING GOOD NUTRITION. Thirty-six million Americans—including twelve million children—don't have access to enough healthy food to thrive. Food insecurity—access to enough food for an active healthy life—exists in one in ten U.S. households. Food banks and food-rescue organizations provide emergency hunger relief to 9 percent of all Americans—about twenty-five million persons.[9]

It's clear that ending hunger has a lot to do with improving health, and that hunger has a lot to do with income. Strategies to alleviate poverty make a difference. But so do the choices that people make when it comes to food. That's where Share Our Strength's Operation Frontline comes in. Operation Frontline helps families with limited resources make healthy meals at home, using a wide variety of foods that are commonly available in stores and from emergency food providers. Instructors teach lifelong cooking skills and provide practical nutrition information and food budgeting strategies. Adult and teen participants receive groceries at the end of each class to practice at home the recipes they've learned.

Volunteers are at the heart of Operation Frontline. Volunteer chefs teach adults, kids, and teens how to cook healthy, low-cost foods; volunteer nutritionists teach them how to make healthy choices; volunteer finance instructors teach adults how to manage money; and support volunteers help facilitate classes by assisting with onsite or offsite class preparation and implementation. During the 2007 program year, Operation Frontline offered hands-on courses to over five thousand low-income adults, teens, and kids. And it has an impact. Nearly 80 percent of participants eat more vegetables after the class than they did before. The average participant eats a wider variety of foods and chooses healthier snacks, and 90 percent of participants say they have improved their cooking skills as a result of the course. Eighty-three percent of participant families report that they have prepared the healthy recipes at home that they tried in class.[10]

ENCOURAGING EXERCISE. It's well known that regular exercise offers important health benefits—everything from improved mental health to a stronger heart.[11] Volunteers help people of all ages and backgrounds realize these benefits when they coach a team or organize a league, lead a walking group, or build a trail.

Children need physical activity for their healthy development, and play is the main way they get it. Active play improves not just their physical health but their social, emotional, and cognitive development as well, according to the American Academy of Pediatrics.[12] Unfortunately, too many children, particularly those in low-income communities, don't have safe places to play.

KaBOOM! and its volunteers are helping to change this. In August 1995, then-twenty-four-year-old Darell Hammond read a story in the *Washington Post* about two local children who suffocated while playing in an abandoned car because they didn't have anywhere else to play. Hammond had grown up in a group home outside of Chicago and spent happy hours at the home's large playground. As a young adult, he had helped build several playgrounds for other organizations. He realized this tragedy could have been prevented, and the idea for KaBOOM! was born.

KaBOOM! organizes volunteer playground builds, bringing together employees of its business sponsors with families in the community to construct state-of-the-art playgrounds. The construction skills of several of its key partners—such as Home Depot— offer an important asset to complement the community knowledge of neighborhood volunteers. As an added benefit, the involvement of community volunteers means that the playground will be maintained. Realizing that teens also need places to play, the organization expanded its menu in 2003 to include volunteer-built skate parks, playing fields, and other play spaces.

Since its founding, KaBOOM! has built over sixteen hundred play spaces and provided online tools, training, and technical assistance to help communities create hundreds of additional volunteer-built playgrounds on their own. With these new tools, KaBOOM! is well on its way toward achieving its vision: a great place to play within walking distance of every child in America.[13]

SHARING INFORMATION AND SUPPORT. Often a diagnosis for a serious disease can be both frightening and isolating for a patient. Doctors can offer treatment options, and families may offer moral support. But the chance to communicate with others going through a similar experience may make a tremendous difference. While they may not consider themselves volunteers, the people who share their stories and offer advice through chat rooms, listservs, online forums, and blogs are offering important assistance to people facing difficult times.

I recall when facing a difficult health decision for my son, Matthew—whether or not to have a cochlear implant that might enable him to access sound—that the parents who participated on the CI Circle listserv provided tremendous insights. They did not impart medical advice, but offered a realistic picture of their own children's experiences as well as practical tips (such as where to find clothing that would securely hold the small processor that Matthew, then age five, would need to wear).

Today, online support groups are available for practically every possible condition; many of them are managed by volunteers who have themselves seen the need to build these connections. For example, BMT-Talk, for people concerned with bone marrow transplants, was started by a young MIT lab manager who had beat back leukemia twice. In the course of managing her disease she had amassed a great deal of information that she wanted to share, and was inspired to create the listserv, which enables individuals to ask and answer questions, find people with similar challenges, and simply communicate with others who can provide empathy and support.[14] Studies of online health support groups point to their value in providing emotional support to women with breast cancer, citing the ability of women to be anonymous and avoid having to "maintain a show of strength" as may be required with family and friends.[15]

The Internet is also full of websites and blogs by volunteers who have done their own health-related research and want to point people facing similar challenges to the resources they have identified. And although users should view these sites with a critical eye, and not substitute for the medical judgment of their own doctors, such sites can make individuals better informed in dealing with the medical establishment.

PROVIDING PRO BONO HEALTH SERVICES. While ideally every American would have access to the health services they need, that's not always the case. Without insurance, people may not be able to find a doctor. Or the specialist they need may not be located within a reasonable distance. Mobile vans, telemedicine, and online services can help, but the nation is a long way from being able to match every person with the professional provider he or she needs.

Volunteer medical professionals can help fill this void by staffing free clinics or offering pro bono services. That was the idea behind Give an Hour™, founded in September 2005 by Dr. Barbara Van Dahlen, a psychologist in the Washington, D.C., area. While the organization's mission is to "develop national networks of volunteers capable of responding to both acute and chronic conditions that arise within our society," currently, the nonprofit is dedicated to meeting the mental health needs of a particularly deserving population: the troops and families affected by the ongoing conflicts in Iraq and Afghanistan. Sadly, more than one hundred thousand combat veterans have sought help for mental illness since the start of the Iraq war, and as many as one in four soldiers who have served in Iraq display symptoms of serious mental health problems such as depression, substance abuse, and post-traumatic stress disorder. Their families also pay a price—one in five married service members has filed for divorce since September 2001, and more than thirty-five thousand families have faced the loss or injury of a loved one in Iraq or Afghanistan.

Since its founding, more than forty-four hundred Give an Hour volunteers have provided more than $1.7 million in free services. Give an Hour works like this: mental health providers register with the organization and offer an hour a week of pro bono counseling. Individuals in need of services search the provider list and find the help they need. Once they have been served they are given the opportunity to provide confidential feedback, and they may look for volunteer opportunities that enable them to "give back" as well. While the military offers counseling, many military personnel feel that seeking mental health services will jeopardize their career. Operating outside the military, Give an Hour has created a confidential way to serve military men and women. In addition, the organization provides services to those not eligible to receive health care from the military system, including significant others, parents, and siblings.[16]

AGING

Seniors in Severna Park, Maryland, the coastal area along the Chesapeake Bay, know that if they need help, they can call Partners In Care and a volunteer will be there. "Partners In Care helped me because I had felt at one time I should go into a senior citizens place. But I didn't want to let my house go," says Della Jackson. When difficulty walking made it hard for her to reach her car, three Partners In Care volunteers installed a handrail. "I had tears when I received this," Jackson says. "They are very wonderful people. Thank God for them."[17]

Partners In Care is an exchange program that connects frail elderly and disabled adults with neighbors who volunteer their time providing transportation, home repairs, and other services that enable them to remain in their own homes rather than go to nursing facilities. These volunteers are entitled to draw on other participants for what they need. For example, Helen, a sixty-five-year-old woman, might offer rides to Jackie, earning hours in her own bank. Helen uses her hours to have John fix the loose bricks in her front walk. John uses the hours he earned to get help for his ailing mother, who needs someone to check in on her on weekends when John is out of town. "Having credits in the 'bank' makes it easier to ask for help when it is needed," according to Partners In Care.[18]

What began as a kitchen-table nonprofit has developed into a vital resource with twenty-six hundred participants currently exchanging more than twenty-five thousand hours of service each year in four communities across Maryland. The exchange concept makes it easier for many people to ask for help because it doesn't feel like charity. Many volunteers who have logged hundreds of hours driving their neighbors to appointments or working in the used-clothing boutique or other projects run by the organization expect that when they need help, they will have earned it.[19]

Partners In Care is a "Time Bank," a concept developed in 1980 when Edgar S. Cahn, co-founder of the National Legal Services Program and founder of the Antioch School of Law, dreamed up "Time Dollars" as a new currency to offset cuts in government spending on social welfare. Around the world, hundreds of Time Banks are in operation, ranging in size from as few as a dozen members to more than eight thousand. Service exchanges are coordinated through Time Banks, and the amount of Time Dollars that members earn and spend can be recorded using Time Bank software. The strongest Time Banks also connect members through group activities, such as classes, potluck dinners, or other social events. They may also collaborate with community organizations—allowing members to buy things they need with Time Dollars or to earn Time Dollars by volunteering with the organization or other nonprofits.

Research has found Time Banking to be an effective way to engage people in service to others, including those who have never before volunteered. When well implemented, studies show, Time Banks deliver "important services to frail elderly people that weren't being delivered elsewhere."[20] An evaluation conducted by the University of Maryland established that Time Bank schemes succeeded in attracting people who don't normally volunteer, keeping older people healthier, and fostering volunteer retention.[21]

"Often you can't buy what you really need," says Mashi Blech, who runs the Visiting Nurse Service of New York Community Connections Time Bank in Manhattan. "You can't hire a new best friend. You can't buy somebody you can talk to over the phone when you're worried about surgery." But you can buy these services with Time Dollars.[22]

How Service Helps

"Aging in place" means being able to grow older in your own home without having to move out of a familiar community away from people you know. Most homeowners over the age of fifty prefer to remain in their homes, yet most older adults will require special housing at some point.[23]

Within twenty years, as Baby Boomers enter their retirement years, almost one out of five Americans (seventy-two million) will be sixty-five or older. Seniors over age eighty-five—the cohort most likely to need daily assistance—will continue to be the fastest-growing segment of the U.S. population.

Our social services systems could easily be overwhelmed by this "age wave." By 2020, twelve million older adults will require some type of care. Unfortunately, this surge in need is paralleled by an equally dramatic drop in the availability of younger friends and family members available to provide the needed assistance. In 1990, there were eleven potential caregivers for each person needing help. By 2050, that ratio will be only four to one.[24]

As a society, we have compelling reasons for helping older adults "age in place" while staying actively involved in their communities. Studies show a strong association between social engagement and positive health outcomes among older adults—an association that holds true even for risk of developing dementia, a primary cause of need for extensive long-term care, either in the home or in a care facility. Moreover, seniors who can access the support they need to continue living in their own homes can significantly delay nursing home placement or avoid it altogether, relieving the unsustainable pressure on state and federal Medicaid budgets. Since nursing home care now costs $70,000 or more per year, most seniors quickly "spend down" to Medicaid eligibility, making Medicaid the primary payer for 65 percent of America's nursing home residents.[25]

To "age in place," most seniors eventually will need a support system that helps them with "activities of daily living" (such as bathing, dressing, eating) or "instrumental activities of daily living" (for example, shopping, preparing meals, bill paying, transportation). Eighty percent of this care is now provided by families. Although this care is unpaid, it carries significant cost to families and society. Over 60 percent of family caregivers have full- or part-time jobs, and more than 40 percent also care for children. These dual, sometimes conflicting responsibilities affect caregivers' attendance at work, stress levels, and career prospects. Experts estimate that the annual cost to U.S. employers in terms of this lost productivity alone is $29 billion.[26]

Large numbers of older adults live far away from their families and have no nearby relatives who can meet their day-to-day needs. In other cases, elderly parents are reluctant to ask their adult children or other family members for assistance, either because they do not want to be a "burden" or because they know their children are already struggling to balance the demands of full-time jobs and childrearing responsibilities. A supplementary system of support is badly needed, both for seniors who only need occasional help to maintain their independence and for seniors who have a regular source of home care but cannot find or afford the extra help they need to continue living at home.

Anyone who has struggled to get the lid off a jar or program their DVR knows how frustrating it can be when the chores of daily life become a challenge. As discussed in Chapter Two, the simple act of serving others can improve the mental and physical health of older adults—that's part of the idea behind Partners In Care and other Time Banks for older adults. There are many other ways that volunteers can help frail elderly and disabled people remain independent—from offering companionship and healthy meals to safety checks and help with repairs. Often these services are out of financial reach for seniors on fixed budgets—if they can be bought at all. By staving off the need for costly care settings, volunteers can make an important contribution not just to quality of life for the elderly but to the nation's health care bill.

PROVIDING CARING COMPANIONS. Like the neighbors who help others through Partners In Care, volunteers can perform many services that older people need to remain independent. One of the most important is companionship.

One of the longest-running federal service programs, Senior Companions began as a pilot program in 1968. A few years later, President Richard Nixon called for a volunteer program to enable older persons to help other older people. Senior Companions was born in 1974, pairing people aged sixty-plus with seniors who needed assistance.

Today, sixteen thousand Senior Companions serve fifty-eight thousand frail adults, mostly on a long-term basis. Studies have documented that the program reduces depressive symptoms reported by clients and their families when compared to older adults on the waiting list for services, as well as helping with the daily lives of those served and the ability of their families to remain employed.[27]

OFFERING TELEPHONE REASSURANCE. Sometimes what people need to remain independent can be provided with a simple daily phone call to make sure a person living alone is okay. Friends and family may check in, but can easily be distracted by daily demands. Commercial services featuring a computerized call are on the market. But often the kind of systematic check-ins that offer both a friendly voice on the end of the line and the comfort of knowing that if you don't answer a daily call someone will find out why are far more valuable.

Portage County RSVP in central Wisconsin runs one of many volunteer programs around the country that offer "telephone reassurance." RSVP volunteers, who are themselves older adults, participate in Telecare, calling seniors each weekday to check on their well-being, referring any concerns to family members, staff, or emergency services. In Portage County, of the nearly one thousand people over 85, 17 percent live below the poverty line and 41 percent live alone. For many of these older adults, the Telecare volunteer call is the only human contact they have all day.[28]

SUPPLYING INTERGENERATIONAL SUPPORT. Over the past century, older and younger generations have become increasingly segregated. No longer do grandparents live with their children and grandchildren. Senior communities have become more and more common, and young people often don't benefit from knowing older adults. As Generations United points out, as a result, "the old do not have relationships with the young, the young do not understand their elders or the aging process."

In fact, just as older adults have much to contribute to young people, youths have much to offer seniors—from technology skills to dog-walking assistance to simple friendship.

Sometimes the best ideas come from the young people themselves. When Manateens was founded on the west coast of Florida in 1994 by then twelve-year-old Laura Lockwood, the program struggled to find organizations willing to take on the young volunteers. As a result, the teens created their own projects, a hallmark of the program today that engages more than half of the teens in the county. For example, Shannon Walsh, the 2005 Manateens president, read an article in the newspaper about low-income elderly people who cannot afford to buy pet food and often end up sharing their own meals with their pets. Walsh dreamed up PAWS—a "Meals on Wheels" program for seniors' pets. The teens collect donated pet food and deliver it once a month to program participants. The Manateens have found other ways to support the seniors in their community. Their Home Safety for Seniors project sends teams of youths to the homes of older adults to look for safety hazards and deliver $100 in free products from Lowe's, while the teens' "Adopt a Grandparent" program calls on the young volunteers to include a senior in their daily lives.[29]

POTENTIAL FOR TRANSFORMATION

America's health crisis begins in backyards and houses and extends all the way to the hospital. To make America healthier and reduce the costs we pay for health care, we need to change behavior, build community knowledge, screen for common conditions, and connect everyone to health care with the insurance to pay for it. Service can be a significant part of this effort. Programs such as Community HealthCorps and KaBOOM! already operate on a large scale, but not in every community that needs them. Others offer tested local solutions to problems common to communities everywhere, but no system spreads them beyond a few sites.

A similar situation exists in the field of aging in place. A large percentage of the growing number of elderly adults could remain independent for far longer with a ramping up of service. The result would not only be a better quality of life for seniors, but a savings to the nation of billions of dollars. It's time to make service by and for older adults part of our national strategy to transform America into the nation we want to see.

CHAPTER SIX

Helping People and Communities in Distress

POVERTY

Montgomery County, Maryland, a close-in suburb of Washington, D.C., is home to some of the wealthiest towns in the country. But it also encompasses some of the poorest neighborhoods in the region. The last census revealed that the suburbs of America, even wealthy ones, house nearly 40 percent of the poor, and suburban poverty looks different from many enclaves of urban poverty. In Montgomery County, where nearly a third of residents are immigrants, low-income families come from all backgrounds. They speak nineteen languages among them. Neighbors don't know one another. And that makes it hard for community leaders to build ties across ethnic groups. As a result, low-income people have little voice in the schools and have difficulty accessing the services set up to help them.[1]

Frankie Blackburn, a long-time civic leader and community organizer, had an idea to shake things up in the Silver Spring area of Montgomery County. An area with rapid development, Silver Spring had many renters who had no political voice. Nor for the most part were low-income families engaged in the schools that served their children. Rather than define an agenda and enlist the community to put muscle behind it, Blackburn wanted the agenda to come from the people themselves. But how to do this? Because of the diversity of the community and its history of isolation, her organization, IMPACT Silver Spring, could not simply tap into an established network of neighborhood or ethnic leaders. Thus began a ten-year effort to seek out and develop leaders who could change the balance of power in Silver Spring.

When the head of the local Department of Health and Human Services (DHHS), Uma Ahluwalia, asked for help establishing a network of community-based centers, Blackburn had a powerful reason to tap into the community to find a larger circle of indigenous leaders who might not have run for PTA president, much less City Council, but who could serve as "community connectors" for the new centers. DHHS wanted communities to know about the services government provides but knew that for many recent immigrants, the location of facilities, lack of knowledge, or misconceptions about government services kept them away. For example, many immigrants believe that if they seek help for their family, their children will have to join the military when they turn eighteen. When families don't seek help, the problems they face can grow worse. As Ahluwalia told *Washington Post* columnist Neal Peirce, putting up homeless families costs $110 dollars a night, and it often takes forty to sixty days to find them a new place. "If I can stop that $5,000 bill by providing rental assistance and back rents, I have saved a lot of money," not to mention saving children the destructive experience of living without a real home or with frequent school moves.[2] Neighborhood centers, staffed by people knowledgeable about the community, could save the county money and prevent many families from falling into even worse circumstances.

Blackburn set out not just to find community connectors but to build a system of outreach and mutual support that could change circumstances for low-income families in the area. To build this system would take more than a notice in the local paper or a flyer at the grocery. Blackburn developed a simple volunteer-centered model that fit both her limited budget and a need for culturally competent help. Her organization, with the assistance of a half-dozen AmeriCorps members, would recruit community volunteers to knock on doors in targeted neighborhoods. They would engage residents in conversations to find out what their needs were, as well as what they might have to offer others. Those who showed interest would be invited to a "Neighbors Exchange" dinner, where they would hear about opportunities such as a financial literacy program or job services. Some would be asked to join the door-knocking effort. Others might be convinced to host a "Neighbors Circle," a series of gatherings over meals for a group of eight or ten people who might become a community of mutual support, sharing child care, job leads, cooking, or rides. And a few would emerge as leaders, who might help DHHS establish centers in their neighborhoods and carry forward the critical role of weaving these networks of mutual support among neighbors.

The evening of the first Neighbors Exchange, the IMPACT team nervously arranged the basement room of Mercy Seat Chapel where they would hold their dinner. They prepared two small rooms for child care and checked translation headsets. A team did a last-minute door-knocking in nearby apartments. By 7 P.M. the room was full with more than fifty people from different walks of life. The vast majority were Latino or African immigrants, with a few Asian immigrants and African American families. After an exercise to help neighbors find and meet each other, the group was invited to join one of four circles, on finding a job, on access to health care, on credit and savings, or on emergency services. Several people picked up job leads from other neighbors; a few others found they had the same problem—they had lost their homes to foreclosure and were now renters. At the end of the night, the facilitator invited people to shout out one word that described how they felt about the experience. "Empowered!" "Connected!" "Informed!" "Happy!" were the responses.

Before heading home, Blackburn's team compared notes—Who would make a good door knocker? Who could be a Neighbor Circle host? Satisfied, the group departed, confident they had found a powerful way to unlock the power of community.[3]

How Service Helps

Forty million people, including fourteen million children, live in poverty in America.[4] While often the stereotype of urban poverty pervades, more poor people live in the suburbs than in the inner city, and rural areas have a poverty rate close to that of inner cities.[5] Although the face of poverty—and strategies to combat it—may vary, it often comes with a host of common problems, including exposure to gangs and crime, run-down neighborhoods, widespread substance abuse, and an environment that repeats the cycle for the children who grow up there.

Government does many essential things to help low-income people in America, from providing income supports and food stamps to job training and adult education. Government programs have helped to greatly reduce poverty during periods of U.S. history and for specific populations, and have helped to fuel private sector growth that brings opportunities. But government alone won't end poverty in America. Helping families find their way out of poverty requires a complex ecosystem of public and private sector supports, from a thriving business sector that provides good jobs with benefits to a healthy set of nonprofit and education organizations that can prepare people for work, make available decent housing and the services families need at affordable prices, and, with government, provide child care and other work supports and a safety net for people who can't make it on their own.

Often these factors work together. A private sector base of jobs helps support thriving nonprofits, better schools, and middle-class housing, whereas a weak local economy makes it almost impossible to support healthy nonprofit organizations, schools, and neighborhoods. In much the same way, strong social capital—the ties that connect people to one another—helps people succeed economically, whereas weak social capital makes it hard for people to find jobs, services, and other supports that help them help themselves.

If Frankie Blackburn is successful, she will have found a way for the low-income communities of Montgomery County, Maryland, to build their social capital—not only to increase their political voice but to find jobs and shape the services that local government and nonprofit agencies provide. Service can also help in other ways, including the actions described in the following sections.

HELPING PEOPLE FIND THE SERVICES THEY NEED. Even when help is available, people don't always access it due to lack of awareness or misconceptions. Connecting people to services is often a labor-intensive process. The Neighbors Campaign is one model to build connections that benefits from the community credibility its volunteers represent. LIFT, formerly known as National Student Partnerships, offers a different model. LIFT deploys trained college student volunteers in five cities to work one-on-one with community residents, coordinating access to employment opportunities and social services, including job training, housing, health care, child care, and transportation.

Maria is one of the thirty thousand people who have been helped by LIFT volunteers. She first came to LIFT in Somerville, Massachusetts, to update her resume after losing her job. She appreciated the extra caring the volunteers offered. "They did so much more for me here than anywhere else I have visited," she says. "They really care about their clients, I can feel that." With the help of LIFT volunteers, she soon secured part-time work at Massachusetts General Hospital. When her landlord decided to increase her apartment's monthly rent, Maria could not afford the increase—already more than half her income went for rent and utilities—and she was soon handed an eviction notice. After fifteen years of living in one place and with no money for moving expenses, she turned to LIFT in tears at the prospect of homelessness. Volunteers advised her about her tenant rights, helped her obtain volunteer legal help, and accompanied her to court appointments, enabling her to obtain an extension on her move-out date and settle outstanding payments with her landlord. LIFT helped Maria obtain housing benefits, locate a clean apartment in a safe neighborhood for significantly less than her old apartment, and obtain financial assistance for the first month's rent and security deposit from Catholic Charities and the Somerville Homeless Coalition. Maria credits LIFT as her support system while navigating the stressful and confusing eviction process. "They helped me mentally, physically, emotionally, financially, and even spiritually. I can't stress this point enough, they were just there."

Maria moved into her new apartment in July 2009. She still struggles to make ends meet, but LIFT volunteers have helped her establish a monthly budget and payment plans with her bank to make living expenses more affordable. Reflecting back on her challenges of the past two years, Maria says, "I lost my car, lost my job, got a divorce, and then lost my apartment. Since LIFT, I feel like I got my life back. I turned my life around 180 degrees. I worked very hard to get where I am today, and I did it with LIFT."[6]

EXPANDING THE HELP AVAILABLE. Finding available services is a challenge in most areas, but it can be even harder if you live in a community where few exist. That was a finding of a report I worked on for Save the Children, documenting the relationship of weak community institutions with child poverty in rural America.[7] But it can be equally true in urban and suburban areas.

VISTA (Volunteers in Service to America) was created as part of the 1960s War on Poverty to build the capacity of grassroots organizations to help low-income people and has played an important role in building the nonprofit sector in America. Now part of AmeriCorps, VISTA has engaged more than 170,000 adults in full-time service since 1964.

Over the past decade, AmeriCorps*VISTA members have helped to establish microcredit programs, mentoring programs for children of prisoners, rural-development programs, and a host of other services that reflect both innovative and time-tested poverty alleviation strategies.

For example, the New York City Coalition Against Hunger has sponsored an AmeriCorps*VISTA team since 2002. The VISTA members have started community gardens, helped small community feeding agencies write grants and recruit volunteers, supported agencies enrolling families in the food stamp program, increased the use of food stamps at farmers' markets, and connected varied social service and feeding programs for joint projects.[8]

The former executive director of Asian American LEAD (AALEAD), founder Sandy Dang, credits VISTA with helping the community-based youth organization expand from Washington, D.C., to areas in suburban Maryland. Founded in 1998, AALEAD promotes the well-being of low-income Asian American immigrant and refugee youths and their families through education, leadership development, and community building. In 2002, the organization purchased a building to house its Washington, D.C., program, and began to plan for expansion to other parts of the Washington metropolitan area. With the help of six VISTA members—four of them bilingual—AALEAD opened its Maryland office in 2006.[9]

TEACHING IMMIGRANTS TO SPEAK ENGLISH. Not being able to speak, read, and write in English is the biggest barrier to immigrants' ability to lift themselves out of poverty through employment and to communicate with teachers, health care providers, landlords, and others. English is also critical to passing the U.S. citizenship exam. Twenty million adults are limited English proficient, and studies suggest that only a small percentage of the need for English classes is being met.[10]

Volunteers have long served as English as a Second Language (ESL) teachers and teacher assistants, making up a significant portion of those engaged in this effort. In New Orleans, AmeriCorps*VISTA members serving through Tulane University rebuilt the Hispanic Apostolate's ESL program after Katrina and secured permanent space at Tulane University to hold evening classes. They created new sites at a local charter school and a community center for immigrant laborers, and recruited seventy Tulane students, primarily from Latin American Studies and Spanish departments, to serve as teachers and site facilitators.[11]

EXPANDING ACCESS TO AFFORDABLE HOUSING AND IMPROVING THE PHYSICAL NEIGHBORHOOD. Substandard housing and blighted neighborhoods are too often symptoms of poverty that also help to perpetuate it. In the United States, ninety-five million people, one-third of the nation, have housing problems, including payments that are too large a percentage of their income, overcrowding, poor-quality shelter, and homelessness.[12] According to the National Law Center on Homelessness and Poverty, more than three million people experience homelessness annually.[13] In the face of this vast problem, the efforts of volunteers may seem unimportant. However, as a piece of a larger strategy addressing the root causes of poverty, volunteer efforts directed at increasing the supply of affordable housing can help move tens of thousands of families from hardship to permanent home ownership.

Habitat for Humanity is well-known for engaging volunteers to build "simple, decent housing" alongside low-income homeowners. Not a giveaway program, Habitat asks homeowners to make a down payment and monthly mortgage payments and to invest hundreds of hours of their own labor into building their Habitat house and the houses of others. Their monthly mortgage payments are used to build still more Habitat houses.

While it had traditionally depended on volunteers, Habitat for Humanity International was one of the first nonprofits contacted by the Corporation for National and Community Service in the early days of AmeriCorps. As part of the first class of AmeriCorps members around the country, Habitat inducted 122 members to serve at five affiliates around the country. Affiliates soon found that the addition of AmeriCorps greatly amplified their impact. In Michigan, for example, Habitat affiliates had been unable to increase their production beyond one house per year. With the help of AmeriCorps, Michigan affiliates increased their production exponentially, building five hundred homes with twenty thousand volunteers in a half-dozen years. In the 2009 program year, over five hundred AmeriCorps members at affiliates all over the country helped build nearly two thousand houses and recruit and retain nearly two hundred thousand community volunteers.[15]

For nine years, on and off, I lived with my five siblings and my mother in a one-bedroom trailer where the tub was falling through the floor. I lived in constant fear that I would come home from school to find the trailer crumbled into heaping piles of rubble.

My Habitat home means security because I know it's healthier, I know that I can always come home and that Habitat for Humanity cares about what happens to my family. In our one-bedroom trailer, a whisper in the bedroom at the back of the house could be heard in the kitchen at the front. When winter came I'd huddle with my two sisters under a pile of blankets, shivering if so much as a toe broke free. In summer four of us sat in a circle, under the biggest tree, while taking turns fanning the lucky one who rested in the center.... Inside the trailer there were holes in the rotting floor. One hole under our bunk beds allowed cold air and creepy crawlers in. After we moved to our remodeled, four-bedroom, two-bath house I was relieved to find heating, air conditioning, no holes, and one roommate instead of five.

I don't dream anymore about coming home from school to find my house condemned, with a huge wrecking ball quivering to turn it into scraps. It's true that I'm a born worrier, but now I don't worry about a safe home. Sure my home gets dirty and Mom might consider my room a disaster zone, but I love my home. Sometimes I start walking to school, panic, turn back and check to make sure the coffee pot is off. I know that Habitat follows guidelines and meets safety codes the trailer would never pass. I know they put more love and care into my family's house than billionaires could buy.

Source: Josephine Pacheco, Winner, 2008 Youth Essay, Contest for Habitat homeowner children[14]

Houses, of course, don't exist in a vacuum. The neighborhood around them determines their value and often the quality of life for the people who live in them. The Alliance for Community Trees (ACT), with the hope of improving the environment while supporting livable communities, tackles one part of the challenge of building healthy urban neighborhoods. Many cities have lost more than a third of their forest canopy in recent decades. ACT's NeighborWoods trains local community organizers to lead volunteer tree planters and connects them through an online community so they can collaborate and share success strategies.

Baton Rouge Green is one local partner. According to Iman Fahmee Sabree, it all started when he and other business owners and residents from the community began to take a closer look at Washington Street, where crime had gotten out of control: "Drug dealers, drug users, and prostitutes were operating in broad daylight with no fear — many were young kids hiding from their parents — and the vacant houses and lots were being used as drug and sex dens." Sabree and other community leaders gathered to discuss how trees and flowers in other communities had been transformational. "You could see in people's faces a certain sadness and fear just disappear. People began talking with each other, came out more . . . . That was the beginning," he noted. To transform their own neighborhood, the group planted crape myrtles and colorful flowers along the street, in front yards of houses, in vacant lots, and at local businesses. They also put in picnic tables and built brick flowerbeds. "It didn't take long before neighbors started coming out to the picnic tables playing chess and checkers, criminals stopped coming out as much, new customers even started coming to the barbershop and the other businesses," Sabree observed. "Owners of non-vacant as well as owners of vacant properties now plant trees on their property . . . . When the trees are in full bloom, it's just beautiful. Baton Rouge Green started the community going with trees, but business owners, neighbors, and the interfaith collaborative have expanded the re-greening work."

As a result of the effort, according to Sabree, crime is down compared to similar neighborhoods and the value of property is up. "It just makes sense that in the nicer neighborhoods things are more beautiful, because people take care of their surroundings. And that's not a welcome environment for crime," notes Sabree. "These efforts are leading the neighborhood back to a time when it was a close-knit community, when neighbors looked out for each other."[16]

COACHING SMALL-BUSINESS OWNERS IN LOW-INCOME COMMUNITIES. Ultimately, reducing poverty in America requires creating more living-wage jobs and ensuring that more Americans have the skills and abilities to obtain and keep such jobs. Small businesses constitute 99 percent of inner-city establishments and account for more than 80 percent of inner-city jobs. In addition, entrepreneurship is a critical pathway to the middle class, as business ownership is second only to homeownership in contributing to household wealth.[17] Unfortunately, half of small businesses fail in the first five years, according to the Small Business Administration. The support of skilled volunteers who are seasoned entrepreneurs and business consultants can make all the difference.

In 2002, when the Clinton Foundation set out to support the economic development of Harlem, where President Clinton opened an office after his presidency, the help of volunteer business mentors from Booz & Company, New York University's Stern School of Business, and the New York chapter of the National Black MBA Association was part of the plan. Since then, the broader Clinton Economic Opportunity Initiative (CEO) has expanded its reach to help more entrepreneurs succeed and individuals and families to join the financial mainstream. Over the years, CEO has provided more than seventy-two thousand hours of pro bono consulting services worth more than $15 million to New York City area entrepreneurs. In 2007, in partnership with *Inc.* magazine, CEO began building mentoring communities in several cities nationwide, including Oakland, Chicago, New York, and Newark (New Jersey), by pairing inner-city entrepreneurs with successful business leaders and entrepreneur mentors through the Entrepreneur Mentoring Program. Over the course of the program, mentors help entrepreneurs develop a better understanding of their business and industry, become better leaders and sharpen their business acumen, and make better decisions on the critical issues facing their company.

In addition, the Clinton Foundation partnered with Zagat Survey to create the first-ever *Spotlight on Harlem* neighborhood guide, highlighting 323 of Harlem's restaurants, nightspots, shops, and attractions with ratings and reviews that are based on the collective opinions of thousands of surveyors who voted at ZAGAT.com.[18]

Prisoners returning to the community are a population in particular need of business consulting help. It's not easy for ex-felons to find jobs, and without economic alternatives, returning to crime may be their only option. The national recidivism rate is above 60 percent. With one out of a hundred Americans in prison today—or a total of 2.3 million people, a population exceeding those of fifteen states—Americans spent $49 billion on incarceration, or $21,000 per inmate annually. When $1 out of every $15 of state budget funds is relegated to corrections, other budgetary needs (such as education and transportation) are squeezed out.[19]

Former Wall Street investor Catherine Rohr founded the Prison Entrepreneurship Program, or PEP, in 2004 when she toured a prison and noticed that executives and inmates had more in common than most would think. "They know how to manage others to get things done. Even the most unsophisticated drug dealers inherently understand business concepts such as competition, profitability, risk management and proprietary sales channels," observes Rohr. She wondered what would happen if inmates who were committed to their own transformation were equipped to start and run legitimate companies.

Rohr left behind her New York career, moved to Texas, and started a one-of-a-kind "behind bars" business plan competition. Her efforts were geared toward channeling the entrepreneurial passions and influential personalities of the inmates—intentionally recruiting former gang leaders, drug dealers, and hustlers. The overwhelming response of fifty-five inmates and fifteen executive volunteers to judge the business plans and presentations was the catalyst to launch the Prison Entrepreneurship Program. By June 2009, with the help of more than a thousand business volunteers, PEP had produced staggering results, including a return-to-prison rate of less than 10 percent, an employment rate of 80 percent within thirty days of release, and a rapidly growing network of entrepreneurial startups. Their experience with PEP doesn't consist of only receiving benefits; its graduates are also donors to the program, while others have signed on to PEP's employee team to contribute their skills to help others.[20]

RECRUITING THE NEXT GENERATION OF COMMUNITY-DEVELOPMENT PROFESSIONALS. Community-development agencies help to change distressed neighborhoods into thriving communities. The people who lead this effort need to possess a special blend of community knowledge and community organizing and other skills.

For LISC (Local Initiatives Support Corporation), a national network of community-development organizations, AmeriCorps has offered not only the benefits of full-time help but a network of future leaders in training. LISC's diverse AmeriCorps team includes both college graduates and residents of the low-income neighborhoods its member organizations serve. They help individuals become homeowners, establish after-school education programs, and organize crime-watch groups and tenant associations. The experience immerses members in the world of community development and shows the many professional paths it offers. According to LISC, the "AmeriCorps experience is to community development what medical school is to health care. It's where the industry's future leaders are groomed."[21]

DISASTER

The Lower 9th Ward, years after the New Orleans levees broke, almost looked like a subdivision about to be built. The roads and street signs were there, and lawns where houses should be. Sometimes there was a concrete foundation slab, or a pile of sticks that once made up a house. On the outside walls of houses were symbols painted in bright orange—circles with numbers signifying the identity of the search unit that looked in the house for people or bodies and the number of each that they found. In through a hole that must once have been a window, one could see jumbled furniture, a kitchen sink torn from the wall. On the floor, a water-stained gray-leafed paperback.

In the days that followed Hurricanes Katrina and Rita in 2005, more than eighteen hundred people were killed in floods across the Gulf Coast. Eight hundred fifty thousand homes were damaged or destroyed, two hundred thousand in New Orleans alone.[22] An estimated ten million people were affected across an area the size of Great Britain, and more than $110 billion in damage was inflicted.[23] Floodwaters covered three-quarters of the city of New Orleans.[24]

This tragedy exposed what was wrong with our systems for disaster preparedness, response, and recovery. It also revealed what was right. One thing that was right was the crowded bunkroom in what had been the recreation hall of the First Street United Methodist Church. Located in the heart of Central City, First Street Methodist was founded for slaves in 1833 in a low-lying area of New Orleans. While it weathered the storm with minimal roof and flood damage, houses in the economically depressed area around it fared far worse. Reverend Lance Eden and most of the parishioners lost their homes in the storm.

In the weeks and months that followed the hurricanes, forty-five million Americans came forward to help. Half a million made the trip to the Gulf to do what they could in person.[25]

One of them was Kellie Bentz, a young member of AmeriCorps Alums, who joined the HandsOn Network staff in January 2006 for a six-week stint to help set up a base camp for volunteers. She stayed three-and-a-half years, becoming the director of HandsOn New Orleans.

Bentz and her colleagues found not just destroyed homes and abandoned businesses but a decimated volunteer infrastructure. Reverend Eden offered the recreation and dining halls of the church to serve as a base camp for the thousands of volunteers making their way to New Orleans. Bentz and her team worked quickly to build a hundred bunkbeds, crammed into such a small space that there was barely enough room to walk between them. Outdoor showers, a tool shed, and a work-assignment bulletin board completed the base. Teams of AmeriCorps members from the National Civilian Community Corps came to lead the volunteers that would serve under Bentz's direction. Ready for action in March of 2006, spring breakers from St. Bonaventure University in New York filled every bed on the first night.

Early on, the volunteers gutted houses. Day after day they carried out water-soaked mattresses, ruined sofas and carpets, unrecognizable debris. They then knocked out drywall, taking the walls down to the wooden studs that framed each room. Then for days on end the team would remove mold from the walls, using toothbrushes to get every spore. It was hot, tedious, uncomfortable work that required full-body suits and face masks for protection. After a long day of work came dinner in the church dining hall and sleep in the bunkroom. And then they were up early to do it all over again.[26]

In the first year, twenty-seven hundred volunteers came. In the years that followed, the work changed from demolition to construction. HandsOn New Orleans, working closely with Habitat for Humanity, Rebuilding Together, and a host of local organizations that were part of the Greater New Orleans Disaster Recovery Partnership, continued to host streams of visiting volunteers, directing them not just to rebuild housing but to man volunteer projects that might have been done by local people in other, less desperate circumstances. Soup kitchens, school libraries, and animal shelters all needed volunteers as people slowly returned to their communities. Keeping these doors open was as important to the recovery effort as the reopening of local businesses and repair of people's homes.

How Service Helps

In the past decade, more than forty-five disasters have been declared in the United States each year.[27] They may be manmade—in the case of terrorism, hazardous spills, or arson leading to large-scale wildfires—or they may be naturally occurring. Many scientists predict climate change will increase the number and severity of hurricanes, and population growth will increase the number and impact of manmade disasters. Large-scale emergencies can occur in any state, in any community. And as Hurricanes Katrina and Rita illustrate, the human toll they take can be devastating. At the same time, tens of thousands of smaller-scale emergencies occur every year, in every community. To the people they affect, they are no less traumatic.

HandsOn New Orleans and other volunteers provided a substantial labor force that was badly needed after Hurricane Katrina. However, volunteers are also critical to both emergency preparedness and response.

RESPONDING TO DISASTERS. Volunteers have long responded to disasters, informally and through organized efforts. The American Red Cross is the largest disaster response organization in the United States, organizing both trained volunteers and paid staff to provide relief and other assistance. Founder Clara Barton as a child had nursed her brother to health after a serious fall; as an adult, she pioneered a role for volunteer relief workers on the battlefield during the Civil War. Under her leadership, the American Red Cross was launched in 1881 to continue this support.

In 1905, President Theodore Roosevelt signed a congressional charter authorizing the American Red Cross to provide emergency assistance when disaster strikes. Since then, Red Cross workers and volunteers have been on the scene of every major disaster, starting with the San Francisco earthquake of 1906, which killed seven hundred people.[28]

Today the Red Cross disaster response human resources system (DSHR) includes hundreds of thousands of individuals trained to respond to disasters nationwide, 96 percent of whom are volunteers. When a major disaster strikes an area, the local chapter rarely has enough trained personnel to provide adequate response. The DSHR program provides assistance by sending trained volunteers from chapters in other parts of the country to assist the local chapter. For example, according to *Blood, Sweat and Tears* by Michele Turk, in the wake of Hurricane Katrina, the Southeast Louisiana chapter of the American Red Cross "had four to six feet of water and remained uninhabitable for months. In addition, thirty percent of . . . staff left town." The forty staff members and volunteers who remained, some of whose homes had been destroyed, "are some of the heroes of the storm," according to Kay Wilkins, CEO of the chapter.[29] "They had great courage." With the assistance of DSHR volunteers, ultimately the American Red Cross staffed more than a thousand shelters in twenty-seven states after Katrina, housing a record one hundred eighteen thousand evacuees in one night and serving twenty-five million hot meals in three months.[30]

Disaster response volunteers offer a wide variety of skills needed during a disaster, including first aid, communications, logistics, and mental health counseling. Virginia Stern, profiled in Turk's book, was among the fifty-five thousand Red Crossers who responded to the September 11 terrorist attacks. A retired social worker, Virginia had signed up for a disaster service course just months before the attack. She could see the World Trade Center from the corner by her apartment. Even before the towers fell, she had left her house and made her way to the Red Cross center in the neighborhood. "As a mental health worker in a crisis, there's not much to *do*," she recalls. "You don't go eliciting feelings, you don't ask probing questions. What you do is offer the families or friends the sense that they're not alone, that there are people who care, that people are taking care of the situation, and that they will get information as soon as its available."[31] The relief workers themselves also may need support. In the book, Stern recalls a crane operator who approached her on break on the *Spirit Ship*, which had been set up to provide meals and a place to rest for workers at Ground Zero. "You know what happened today?" the man told Stern. "I found a leg from the knee down." Notes Stern, "he was as surprised by what he said to me as I was—he didn't plan to talk about it, but he couldn't keep it in . . . . We started talking about how the family of the person whose leg he found is probably wondering what happened, and now they would be able to know. We talked how this was a 'gift' for family members because they could begin the healing process. Afterwards he felt more in control of himself and more able to go back to operating the crane."[32]

REBUILDING COMMUNITIES. Once the initial crisis passes, usually in a matter of weeks or months, emergency response volunteers move on and the recovery process begins. This typically includes the rebuilding of structures damaged or destroyed in the crisis.

In New Orleans and other Gulf Coast communities, national service has been an important part of the recovery process. The story of HandsOn New Orleans echoes that of other organizations that rose to the occasion to respond to the tragedy. In St. Bernard Parish, just outside New Orleans, local officials called on AmeriCorps*NCCC to help muck out houses. Initially, the team worked twelve-hour days but was able to complete just ten homes in a week. A larger workforce clearly was needed, so in December 2005, the team turned to setting up and running a volunteer operation, successfully building the capacity to take on twenty-five hundred volunteers a day and increasing the number of houses completed each week twenty-fold, to two hundred a week.[33] In Pass Christian, Mississippi, the AmeriCorps St. Louis Emergency Response Team spent a year stocking and distributing donated goods; opened an information and referral center for residents to locate assistance; helped hundreds of residents muck out and repair their homes; and operated a tent-style housing facility for displaced residents. When the facility was no longer needed, the team transformed it into a base camp for out-of-town volunteers so they could house and lead an additional twenty-four hundred volunteers from across the country.[34]

HELPING RESIDENTS RECLAIM THEIR LIVES. Rebuilding after a disaster isn't limited to physical structures. Individuals affected by disasters often require a wide range of assistance to help them rebuild their lives.

For example, in the aftermath of the 2005 hurricanes, affected residents faced myriad legal needs. They needed help filing insurance and FEMA claims, as well as appeals when their claims were denied. As Gulfport resident Sammie Gray put it, "How did I apply for FEMA relief when I have no electricity and no computer and they do not take handwritten applications?" As time passed and the housing supply was greatly diminished, landlords doubled and tripled rents and sought to evict tenants in favor of new residents whom they could charge higher prices. As a result of the hurricanes, the criminal justice system collapsed, leaving hundreds of people imprisoned without proper paperwork or access to counsel.

Navigating these legal challenges was daunting, especially for people with limited education or incomes. Many local attorneys were displaced, and the few public interest legal organizations able to assist local residents were greatly stressed. To respond to the crisis, a group of law students formed the Student Hurricane Network in October 2005 at the annual conference of Equal Justice Works, a Washington, D.C.–based national public interest law organization. Hundreds of volunteer law students came to Mississippi on breaks to reach out to people in ravaged communities, research legal remedies, and help at legal clinics. Mississippi Center for Justice executive director Martha Bergmark calls it the echo of the civil rights movement. "Law student volunteers brought an enormous amount of energy and passion, and made a difference in the lives of Mississippians all across the Coast. They also took their experiences with them—back to school and into their careers—whatever they decide to do and wherever they decide to work. They will also take a renewed awareness of the injustice, inequity and racism that still riddle this country. Even more important, they will take the conviction that they can make a difference."[35]

Equal Justice Works placed ten AmeriCorps attorneys and 106 AmeriCorps law student members in the Gulf. The AmeriCorps attorneys focused on recruiting law students and volunteer lawyers to manage a statewide emergency hotline in Louisiana, help residents in Alabama to overcome legal barriers to secure permanent housing, assist New Orleans residents filing for bankruptcy, and respond to legal needs in Mississippi.[36]

Crystal Utley was an Equal Justice Works AmeriCorps member. A native Mississippian, Utley was practicing insurance law in South Carolina when Hurricane Katrina hit the Gulf Coast, ripping the roof off her mother's restaurant. "It was too difficult to watch my home state suffer from afar," she recalls. As an AmeriCorps member, Utley was placed at the Mississippi Center for Justice, where she became immersed in hurricane-related legal issues. In addition to assisting clients directly, she advised more than four hundred fifty pro bono attorneys and recruited a hundred twenty law students to help people affected by the hurricanes.[37]

Utley and her team helped people such as a sixty-three-year-old wheelchair-bound woman whose home was destroyed. An unscrupulous landlord rented the client a trailer he'd received from FEMA, which is against the law. Although she paid the rent, the landlord didn't pay electric and water bills and she lost service. FEMA's response was to remove the trailer, which would have left the client homeless. Utley and the pro bono attorneys worked successfully to get her a trailer of her own from FEMA.[38] In another case, Utley came to the aid of a widow from Moss Point, whose mortgage lender threatened to foreclose on the home she shared with her four grandchildren. Utley explained to her client that the state had declared a moratorium on foreclosures for hurricane survivors and gave her step-by-step instructions on how to file for an injunction against the lender. She warned the client that some lenders don't give up. Sometimes, said Utley, "it takes a phone call from me to say, 'I just want to make sure that you're aware that this has been filed, and if you continue, you'll be in contempt of court.'"[39] After the moratorium, the landlord continued to pursue foreclosure, but Utley's team was able to negotiate with the lender to reinstate the loan.

PREPARING FOR DISASTERS. Preparation for disasters can minimize the human cost of sudden large-scale emergencies. Poor preparation made Katrina more a story of recovery than of proper planning and response. In contrast, Florida, no stranger to hurricanes, offers a model of what is possible. By learning from past crises, leaders in Florida have built a comprehensive volunteer system to complement professional emergency response mechanisms.

Volunteer Florida, the Governor's Commission on Volunteerism and Community Service, serves as the state's official lead agency for managing volunteers and donations during emergencies. According to Wendy Spencer, the chief executive officer of Volunteer Florida, the success of a volunteer effort depends on preparation, including planning, training, and building partnerships. It also means continuously improving systems. "We learn countless lessons every time a disaster hits," notes Spencer.[40]

In the wake of 9/11, the Bush Administration created the Freedom Corps, which included a heavy emphasis on emergency preparedness. According to Freedom Corps's first director, John Bridgeland, it was clear that volunteers could support professionals in important ways, and that in fact, they were a critical part of an effective emergency response infrastructure. In 95 percent of all emergencies, bystanders or victims themselves are the first to provide emergency assistance or perform a rescue. Bridgeland pushed for the creation of Citizen Corps, to encourage Americans to help prepare themselves and their communities. These councils educate the public, organize volunteer opportunities, and share information so their best efforts can be replicated.[41]

One function of Citizen Corps is to promote the Community Emergency Response Team (CERT) program, to train ordinary citizens in basic disaster response skills, such as fire safety, light search and rescue, team organization, and disaster medical operations. Inspired by Japan's extensive earthquake preparedness system, which trains entire neighborhoods to respond to earthquakes, CERT was begun at the instigation of the Los Angeles Fire Department. The work of the L.A. planning team took on more urgency after a major earthquake struck Mexico City in 1985, killing more than ten thousand and injuring more than thirty thousand. Mexico City had no training program for citizens prior to the emergency, but large groups of volunteers organized themselves to search for survivors. Although they saved more than eight hundred people, more than a hundred volunteers died during the fifteen-day rescue operation. The following year, the City of Los Angeles Fire Department developed a pilot program to train the leaders of a neighborhood watch organization in disaster response. A few years later, with the new program widespread across Los Angeles, FEMA decided to take the concept nationwide.[42]

Using the training learned in the classroom and during exercises, CERT members can assist others in the event professional responders cannot help. John Bridgeland describes CERT as "the intersection of professionals and volunteers."[43] Volunteer Florida became an enthusiastic supporter of Citizen Corps and CERT training. More than twenty-two thousand Floridians were CERT trained in just six years. "It typically takes three to thirty minutes for professionals to respond to an emergency. Those are critical minutes," according to Wendy Spencer. "Instead of having to train people on the fly in a large-scale crisis, it is so much better to prepare them through CERT. The more people are CERT trained, the safer the environment. And ultimately, the better we become at stabilizing a situation until first responders can arrive."[44]

In the wake of a high-profile disaster, volunteers come forward in large numbers. As the experience of the Red Cross demonstrates, with proper preparation, they can play important roles. However, "unaffiliated" untrained volunteers can easily overwhelm local systems, particularly in the face of a major disaster. Without local coordination, "you have a disaster within a disaster as well-intentioned volunteers just start providing aid in some ways that are not effective or efficient," according to Spencer. The answer, however, is not to turn them away but rather to prepare for them. A local volunteer center, government volunteer coordinator, or volunteer coordinator at a nonprofit organization can be tapped to coordinate these volunteers, including educating other organizations, conducting community outreach, developing a volunteer referral plan, arranging for transportation, and writing a public information plan. They can set up and operate a reception center for volunteers, and be prepared to register and deploy them in support of local emergency response efforts.

AmeriCorps figures prominently in Volunteer Florida's disaster plans as well. As part of their commitment to service, all AmeriCorps members supported by Volunteer Florida are required to obtain disaster training. In some cases, AmeriCorps members play a critical role supervising unaffiliated volunteers. In others, they bring special skills. The fact that they are part of a national program also makes a difference. "Seeing these young people with the AmeriCorps logo lets people know they're part of something like the Peace Corps," according to Spencer. "People are often more comfortable with a 'branded' large organization. AmeriCorps members' sustained commitment to service, day in and day out, provides great assurance to survivors that they will be there for the long haul."[45]

Florida also worked to implement the American Red Cross "building Disaster Resistant Neighborhoods" model to encourage homeowner associations to help their members prepare for potential disasters, and expanded the network of volunteer centers across the state to match those who want to serve with opportunities to make a difference.

One of these volunteer centers serves Manatee County, where youths in the Manateens program play a significant role in disaster preparedness. Disaster-related projects are popular with the teens (second only to animal causes). The Manateens have invented dozens of programs, including the *Pets in Emergencies Guidebook*, which identifies pet-friendly disaster shelters, and Nosey Neighbors, which introduces neighbors to one another through block parties and surveys them regarding their special needs and skills they can share, including those relating to possible disasters. As part of the county's disaster response plan, Manateens offer CERT training as well as CPR, and take responsibility for managing the Volunteer Reception Center after disasters.[46]

The record-breaking 2004–2005 hurricane seasons put Volunteer Florida's system to the test. Florida experienced seven hurricanes and one tropical storm that brought widespread destruction across the state and together caused more than $61 million in damage. In addition, Florida provided assistance to Mississippi and Texas after Hurricanes Katrina and Rita affected those states.

Linking 140 relief agencies with local needs, Volunteer Florida oversaw the work of 252,000 volunteers who served twenty million meals, fielded eighty-three thousand calls to the volunteer hotline, distributed thirty-five million bottles of water and 1.4 million bags of ice, and tarped thirty-five thousand roofs. "Without a doubt, our collective ability to effectively respond to these storms is directly attributable to the maximization of volunteer and donated resources," confirmed Spencer. "Voluntary, community, and faith-based organizations are keys to our success in meeting the needs of disaster survivors."[47]

POTENTIAL FOR TRANSFORMATION

Disaster work begins with preparation—an effort by a whole community to make sure community-wide plans are in place, that individuals, organizations, and businesses are aware of them and have made appropriate preparations, and that local teams are CERT trained and otherwise prepared for a large-scale emergency, including the influx of large numbers of people from outside the community who want to help. Volunteers play a critical role in all of these efforts, and if they are trained and prepared, in the response to disasters as well. By making full use of these human resources, we can ensure that every community is prepared for the worst.

Whether a neighborhood suffers from long-term urban decay or a sudden emergency, volunteer and national service can also help sustain a rebuilding process, creating physical changes to housing, parks, and sidewalks as well as meeting human needs that put the people who live there on a path to economic security. By engaging people from the community, these efforts have the trust of local people and greater staying power.

Imagine these sets of services in every neighborhood. Anchor institutions and connected neighbors, who can offer a hand up to anyone who needs it. Clean streets and green parks. The commitment of everyone who lives there to give back and stay engaged to protect their gains. It's happening in spots across the country, but in no place at scale. Service can help this vision take hold everywhere in America.

CHAPTER SEVEN

Protecting the Environment

CONSERVING ENERGY

A light bulb went on in Avery Hairston's head. As a middle school student, he had seen Al Gore's slide show, *An Inconvenient Truth*, and it had made a deep impression on him. Later, Avery saw an advertisement by Starbucks in the *New York Times* that said if every person who received the newspaper changed one light bulb to a compact fluorescent light (CFL) bulb, it would be the equivalent of taking eighty-nine thousand cars off the road. That gave him an idea, perfect in its simplicity: he and his friends would raise money to buy light bulbs that they could use to "relight" New York City's housing projects. Not only would the effort save the residents money, it would raise awareness about CFLs, which last ten times longer than conventional bulbs and use roughly two-thirds less energy.

Avery and his friends turned to the social networking website Facebook to recruit others, and in less than thirty days, they had over five hundred members. He and his friends secured donations of light bulbs and help in developing a website that shared the simple steps anyone could take to "relight" a building and featured a map (using a Microsoft map mash-up) that allowed people to register their teams and post their accomplishments. It was a hit. Relight went national, adding materials for teachers and expanding the map to the rest of the United States.

By 2009, ninety-four RelightUS.com teams had adopted 629 addresses, changed 112,476 bulbs, eliminated 22,039,251 pounds of CO_2 emissions, and saved $5,555,046 in energy costs. But Avery is humble about his accomplishments, which he sees as part of his civic responsibility. "I don't want to be part of the generation that made the wrong choices and kind of let down everyone in the future."[1]

How Service Helps

The vast majority of scientists now agree that climate change is real and attributable to human activities such as burning fossil fuels and clearing forests, as well as methane gas resulting from garbage and livestock. We are already seeing the results: glaciers are melting, plants and animals are being forced from their habitats, and the number of severe storms and droughts is increasing. And this could worsen: deaths from global warming will double in twenty-five years, to three hundred thousand people per year; global sea levels could rise by more than twenty feet; the Arctic Ocean could be ice free in summer by 2050; and more than a million animal species worldwide could be driven to extinction by 2050.[2]

Much of the public debate about climate change has focused on international treaties and domestic energy policy—debates with high stakes for the economy and implications for our foreign policy. There are, however, many ways for ordinary citizens to make a difference. As Avery Hairston discovered, changing a single light bulb can have an impact. Widespread education efforts; green building; and home, school, and office energy conservation projects are all essential parts of any serious effort to reduce energy consumption. In each of these areas, volunteer and national service are core strategies.

CHANGING BEHAVIOR TO REDUCE ENERGY CONSUMPTION. It doesn't take an engineering degree to reduce your energy consumption. The car you drive—or your decision to carpool, bike, walk, or use public transportation when possible—matters. So do the appliances you choose, the temperature on your water heater, and whether you turn your computers and other electronics off when not in use. Motivating Americans to take simple steps to reduce their energy footprints is a task easily taken on by volunteers, and can be particularly effective when someone they know makes the "ask."

Young people are natural messengers, and many service-learning programs address environmental issues—from college courses analyzing energy alternatives to elementary classes that compare the environmental impact of biking to driving. And they welcome the opportunity: over 80 percent of American teens are bothered by the fact that the United States represents one of the world's leading sources of pollution, and more than half (54 percent) are strongly bothered by it. Indeed, a majority of teens (61 percent) actively agree that their generation will be more environmentally responsible than older generations.[3]

Earth Force offers training and support for teachers who want to incorporate environmentally focused service-learning opportunities into their courses. For example, the AP Environmental Science students at Northwest Pennsylvania Collegiate Academy enthusiastically took on the challenge of educating their community about energy conservation. With the help of Earth Force teacher Doreen Petri and support from the Pennsylvania Department of Environmental Protection, they conducted an energy audit, then developed and implemented a plan to cut energy consumption in their school, which they continue to monitor. In addition, they have traveled to the local elementary school to help the younger students conduct their own energy audit. National surveys of Earth Force students show that 86 percent of students report a better understanding of environmental issues and 81 percent said they felt their project made a difference.[4]

Neighbors can also be good messengers. The Operation Energy Save toolkit offered by AARP for free on its Create The Good website shows how to save on energy costs and organize a service project in your own community.[5] The Green the Block campaign, led by the Hip Hop Caucus, Green For All, and a coalition of over seventy organizations, takes energy conservation campaigns into neighborhoods that aren't often the focus of environmental projects. For example, in honor of the September 11 National Day of Service,

The Berkshire School in Massachusetts already had won recognition for its recycling efforts from the National Wildlife Federation for Campus Ecology. But school leaders wanted to take their efforts to "green the school" to the next level. The school experimented with making biodiesel out of kitchen grease from the dining hall. Successful, the school set the goal of producing fuel to power its "guzzling fleet of machinery," including lawn mowers and utility vehicles. By switching from petroleum-based commercial fuel to student-manufactured biodiesel, the Berkshire School will reduce emission of harmful gasses and lower fuel costs. Its efforts won it recognition as a finalist in the Student Conservation Association's "Green Your School" contest.

Source: "Production of Bio-diesel," http://www.thesca.org/contest/green-your-school-finalists/production-bio-diesel, accessed December 1, 2009.

Douglass High Students in Tennessee "greened the block" of their North Memphis neighborhood by delivering to residents packages of compact fluorescent bulbs, faucet filters, and switchplate insulation donated by the local utility.[6]

INSTALLING GREEN TECHNOLOGY. Changing a light bulb is a task that almost anyone can do. Installing solar panels takes a bit more skill. Not only can solar energy reduce carbon emissions, it can save homeowners thousands of dollars on their energy bills. But the cost of such systems may be out of reach for the low-income families who are the most likely to be hard hit by high energy prices, utility rate shocks, and polluting power plants.

Grid Alternatives, founded in 2001 by Erica Mackie and Tim Sears, two engineering professionals, offers a model for bringing solar energy to low-income families. Working in partnership with local governments and nonprofit housing developers, Grid Alternatives trains and leads teams of community volunteers to install solar electric systems for low-income clients who contribute "sweat equity," either by participating in the installation process or helping to spread the word to others. Project days are like "renewable energy 'barn raisings,'" according to Grid Alternatives, bringing together diverse individuals—environmentalists, job trainees, do-it-yourselfers, and low-income community members. By 2009, more than two thousand people had participated in volunteer installations, and projects have long waiting lists of people who want to help. The program has installed 250 solar electric systems for low-income families throughout northern and southern California, reducing each family's electric bills by approximately 75 percent, which will translate to a total of over $4.13 million in energy generated over the systems' projected life spans. They will also prevent roughly 12,508 tons of greenhouse gas emissions over the next thirty years, the equivalent of planting 17,457 trees.[7]

PREPARING FOR "GREEN JOBS". Analysts show that the "green-collar" sector is growing in the United States. According to the American Solar Energy Society, there are 8.5 million U.S. jobs that involve earth-friendly enterprises and renewable energy sources. That figure could grow by five million in a decade.[8]

Youth corps programs that teach green job skills offer the dual benefits of filling essential jobs and offering low-income youths the chance for a well-paying career path. American Youthworks has been a leader in green job training for more than two decades. Engaging a diverse population (57 percent Hispanic, 21 percent African American, and 22 percent Caucasian), ages sixteen through twenty-six, who are disproportionately poor (88 percent come from low-income households), American Youthworks operates several AmeriCorps programs, including Casa Verde Builders, a YouthBuild program that incorporates the opportunity for corpsmembers to earn their high school diplomas. Casa Verde Builders teams construct affordable five-star award-winning energy-efficient housing in East Austin, Texas, for first-time home buyers. Since 1993, they have built over ninety homes that are 40 percent more energy efficient than the average home. Corpsmembers learn green building techniques, including the importance of landscaping; energy-efficient design; and use of renewable resources, recycled products, and local materials. Environmental knowledge is integrated into the youth corps's curriculum—math, science, and social studies offer opportunities to teach the impact of pollution, waste, recycling, energy conservation, and renewable resources.

Students not only become knowledgeable about environmentally sustainable practices, they also become committed to the cause. According to staff, "Most of our young people are not environmentally sensitive when they start the program. By graduation they are excited about promoting a more sustainable life." Many graduates pursue higher education and careers in environmental fields.[9]

PROTECTING THE ENVIRONMENT

On a windy bluff overlooking San Francisco Bay, it would be easy to overlook the Raven's Manzanita. If visitors were allowed in the area, they might step carefully to avoid the poison oak and be distracted by the dramatic vistas nearby. This unassuming plant, a gnarled, low-growing shrub with waxy leaves, has lived at the Presidio for a hundred years, thriving in the sunlight and magnesium-rich soil and drinking from the fog that so often envelopes the bay. Its forebears might well have offered the native people and early settlers of the Bay Area berries, to be dried and ground into meal or soaked to make a refreshing cider; bark curls, which could be used as a tea for nausea; and leaves that quenched their thirst or served as toothbrushes.[10] But over the years, development shrunk the Raven's

Manzanita's habitat, and the towering trees planted at the Presidio in the late nineteenth century robbed it of the light it needed to thrive on the military base. And now, this single lowly shrub, growing in a secret spot at the Presidio, holds the dubious distinction of being the last of its kind.

Conservationists are working hard to save the Raven's Manzanita and eleven other endangered plants within the Golden Gate National Recreation Area. If they are saved, volunteers will have made a big difference.[11]

Habitat restoration activities are a classic "many pairs of hands" challenge—labor-intensive tasks that can easily be taught but overwhelm the capacity of the limited number of paid professionals working for the Park Service and the Presidio Trust. The core activities of restoration begin with collecting seeds and propagating seedlings, to planting young plants in restoration sites, to weeding invasive plants, to monitoring the results of restoration efforts. Volunteers with the Presidio Trust, the National Park Service, and the Golden Gate National Parks Conservancy partnership help with all of these tasks. In fact, as many as two thousand people volunteer each year at the Golden Gate National Recreation Area helping endangered species, along with an additional twenty thousand other volunteers, serving a total of 414,000 hours in 2009.[12]

How Service Helps

The rich diversity of plant and animal species on the earth is of profound importance to the balance of nature and to human life. In the preamble to the Endangered Species Act of 1973, Congress found that threatened and endangered species "are of esthetic, economical, educational, historical, recreational, and scientific value to the Nation and its people." For example, one in four prescriptions taken in the United States today come from chemicals discovered in plants and animals. Farmers use biological controls to protect their crops from insects, and new uses for plants are found that expand the food supply and meet other human needs. The opportunity to view wildlife creates economic opportunities through tourism. Even more important, each plant or animal occupies a place in the ecological system, supporting the survival of other species.

Due to habitat loss, as well as exploitation of wildlife for commercial purposes, the introduction of nonnative species, and the spread of disease, the rate of extinction has accelerated greatly over what would have occurred in the natural order. In North America alone, since the Pilgrims landed at Plymouth Rock, more than five hundred species and subspecies have disappeared.[13] Human activity harms the environment in many other ways. Due to runoff, dumping, and other hazards, 40 percent of American rivers and nearly half of our lakes are too polluted for fishing, swimming, or aquatic life.[14] Of the over 250 million tons of solid waste generated by Americans every year, only a third is recycled or composted—the rest goes to landfills.[15] The over forty thousand landfills in the United States pose the risk of leaching hazardous waste into groundwater and releasing methane gas, which contributes to global warming.[16] Environmental laws play an important role in reducing harm, but the acts of ordinary citizens can also help—or hurt. The small actions of millions of people can help prevent or reverse environmental degradation. Service supports environmental protection in the following ways.

PLANTING TREES. Many activities that can preserve or restore the environment require numerous pairs of hands and little training. Planting trees is a classic example. Not only do trees beautify our landscape—they remove carbon dioxide from the air, which is key to reversing climate change; filter the air of pollutants; provide habitats and food for wildlife; and prevent soil erosion and pollutant runoff into watersheds. Planting native trees is particularly important to maintaining an ecosystem and preventing unintended harm that sometimes occurs when new species are introduced into an area.

In the Washington, D.C., area, runoff from commercial and residential development poses a great threat to water quality, ultimately harming the Potomac River and Chesapeake Bay. In addition, the high volume of water during a storm causes erosion of stream banks and excessive sedimentation of the bay. Growing Native, a project of the Potomac Watershed Partnership and Potomac Conservancy, engages volunteers to address this problem by calling on local groups to collect acorns, walnuts, and other native tree seeds. In addition to gathering seeds that can be grown into seedlings for planting to restore streamside lands, the program builds awareness and presents an excellent learning opportunity for students to understand the connection between trees and clean water. A popular activity for schools, seed collection enables students to practice identifying different species of trees and learn about watersheds and other topics using tools and curricula provided online by Growing Native. Since the program's creation in 2001, thirty thousand volunteers have collected more than ninety-four thousand pounds of seeds off the ground in Maryland, Virginia, West Virginia, Pennsylvania, and the District of Columbia.[17]

ENCOURAGING RECYCLING. One simple way to reduce the problems created by landfills is to decrease the amount of material that is discarded. Reducing consumption, recycling and buying recycled materials, and composting are all simple ways that everyone can help. So is reuse of unwanted items—donation programs for reuse or resale not only contribute to the economic health of the people who receive them and the organizations that manage these programs, but also decrease landfill waste.

Freecycle takes reuse to a new level by using the Internet to obviate the need for an intermediary to collect and distribute used goods. Freecycle is the brainchild of Deron Beal, who worked with a small nonprofit organization that provided recycling services in Tucson, Arizona, to downtown businesses and transitional employment to residents. He found it cumbersome to find nonprofits that could use the donated goods and decided to email friends and nonprofit organizations inviting them to join a "Freecycle Network." Through the network, members could post to a listserv any item they did not want to find it a new home. At the same time, a member who wanted an item could ask for it. From sofas to electronic equipment, clothing to houseplants—anything that would otherwise become public waste is eligible. Since 2003, Freecycle has spread to eighty-five countries, with nearly five thousand local groups representing nearly seven million members. As a result, the organization estimates that it keeps over five hundred tons a day out of landfills.[18]

RESTORING POLLUTED AREAS. Four centuries ago, Captain John Smith sailed up the Anacostia River, in what would one day become Washington, D.C.[19] According to the National Resources Defense Council, the Anacostia was the "central artery of a watershed that straddles both wooded hills and coastal flats; its shores were cloaked with lush forests and rich tidal wetlands." It was "a thriving hub of Native American culture" and "teemed with shad, white and yellow perch, herring and other fish that were a staple food of the local Nanchotank people."[20]

Today, the Anacostia winds through the poorest part of the District of Columbia and is one of the most polluted rivers in the nation, with sewage, industrial pollution, and trash rendering it unusable for swimming or fishing.[21] These challenges are not unique to the Anacostia, but can be found in urban water bodies across the country.

In recent years, advocacy by nonprofit organizations and efforts by local partnerships have begun to reverse the effects of centuries of neglect, targeting the local sewer authority and development policies. However, advocates call on citizens in the Anacostia watershed to take steps as well—to minimize water use, discourage use of pesticides, and clean up other polluting substances that could end up in the river, from pet waste to motor oil.

The Earth Conservation Corps is a youth corps that engages local young people from the crime- and drug-infested local area, ages seventeen through twenty-four, in cleaning up the Anacostia River. The corps cleans the Anacostia River and its tributaries of trash and debris, rebuilds the shoreline, creates community access trails, and plants trees. In the last decade the corps has been responsible for reintroducing bald eagles to the Anacostia watershed, transforming three city dumps into city parks, and restoring two abandoned "Brownfield" buildings into environmental education centers. The Earth Conservation Corps also participates in the Riverkeeper program, pairing corpsmembers with the Anacostia Riverkeeper to speak for the community on environmental justice, education, and outreach on Anacostia River issues and to regularly patrol the river and its tributaries. The Riverkeeper program and youth corps engage local students and thousands of volunteers to plant trees, remove invasive plants, test water quality, and remove trash to increase awareness and build a community-wide ethic for stewardship.[22]

POTENTIAL FOR TRANSFORMATION

With the urgency around the global climate crisis and other threats to the environment, we can't afford to leave volunteer and national service out of the toolbox. Public policy solutions are critical, but so are the actions of individuals—from the skilled professional who can install a solar panel to a young student who can collect seeds, help "green" a school, or educate the neighborhood about conservation.

Technology creates opportunities to engage millions of people in their own communities, including making available "how to" options that can easily be downloaded or accessed online so that everyone can help. Youth corps can train young people to fill green jobs that could otherwise face shortages. A serious investment in any of these strategies could yield a major impact.

CHAPTER EIGHT

Inspiring and Sustaining Innovative Solutions

I n the mid-1990s, when Geoffrey Canada began building a ground-breaking new organization to break the cycle of poverty in Harlem, he needed a way to hire "the army we needed and could afford." AmeriCorps offered him that army. His "Peacemakers," as he termed the AmeriCorps members, were young adults, many from the neighborhood or places just like it. Some had college degrees, but others were in transition. While many people at the time thought of these young people as part of the problem, Canada saw them as the solution to his challenge. What's more, they were welcomed into the public schools by teachers who were wary of outsiders but struggling to keep order in their classrooms.

Over a decade later, the Peacemakers are an integral part of the acclaimed Harlem Children's Zone. They serve in seven schools, including the Promise Academy Charter School run by HCZ and HCZ's preschool. Each Peacemaker is assigned to a classroom, to calm down kids who act out or offer one-on-one help to struggling students. They serve under the direction of the teachers, who "value their support to a fault," according to one assistant principal. After morning classes, they keep recess fun and structured, and when the closing bell rings, they run the after-school program.

Starting their day at 7:45 A.M., the Peacemakers don't quit until the last child goes home at 6:30 P.M. But their efforts don't end there. They are role models in the community 24/7, and are at the core of the organization's community-building efforts. When HCZ's corporate partners want to pitch in to beautify a park or rehab a building, the Peacemakers lead them. Peacemakers volunteer for weekend playground duty so the neighborhood children can play safely, and chaperone trips so children can have experiences beyond their block. They're active even on Christmas Day, when HCZ teams deliver gifts to low-income children around the city who wrote to Santa hoping their wishes would be granted.

Those Peacemakers who complete their terms of service earn Segal AmeriCorps Education Awards to pay for college or graduate school. Those who do well are asked to stay for a second year. The best are invited to join HCZ's staff. Because they have been exposed to the organization's work at the ground level, "they continue to be the carriers of the culture," notes Canada. "They understand our mission." Today, five out of sixteen senior managers and twenty additional HCZ management staff are former Peacemakers.[1]

SERVICE AND SOCIAL INNOVATION

HCZ's experience with AmeriCorps is a story that is largely untold but not uncommon. Hundreds of innovative nonprofits struggling for resources have found the answer to their human resource and sometimes financial needs through AmeriCorps. Habitat for Humanity, Citizen Schools, Jumpstart, and other breakthrough nonprofits have made AmeriCorps central to their delivery systems and found a feeder system for road-tested staff in the process.

The strong connection between service and social innovation is not a coincidence. Social innovation as I talk about it means a system- or field-changing insight tied to activities that apply the insight to a problem. It also implies improvement over traditional methods of addressing the problem on a substantial scale—often in the form of better outcomes or use of resources. Not every service program is innovative, and not every social innovation involves service. However, there is a strong relationship between the two, relating to the structure and availability of capital markets in the nonprofit sector, and the unique way that service interacts with them (Figure 8.1).

It's easiest to explain this by comparing social innovation to innovation in the world of business. To simplify a complicated topic, think of it in this way: in the business world, when an inventor has a new idea, she seeks seed funding, often from friends and relatives but sometimes from venture capitalists or other investors, to build a prototype and test it. If it is successful, additional financing may become available from investors hopeful that they will receive a return on their investment. Each stage of financing takes the company to a new level, and eventually, the business may "go public," offering shares on the stock market, raising new growth

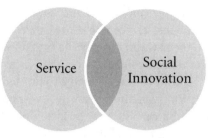

Figure 8.1.   The Relationship of Service and Social Innovation.

capital and enabling early investors to realize a profit. Successful companies can fund subsequent inventions using their own financial capital, creating a cycle that supports innovation over the long term.

Now consider the nonprofit sector. When an inventor has a new idea, if he is lucky he may obtain funding from friends or family, but chances are no financial resources will be available. The inventor is likely to try out his idea using volunteer labor—his own and that of his friends and colleagues. Most charitable endeavors never make it past this phase.

If the effort is successful and the inventor is committed to it, he may create a formal nonprofit organization by registering with the Internal Revenue Service (IRS). Even this is no guarantee of success—more than 70 percent of nonprofits registered with the IRS have no paid staff.[2] However, the tax-exempt status granted by the IRS enables the organization to seek tax-deductible financial donations to cover operating costs. This financial capital often comes from individual donations and occasionally from foundations, and typically comes in the form of modest program grants, not substantial operating capital.

If significant financial capital is available, sometimes an organization will choose to professionalize its workforce, turning to paid employees rather than volunteers to carry out its mission. In other cases, the organization will continue to use volunteers as its main delivery system—in essence, this form of human capital reduces the amount of financial capital needed. It's important to recognize that even in these cases, financial resources are usually essential to pay for staff, office space, and other expenses relating to managing the organization, including recruiting, training, and supervising volunteers. Sometimes financial capital comes from philanthropic or government sources, or even earned income that the organization obtains through "fee for service work" or other income-producing efforts when someone is willing to pay the organization for goods or services. However, while business success funds growth, that is not often the case in the nonprofit world. Due to limited capital markets, it is often difficult for even the most effective nonprofit organizations to grow beyond a certain size. In fact, since 1970, more than 200,000 nonprofits have opened in the United States, but only 144 of them have reached $50 million in annual revenue, according to research by the Bridgespan group.[3]

With this understanding of nonprofit capital markets in mind, the relationship of service to social innovation becomes much easier to appreciate. For example:

- *Many social innovators begin their efforts as volunteers*—for the simple reason that there is very little financial capital available for true startups in the nonprofit sector and it's hard to get paid to test a new idea. Social innovators often recruit other volunteers, again as a type of "capital" that comes in the form of human rather than financial resources and is easier to access.

- *Service as a strategy for program delivery can itself be an innovation,* particularly in a field that has been highly professionalized. In these cases, the service provided by volunteers and national service participants offsets the need for financial capital. It is also worth noting that many innovators who do not use service as their primary delivery mechanism do engage volunteers for other purposes—meaningful engagement of potential champions is an effective way to build an organization's social capital, which leads to all other forms of capital.

- *The Corporation for National and Community Service, the federal agency for service, has provided not only human capital to innovative organizations (in the form of VISTA members who build nonprofit capacity), but also financial capital that supports the engagement of volunteer and national service participants.* This financial capital is critical to organizations that employ nontraditional approaches that make it difficult for them to access other government funding streams, even if their outcomes are superior to other providers.

- *Many people who volunteer or serve in national service programs become aware of and committed to solving problems, and go on to become innovators.* The rich knowledge that comes from direct interaction with a community can inspire practical solutions to problems. The fact that the person performing service is typically *not* a professional in the field frees him or her to think differently about solutions, and the knowledge and social capital such people bring from other experiences (such as a business background) provides both insights and useful assets to the endeavor.

The experience of LIFT illustrates all of these points.[4] LIFT, discussed briefly in Chapter Six, runs centers where low-income clients with needs can get assistance navigating the vast and confusing network of programs and opportunities that can help them find jobs, secure safe and stable housing, make ends meet through public benefits and tax credits, and obtain services such as child care and health care. LIFT was created by Yale undergraduates Kirsten Lodal and Brian Keiter in 1998, but its roots, according to Lodal, go far deeper. Lodal was involved in service from an early age due to her family's public service background and school service requirements. As a senior in high school, she volunteered at the Children's Defense Fund during consideration of President Clinton's welfare reform plan, and at a Head Start center that served homeless children. Both experiences exposed her to the challenges faced by families in poverty, and the role of programs in helping them.

Lodal continued her volunteer work in college, where a rich mix of service opportunities engaged willing students. "There were fifty-six competing tutoring and mentoring programs on campus," she recalls. Through her volunteer work at a local school, she "kept coming back to the same feeling—as important as tutoring and mentoring were, there were issues that no one was addressing, the root causes of the challenges the kids faced." She took on the cases of several parents at the school to see if she could help, and talked to social service providers, community leaders, and government officials in New Haven, exploring whether there was a way that they could engage volunteers on campus to solve these problems. The resulting model became the foundation of LIFT, then called National Student Partnerships.

Housed in donated space in a YMCA, LIFT deployed energetic and idealistic college student volunteers to work one-on-one with low-income people to help them solve their own problems. Often resources were available to assist these people but they did not know about them, or could not access them. The students received extensive training and had access to computers, phones, and information about services that were available. Lodal found a ready stream of volunteers among the students, and no shortage of need among people in the community.

Once the model was established and working, Lodal's team explored opportunities to expand the program to other schools and cities. While she was convinced that students would readily sign up to volunteer, expansion would require stable, full-time coordinators to recruit them, raise funds, and put in place other systems that would be needed. Most government poverty programs were out of the question—as a small startup dependant on volunteers, LIFT could not access the substantial funding that flowed to professional providers. Foundations were similarly risk-averse, and not forthcoming with "big bites" of funding to expand the innovative program, which "worked against the grain of how professional social services are provided," according to Lodal.

One government program, however, seemed tailor-made for LIFT—VISTA (Volunteers in Service to America). VISTA, which is now part of AmeriCorps, was originally proposed by President Kennedy as a domestic Peace Corps that would engage Americans in fighting poverty through full-time service. VISTA volunteers by design are "capacity builders"—people who help nonprofit organizations grow, build systems, and engage others as donors or volunteers. It was just what LIFT needed, and fortunately, VISTA staff "were willing to take a bet on a promising model that was volunteer-driven," awarding the young organization nine full-time VISTA slots, one for each new site.

LIFT filled its VISTA slots with student volunteers who were graduating but wanted to stay involved with the program. They worked wonders—dramatically increasing the volunteers recruited by 450 percent over previous years and in just six months increasing the services provided by 68 percent. The VISTA members enabled the centers to be open year round, rather than opening and closing on the basis of the "lumpy academic calendar," according to Lodal.

A few years later, LIFT successfully applied for AmeriCorps funding, further expanding the sites' stability and capacity, and built up professional expertise by hiring staff with master of social work degrees to train the AmeriCorps members and volunteers and take on the more complex cases.

Today, LIFT continues to expand, using highly trained volunteers as its main delivery system, with AmeriCorps members supporting their work alongside professional staff. In 2009, LIFT operates in twelve local sites, engaging more than five hundred volunteers to assist nearly six thousand clients.

The organization has continued to innovate with the help of volunteer and national service. For example, a former student volunteer and later VISTA member not only helped to start the organization's Somerville, Massachusetts, office but also pioneered the organization's tax and benefit counseling program. In Washington, D.C., when the local housing authority refused to provide a list of landlords that would accept Section 8 housing vouchers, LIFT was undeterred. "Imagine what it is like traveling all over town with your kids in tow, using your last dollar on bus fare, trying to find an apartment that will take you," observed Lodal. The organization enlisted a volunteer, "an intrepid student at Georgetown," to build the database himself, which they shared with other organizations. "It made no sense that the housing authority wouldn't do this," noted Lodal. "We do things differently, scavenge for resources, and engage energetic and optimistic people."

According to LIFT, whenever the organization has explored replacing its volunteers with professionals, it has rejected the concept. Cost is a factor—the program's per unit costs are a fraction of those of comparable social service organizations. But something else would be lost. In addition to tracking outcomes relating to service provision, LIFT monitors customer satisfaction—and has consistently found that the people it helps appreciate the extra caring provided by student volunteers. And the organization would lose a key benefit—the chance to influence young leaders at a formative period of their lives. Already LIFT alumni can be found at the federal Department of Health and Human Services, the IRS, and other influential policy positions. One student volunteer has gone on to lead a prominent anti-poverty organization's first-ever advocacy effort, organizing tax outreach volunteers around a policy agenda.

Service and Social Innovation Throughout American History

Over the history of the United States, important social innovations have begun with the work of volunteers, often because no other source of capital was available. The efforts of volunteers have led to the creation of whole professional fields or American institutions. Fire departments, police departments, public libraries, and social work began with volunteers. So did adult education, the Morse code, and baseball.

Consider the birth of fire departments in the United States. Throughout colonial times, fires were fought by volunteers, typically in an ad hoc fashion. In 1648, the city burghers of New Amsterdam (later New York) appointed eight prominent citizens to the "Rattle Watch." These men volunteered to patrol the streets at night carrying large wooden rattles, which they would spin if they spotted a fire. Responding citizens would form bucket brigades. Benjamin Franklin pioneered the idea that an organized volunteer effort would be more effective. In 1736, he organized "a company of thirty volunteers who equipped themselves with leather buckets and bats and baskets." The concept was an immediate success, and within a few years, every Philadelphia property holder had joined up and the idea spread rapidly up and down the coast.

In other cases, volunteer efforts have led to for-profit businesses. Commercial broadcast radio, for example, was born when an engineer, Frank Conrad, began experimenting with broadcasting radio programming from his Pennsylvania home in 1916. A child prodigy, Conrad ended his formal education after seventh grade, going to work for Westinghouse at age sixteen. Conrad was surprised to discover that his broadcasts were attracting an audience of ham radio operators. To fill airtime, he broadcast music, first by his sons and then with borrowed records from a local music store, which lent the albums in exchange for an on-air plug. In response to listener demand, Conrad announced that he would broadcast for two hours on Wednesday and Sunday nights at 7:30 P.M. The station became a family volunteer project, with Conrad's sons stepping in as announcers, reporting football scores and providing other talk programming. Seeing the popularity of Conrad's volunteer broadcasts, Westinghouse recognized the potential market and began manufacturing receivers for consumer purchase. By 1920, the experiment was successful enough for the Westinghouse company to open a commercial station, KDKA in Pittsburgh.

The great nonprofits of the late 1800s and early 1900s, many of which are still going strong, similarly started with volunteer efforts. For example, the Boys and Girls Clubs of America got its start before the Civil War, in Hartford, then a mill town, where mothers and fathers worked in factories, leaving boys unsupervised in the streets. One winter afternoon, Elizabeth Hamersley and sisters Mary and Alice Goodwin invited a small group of boys into their homes for tea and cake so they could warm up. Surprised at the boys' appreciation and good behavior, the women continued their hospitality and expanded their offerings to include music, dramatics, and books. With support from other volunteers, the women found a suitable place where the boys could meet regularly, at a Congregational church mission in the slums. They held a weekly recreational program for the boys and eventually called themselves "The Dashaway Club."

The program disbanded with the advent of the Civil War, as the boys joined the war effort as drummers or took the factory jobs vacated by adult men who became soldiers. After the war, the club resumed and others began across New England, typically meeting in churches staffed by affluent volunteers. Meanwhile, on Manhattan's lower East Side, Edward H. Harriman, a powerful railroad businessman, founded the Boy's Club of New York in 1876. According to legend, he was inspired to form the club when, as he visited a school for girls, a rock crashed through a window. When told that this was a regular occurrence, caused by the street-wandering boys below, Harriman set out to do something about it.

In 1906, the existing fifty clubs joined together to form a national organization known as the Boys Club of America. Today, 4.5 million boys and girls participate in the Boys and Girls Clubs of America at more than forty-three hundred club locations across all fifty states, Puerto Rico, the Virgin Islands, and U.S. military bases around the world. Volunteers remain an integral part of the clubs, providing mentoring, tutoring, and coaching services, along with other programming for young people.

Sources: S. Ellis and K. Campbell, *By The People: A History of Americans as Volunteers, NewCentury Edition* (Philadelphia: Energize, Inc., 2005); Colonial Firefighting, "Firefighting in Colonial America," http://www.firefightercentral.com/history/firefighting_in_colonial_america.htm, accessed November 25, 2009; Wikipedia, "Frank Conrad," http://en.wikipedia.org/wiki/Frank_Conrad, accessed November 25, 2009; Boys & Girls Clubs of Northwest New Jersey, "About Our Movement," 2009, http://www.bgcnwnj.org/aboutus.asp?ProgID=88.

TODAY'S INNOVATORS

LIFT's story—of using volunteer or national service to resource, at least in part, every phase of its development—is not uncommon.

It's the story of Kiff Gallagher, a singer-songwriter whose previous experience in government and business convinced him to create the MusicianCorps, a national service program to expand access to music education for disadvantaged youths. Gallagher volunteered his time for more than a year to build the program, which was launched in 2009 with twenty-one MusicianCorps Fellows including an accomplished indie folk artist, a civil rights activist turned jazz musician, an award-winning Brazilian singer, and eighteen other multitalented musicians ready to give a year to make a difference for others.[5]

It's the story of Jim McCorkell, the founder of Admission Possible, who saw that low-income high school students lacked the resources to compete effectively for admission to colleges and universities, while at the same time, higher education institutions were interested in admitting students from low-income backgrounds but had difficulty identifying and attracting them. Working out of the spare bedroom in his apartment, in 1999 he recruited a board of directors, put together a business plan and a website, and began fundraising to create a program that would identify low-income high school students with the potential and motivation for college and provide them with ACT and SAT test preparation help; intensive guidance in preparing college applications; assistance obtaining financial aid; and guidance in transition to college. Two years later, Admission Possible moved into an office, Jim hired four part-time employees to work with thirty-five juniors at two high schools, and the organization received its first AmeriCorps grant. By 2009, with support from AmeriCorps, the organization had grown to include twelve Leadership Team members, forty-four AmeriCorps members, and four VISTA members, delivering these services for twelve hundred students and eleven hundred program alums. Overall, 99 percent of the students in the program are admitted to college and 95 percent enroll. To date, the program has an 80 percent college retention rate.[6]

It's also the story of the Emmons sisters, the founders of Educate Tomorrow. Melanie Emmons Damian, a Miami-based attorney, did extensive pro bono work, including serving as a special advocate for children. One of her clients, Antonio, was about to graduate from high school. But when Melanie asked him where he was going to go to college, he told her that he was a foster kid and couldn't continue his education. As one of eight children who grew up in poverty and abuse, Melanie understood that education was the key to success—her mother and grandmother had worked hard to ensure that she and her sisters got good educations. So she looked into Antonio's case and was pleased to discover that Florida provides a free public higher education, living allowance, and health insurance to any child aging out of foster care. The problem was that Antonio—and hundreds of youths like him—had had no idea this help was his for the asking.

The Manateens program, discussed in Chapters Five and Six, demonstrates the creativity of young volunteers when they set out to solve a problem. Operating with extremely limited resources, the Manateens, who range from ages eight to eighteen, frequently invent their own programs in response to a need they have identified. For example, when a thirteen-year-old member, Alycia Bower, read in an article that seven thousand dogs and cats die every year because fire trucks are not equipped with oxygen masks to resuscitate animals, she and her friends invented the "Big Breath, and Bark!" program. With research, the teens found a company in Sweden that produced the masks for $49 a kit, each including three different sizes. They invited community members to donate $60 each which would equip a fire truck with a set of masks in exchange for the name of a pet on a plaque at a fire station. With just two press releases, the students raised enough money to equip every fire truck in the county. They extended their program to include trauma care kits and emergency training for every canine unit in the county—potentially saving the lives of the seventeen teams of dogs working for the sheriff, police, and fire departments. Although each of these dogs is valued at $30,000 due to its training, the county was unable to pay for the kits or emergency training for the dog handlers. Each year Manateens add new projects at the instigation of their members, which number more than ten thousand in Manatee County, Florida.

Source: Interview with Adraine LaRoza, May 27, 2009; Volunteer Manatee, "New Project to Aid Local Canine Teams!" http://www.volunteermanatee.org/news_archive1 .html, accessed December 2, 2009.

Melanie's sister Virginia Emmons had recently returned from serving in the Peace Corps in Niger. Virginia's work with a Miami nonprofit had opened her eyes to the fact that many people who are homeless spent time in the foster system. A little research convinced her that children aging out of foster care were a group in special need of help. She discovered that less than half finish high school, and less than 5 percent graduate from college. Only 17 percent are self-supporting after leaving foster care, and four out of ten are homeless within a year.

Virginia and Melanie enlisted their three sisters to help. They founded a nonprofit, Educate Tomorrow, and recruited volunteer mentors for one hundred youths in foster care who would help them complete high school and enroll in college. In just a few years, Educate Tomorrow mentors established a strong track record, with 95 percent of their students going to college. With help from VISTA members and community volunteers who help with grant writing, fundraising, and other functions, Educate Tomorrow is taking its model to other communities across the country.[7]

SERVICE ALUMNI ENTREPRENEURS

As in the cases of Virginia Emmons and Kirsten Lodal, Peace Corps, AmeriCorps, college service programs, and other service experiences may give a start to social entrepreneurs who find that after their year of service, they want to take on the challenges they have witnessed in innovative new ways. Teach For America has a history of alumni social entrepreneurs who were motivated by their corps experience to develop new solutions to address the root causes of social challenges, and it launched a special initiative to steward more of its alumni in this direction. Teach For America founder Wendy Kopp attributes the large number of education innovators to the "intense conviction and insight they gained" through their Teach For America experience. In addition, the program incorporates into the training that the new teachers receive the notion that at the end of their two-year term, they will ask themselves, "How can you personally have the greatest possible impact on this problem?" Some—almost 50 percent—stay in the classroom. But others choose different paths, including creating new schools or organizations aimed at correcting the injustices they witnessed.

These entrepreneurs are making a difference. They include the founders of the KIPP charter schools, which are widely recognized as a model for education reform, as well as of YES College Prep in Houston and the IDEA Academies in Texas's Rio Grande Valley, which have each produced schools that are among the top one hundred high schools in America according to *U.S. News & World Report*. They also include innovators in other sectors, including the founders of One Economy, which brings broadband service and IT tools to low-income communities; Building Blocks International, a corporate volunteer "Peace Corps"; Credit Where Credit Is Due, a bilingual financial literacy program; and Charity Navigator, a nonprofit rating website.[8]

POTENTIAL FOR TRANSFORMATION

The future of America depends on innovators achieving ever-higher levels of impact in the social sector, as in business. This innovation can come from many sources—nonprofit organizations that look for better ways, businesses looking to make a profit while they make a difference, and academic experts and think tanks that conceive of new ideas. But ordinary citizens who see a problem and find a solution will always be an important source.

Policymakers concerned with advancing social innovation can find a useful tool in volunteers and national service. To maximize the impact of service on the innovation agenda, however, requires investment at several levels:

- Curriculum and support for secondary and higher education students that help them learn about issues, identify solutions, and test their impact. These experiences could become as ubiquitous as the school science fair. They would set some young people on a path to become social innovators, and an even larger number might be motivated to pursue their education with greater commitment. Learn and Serve America is a good source for this funding.

- Support for national service alumni who want to pursue social entrepreneurship. These individuals can benefit from training in nonprofit leadership, as well as connection to networks of people pursuing similar goals. A database of effective models would help ground these inventors in existing practices so they might benefit from others' experience.

- Continued growth of AmeriCorps, VISTA, and other national service programs that provide important financial and human capital for innovative programs linked to service. For example, a VISTA Growth Fund could be created to provide large numbers of VISTAs to high-growth innovative national programs.

Throughout American history service has supported social innovation in all its stages. It remains an important way to inspire future entrepreneurs and an important source of human capital to turn ideas into reality.

CHAPTER NINE

What You Can Do

Imagine a nation that serves. A nation where every year a million citizens serve in full-time national service and a hundred million more volunteer a hundred hours a year in their own communities. Every town has well-trained disaster response volunteers, and every student can succeed because of extra help from a team of AmeriCorps members or committed community tutors. Whole regions are organized to reduce their energy consumption and improve their environment. Whole communities are engaged in healthy behaviors. Older adults live at home rather than in institutions because they have the help they need. Young children enter school ready to learn. Every immigrant is able to become integrated into the community and become economically successful, is able to speak English, and is on the road to citizenship.

With core volunteer and national service support, this nation doesn't have to exist in our imagination—it could be real. And it would change the nature of our communities—people who give their time to solve community challenges would be less likely to turn away when help is needed, less likely to commit crimes, less likely to neglect civic and personal responsibilities. People who know people who are different from themselves would because of these experiences bridge societal divides in important ways. In their jobs, they would make decisions with the understanding of how their actions affect the community. At home, they would know their neighbors, not fear them. More people would become involved politically at all levels, and we would see better, more ethical candidates and an improved democracy.

We could achieve this, but only if individuals and institutions change in specific ways. This chapter discusses the important steps that everyone can take to create this new vision for America, in their roles as citizens, in their jobs, or in the community. These changes are essential if we are to unlock the potential of service to transform America.

First, such changes would bolster the *supply* of people willing to step up to solve our problems. Sixty million Americans volunteered in 2008. Another million are alumni of the Peace Corps, AmeriCorps, and similar programs, and five million Americans are active-duty military, national guardsmen, or veterans. While these numbers might sound impressive, that leaves more than one hundred fifty million adult Americans who have not spent a year or more in civilian or military service and are not currently volunteering in their communities.

However, a supply-side strategy is not enough. We also need to increase the *demand* for volunteers, by spurring the public problem solvers of the nation—policymakers in government at all levels, philanthropists, and the organizations that deliver services to incorporate volunteers into their strategies for action. Many experts believe that the supply of volunteers will expand to fill the demand—especially if the positions available are clearly tied to making a difference.

Finally, our *systems* for connecting volunteers to opportunities and supporting them must be strengthened to handle increased volume, offer better placement mechanisms, and incorporate the programming and tools needed to achieve the desired outcomes, whether the goals are to increase civic participation, teach personal responsibility, or build job skills. Volunteers are not free—they come with a price tag, albeit a modest one, that makes their service impactful.

Here are the changes necessary to bring about the transformation.

INDIVIDUALS

If you are one of those people who have not found a way to make volunteering part of your life on a regular basis, there are many ways to get involved depending on your interests, location, and personal goals. Start there—What do you hope to achieve through your service?

What's your cause? You might find a cause important to your family—your child's school, a local park, older adults in your apartment building. Or you may want to reach beyond your personal network to help children in a struggling school or victims of a natural disaster miles away. Find something that matters to you personally.

What's your availability? Would a regular schedule each week work well for you—maybe a couple of hours during the school day? Or would the occasional weekend project make more sense? Some people take volunteer vacations, while others may take months or even a whole year off between school terms or jobs and serve essentially full time during that intensive period—AmeriCorps is designed to provide this kind of opportunity. Still other people prefer "microtasks"—small efforts they can undertake whenever they have some free time, often at their computers or in their own homes. Service opportunities are available to suit any of these options.

Where do you want to serve? Would you prefer to serve near your home? Near your work? In the outdoors? In an office? At a museum? Across the country or even overseas?

What do you like to do? Some people have a special skill to offer, often a skill they use in their regular jobs. But you may prefer to do something totally different—if you work in an office all day, maybe you want to get your hands dirty or try something new you're not an expert in.

With whom do you want to serve? Do you have a group of friends or family who might join you? Or do you want to use your volunteer experience to meet new people?

What do you want to get out of your experience? While many people want to serve simply to advance a cause they care about or make a difference in their community, it's absolutely fine to serve to achieve other goals. Making friends, learning or practicing new skills, gaining career experience, or staying active are all common and perfectly appropriate reasons to volunteer. As discussed in Chapter Two, some service programs—notably youth corps—are designed to help young people gain their GEDs or diplomas through service, while other service programs are geared to enable students to advance their understanding of academic subjects through service.

If you can answer all these questions, you can begin your search. Today numerous free volunteer search services are available on the Internet. For example, All for Good, launched in 2009 by a volunteer team that included engineers from Google and support from other high-tech companies and nonprofits, enables searchers to enter their location and keywords and receive a list of service opportunities that might meet their needs. It is novel because it allows other sites to use the data free of charge. For example, the Entertainment Industry Foundation's iParticipate website uses All for Good to display volunteer opportunities on a Google map and enables users to invite friends to join them through Facebook.

Dave Mantus, a self-described "geek scientist," knew what it meant to have an adult stir the interest of a child in learning. His own dad was a rocket scientist who designed the legs of the lunar module—the spacecraft that landed on the moon. As a Ph.D. chemist with a pharmaceutical company, Mantus heard a pitch from Citizen Schools at a Massachusetts Biotechnology Council meeting and learned that "there was lots of active support from various industries, except biotech." The call for volunteers to lead low-income middle schoolers in hands-on activities after school "struck a chord" for Mantus, who had always liked teaching. Although he had a busy schedule, he was eager to share his passion for science and felt he could spare an afternoon a week if it meant he might "change the trajectory of a kid."

Mantus convinced a coworker to join him and set about developing a course that he called "It *Is* Rocket Science." Each week they taught aspects of physics, math, chemistry, or aerodynamics through a different "magical thing." The students built rockets and launched them on the blacktop outside the school, froze the air with cold liquid nitrogen, and built a sleeping chamber that could protect an astronaut from radiation. While they might have initially been reluctant to sign up for a science class, the students were wowed by their experiences.

Another option is to contact a local volunteer center, such as a "HandsOn Action" site in your community, which will help you find volunteer projects that align your passion with real needs in your area. You can become trained to become a volunteer leader or use your professional skills to help a local nonprofit organization.

Older adults may look for "RSVP" programs, while youths may participate with a community service club or other volunteer group in their school, college, place of worship, or recreation center. Any of these organizations may be able to point you to service opportunities or engage you in their own projects.

If you live in an area where few service organizations operate, or prefer to work on your own, you can organize your own project and recruit others to join you. "Self-organized" projects have become increasingly popular as social networking sites make it easy to advertise to your "friends" and savvy organizations make tools

Inspired by his volunteer work, Mantus re-upped for another semester, then another, then another. While it has taken time away from his job, he thinks it's worth it: "One of the students came up to me and said, 'All week I've been bored but this was really fun.' It made me feel good to have brightened her week." He believes in Citizen Schools because he has seen its contribution to turning around the middle school where he volunteers, which had been in danger of losing its accreditation. To support the program he has encouraged his company to make financial contributions, joined the curriculum board, and recruited others to volunteer. Citizen Schools appreciates Mantus's efforts as well—he was named the organization's first Citizen Teacher of the Year.

Mantus's advice for others considering volunteering is simple. First, bring a friend because there's "safety in numbers." Planning a project may take time the first time through, but it gets easier after that and it's "never as much time as you think it will be," he says. In fact, he has posted the curriculum he developed online for others to use. But most important, he counsels, "Do what you love to do.... If you're passionate about something it's easy to get kids excited."

Source: Interview with Dave Mantus, October 8, 2009.

available online for those who want to lead an activity rather than join a preorganized project. For example, AARP's site, CreatetheGood.org, tells you "how to" organize a river cleanup, start a walking group, help others prepare for hurricanes, or reduce energy consumption. Do Something, targeted at teens, offers a search function just for youths—none of the suggested projects requires funding, parental involvement, or a car.

To assess whether an opportunity is right for you, measure it against your own criteria. If not enough information is available, don't be afraid to ask questions. And don't be discouraged if a project is full, or if you don't initially find what you are looking for. New opportunities are posted every week, and the potential for self-organized service is unlimited.

If you're particularly entrepreneurial, you may want to develop your own service initiative to meet a need in your community. Before you start, assess what other organizations are doing to meet that need in your own area or elsewhere—too many "social entrepreneurs" end up reinventing the wheel rather than learning from others' experience.

Like many innovators before you, you may find it wise to begin with volunteer labor to test a premise—startup financial capital may be hard to obtain without evidence that your project will actually make a difference. Be sure to think through what you are hoping to accomplish—think about how you will measure success and work on being able to articulate how your effort will accomplish your goals. Share that information with those you recruit—helping people appreciate what they have done for others is an important element of good volunteer management. Keep track of all your "inputs"—the number of volunteer hours, skills, funding, and so on that go into your project—and then measure the "outputs"—what happened as a result. After you have completed the project, do your own assessment of what worked and what didn't.

Jenny Brody, Karen Barker Marcou, and Marla Spindel followed this route when they thought they might take some pro bono cases. All lawyers who had left legal practices to raise their families, the three soon discovered how difficult it was for an individual lawyer to handle pro bono cases due to the lack of resources—such as a place to meet privately with clients—and the costs of online legal research, litigation expenses, and individual malpractice insurance. Also, they missed the collegiality and support of practicing law with partners who could provide backup in an emergency and discuss practice tips and case strategies together. They found that none of the existing legal services organizations offered all of the resources and support non-law-firm attorneys need to provide high-quality cost-effective representation to indigent clients. Suspecting that there were other at-home lawyers who also wanted to do pro bono work, Brody, Marcou, and Spindel founded the DC Volunteer Lawyers Project in January of 2008 with the goal of addressing the unmet family law needs of low-income people in Washington, D.C., by recruiting, training, and supporting volunteer attorneys. The DCVLP's first organizational meeting attracted over thirty lawyers from notices on school listservs and by word of mouth. Since then, the DCVLP has grown to over a hundred volunteer lawyers and provided thousands of hours of pro bono legal services to low-income Washingtonians, winning the team recognition as "Stars of the Bar" by the Women's Bar Association of Washington, D.C.

The DCVLP team has thought hard about how to measure the success of the organization. They believe "the most basic measure is the number of pro bono hours we provide to indigent clients; hours which would not have been donated, and clients who most likely would not have had representation, if the DCVLP did not exist," according to Jenny Brody. The group has hesitated to measure success by case outcomes because in law there are so many factors that affect what happens, including factors over which the lawyer has no control. In cases in which DCVLP lawyers serve as Guardians Ad Litem for children in disputed custody cases, where they represent the best interests of the child, there is no clear "win" or "loss" outcome. However, as Brody points out, "the judge has accepted our Guardian Ad Litem recommendation re: custody in every case the organization has handled so far. The organization also measures the type of experience our volunteers have working with our organization, looking to whether a volunteer who completes a case asks to take another one."[1]

If you are in a position to give a year of your time, consider joining AmeriCorps. AmeriCorps programs are hosted by organizations all over the country and engage individuals, young and old, with all educational backgrounds. AmeriCorps encompasses VISTA, the residential National Civilian Community Corps, youth corps, and a wide range of other programs. You can serve in your own community or travel to another site for a different experience. Full-time AmeriCorps members receive a modest living allowance plus health and child care benefits, and if they complete their term of service, a Segal AmeriCorps education award of about $5,000. Many AmeriCorps programs advertise locally or online for members, and you can search the AmeriCorps.gov site for opportunities.

GROUPS

Many people volunteer through groups they already belong to—their place of worship, school or college, civic club, or youth group, for example. Friends may decide to serve together or an informal group may join together to undertake a service project in honor of an occasion, such as a wedding, memorial, reunion, or national day of service such as the Martin Luther King Holiday or the 9/11 Day of Remembrance. Leaders of these organizations can easily integrate service into their programming and may well find that it strengthens the ties among group members.

The experience will be more meaningful if the service connects with the values and purpose of the organization. As with individuals, groups should consider several key questions to determine what might make an appropriate service project.

What's your cause? A group may have a natural affinity for a cause. A baseball team could offer batting practice to a youth group, a book club might read to children or senior citizens, or bank employees may teach financial literacy. A group might find it a meaningful experience to discuss their interests and identify issues they want to address.

What's your availability and where do you want to serve? Groups will likely want to serve together at a close-by location, either on a regular schedule or through a "blitz" project on a single afternoon. Be sure to survey members about their interests and availability.

What do you like to do? A professional association or union may want to use its members' skills to help others or do something totally different from their normal work. Make sure the group agrees which is the case.

What do you want to get out of your experience? It's important for the group members to process what they hope to achieve through service. It may well be simply to bond together and contribute to the community. An organization may want to increase its visibility, recruit new members, or build professional relationships. Or members may want to develop skills, build their credentials for college or a job, or achieve other goals. It's important to know what the team is hoping to accomplish through a service project before your search.

Once group members have answered these questions, it may be clear which local organizations would provide a good fit. If no one in the group is familiar with local organizations, you can use a search site such as Network for Good to find one. Groups can also use volunteer matching sites, discussed earlier in the individuals section, or can develop a project of their own using tools available online.

Youth organizations may find it particularly valuable to develop their own projects, which will offer important learning experiences. As discussed in Chapter Two, through these experiences young people learn problem solving, teamwork, leadership, and a host of other important lessons.

NONPROFIT ORGANIZATIONS

Nonprofit organizations are the backbone of our civil society and central to the way we shape our culture, help those in need, and advance our knowledge.

Many people know large nonprofits such as the Red Cross or Habitat for Humanity. But in fact, most nonprofit organizations are small groups with no paid staff.[2] Two-thirds have annual budgets of less than $25,000.[3] Volunteers therefore are critical to the functioning of these organizations.

Often organizations are eager to hire paid staff as soon as they are financially able. There is good reason to do so. Paid staff may be able to put in more time than part-time volunteers and may seem to be more accountable—many people might find it hard to "fire" someone who is helping out for free. Organizations may be more selective in hiring a staff person than recruiting a volunteer.

However, just as volunteers should not replace paid staff, nor should the addition of paid staff push out volunteers. As discussed throughout Part Two, there are many good reasons to make volunteers and national service participants part of an organization's strategy to deliver services. They can produce volume—offering many pairs of hands to accomplish a labor-intensive task. Or they can provide skilled assistance that an organization can't otherwise afford. The fact that they are acting as volunteers may itself be important, signaling a degree of compassion and caring that is not necessarily present in paid staff. Recruiting volunteers can help a community take ownership of a project, increasing its long-term sustainability. Volunteers may possess unique community knowledge and credibility, making them the best recruiters, spokespeople, and advisers around.

A second reason for a nonprofit to engage volunteers is spelled out in *The Charismatic Organization*: to build its social capital. Social capital refers to a network of relationships that benefit those who are part of the network. While high levels of social capital pay dividends to society as a whole, the organizations that build these networks experience more direct benefits. For a nonprofit organization, that means a committed community of staff, donors, volunteers, and friends who can provide access to other social networks. These networks lead to other essential forms of capital—financial, human, and political—that allow the organization to increase its impact and influence even more. For example, a recent survey found that on average, people donate ten times more money if they have volunteered in the past year.[4]

Involvement like this knits a community together. It enables people to meet each other and associate the connection with the organization. It invests individuals in a cause; once they have helped to build an organization through volunteering they have a stake in its outcomes. These meaningful opportunities to contribute often inspire volunteers to make financial contributions and support the organization in other ways.

In *Forces for Good*, Leslie Crutchfield and Heather McLeod identify an organization's efforts to "create opportunities for people to *actively participate and to experience* what the nonprofits do [emphasis in original]" as a practice of high-impact organizations: "They make it an organizational priority, carefully crafting a strategy of engagement and deliberately committing the time and resources to create meaningful relationships. And they invest in sustaining these large communities of supporters who share their values and advocate for their cause." Crutchfield and McLeod think of this as a form of experiential marketing that "helps people understand the organization, feel more connected to its values and become active participants." Once this connection is cemented, these individuals can be mobilized to advance the organization.[5]

It's important that service be well-integrated into the nonprofit organization's delivery system. If it is simply an "add-on," the volunteer management function is unlikely to receive the resources and attention necessary for it to be effective. Therefore, a nonprofit leader interested in exploring how to use volunteers should ask the following questions:

Are there tasks that require many pairs of hands that volunteers could be easily trained to do? An organization can extend its reach or enhance its services with extra person power. Planting seeds, reading to kids, knocking on doors, greeting clients, and painting houses all fall into this category. So do cyber-volunteering opportunities that invite people to edit content, review products and services, or share their knowledge. What does your organization need to reach more people or be more effective?

Do you need skilled help that you can't afford? Many people with skills would be willing to volunteer if only they were asked, particularly for a specific time-limited project. Graphic design, IT, public relations, writing, research, nutrition advice, or management consulting might be yours for free with the right outreach. What kinds of expertise could help your organization go to the next level?

Would the people you serve benefit from connections to a broader network, including people unlike themselves? Much evidence supports the idea that "social capital"—the relationships an individual has with other people—represents an important currency. These networks help individuals find jobs, learn how to apply for college, make mutually supportive arrangements, and do other things that can be particularly beneficial for people who have difficulty navigating the world due to language barriers, lack of opportunity, or limited education. How can volunteering change this equation?

Would some extra time and TLC make a difference? Sometimes the very fact that a service is being delivered with a spirit of altruism and compassion changes the quality of the assistance. The roles of mentors, senior companions, "telefriends" who check in with children or older adults who are unattended, and hotline responders are often played by volunteers who can take extra time because they're not on the clock. Are there functions that your organization performs that could be enhanced by extra caring?

Would deeper knowledge of the community and its culture, and the credibility that comes with it, improve your ability to deliver services or change behaviors? People from the community you want to reach are often the best messengers and advisers. Outreach, parent and health education, training, and translation can all be undertaken by volunteers. Do you hope to engage, educate, or otherwise connect with a community, especially one that is tight-knit or distrustful of outsiders, that might be responsive to volunteers from their neighborhood or cultural group?

Would community "ownership" make your efforts more sustainable? A community will often maintain something it has built for itself in a way that doesn't happen when government or an outside group "owns" the project. Green spaces, playgrounds, and community cleanups benefit from following this model. Are you "building something" that will benefit from community ownership?

If you are a nonprofit leader considering the use of volunteers, once roles have been identified, think about what skills and time commitment are needed to perform them. Create a job description as you would for a paid position—spell out the most important tasks and responsibilities, the time commitment, whether it is flexible or fixed, and for how long. It is often a good idea to set an initial term of service, even if a multiyear commitment is desired. That way either party can terminate the relationship amicably if it doesn't work out. It's important to devote resources to volunteer management. Research by the Urban Institute found that the best prepared and most effective volunteer programs are those with paid staff members who dedicate a substantial portion of their time to management of volunteers. In fact, the National Council on Aging RespectAbility program found that for every dollar invested in volunteer management, the nonprofit received almost three dollars of benefit, a return on investment of 200 percent.

There are many ways to find the volunteers you want. If you're looking for individuals, post the description on an online site such as Serve.gov, Craigslist.org, or Idealist.org. If your need is for a short-term, high-volume effort, seek out organizations that might provide them—a HandsOn Network Action Center, religious congregation, higher education institution, local business, or civic group may provide the volunteers you need. Such organizations may also be great places to recruit volunteers of other types, whether short- or long-term. They may be sources of skilled volunteers, or small groups who can take weekly shifts.

If you need consistent, long-term service, consider offering Ameri-Corps or VISTA placements. For example, AmeriCorps members can help to recruit and manage volunteers. And the nature of their year or more commitment may lend itself to certain efforts in which sustained and consistent participation is important. To apply for AmeriCorps or VISTA, visit the Corporation for National and Community Service website, nationalservice.gov, for details. If you are prepared to run your own AmeriCorps program of six or more members, you will apply to your state commission. (Note that you will need to raise matching funds for your program and comply with government requirements.) If you need fewer members or do not want to manage a federal grant, you may want to contact other AmeriCorps grantees in your state to form a partnership or apply for AmeriCorps*VISTA staff through your Corporation for National and Community Service state office.

You can also create your own fellowship or internship program. It may be easier to raise funding for a modest stipend that would make it possible for someone meeting your requirements to serve full time than to manage multiple volunteers or raise enough for a full-time staff person. Give the program a name—for example, name it after your donor—and advertise through Idealist.com and similar sites. Colleges and graduate schools are also good places to look for fellows or interns.

To get maximum value from your volunteers, be sure to do a few things:

- Meet their needs.
- Train them.
- Supervise them.
- Teach them about the organization.
- Show them their impact.
- Engage them in reaching out to others.
- Thank them.

If your organization is not equipped to engage volunteers directly, you may want to consider other options. For example, you may want to make available to others tools or curricula that you have developed. Could volunteers undertake a book drive, food drive, or even something more exotic—collect native tree seeds for reforestation or used computers for refurbishment? Is there a health, energy conservation, or disaster preparedness checklist that you use that volunteers could use with their neighbors, friends, or fellow parishioners? How could self-motivated volunteers advance your mission without draining your staff?

KaBOOM! is a leading innovator that engages volunteers to build playgrounds. Eli Segal and I wrote about its founding in *Common Interest, Common Good,* our book about cross-sector partnerships, because its core business model is partnering with businesses that donate financially and mobilize employees to create playgrounds in low-income communities alongside neighborhood volunteers.[6] But after years of developing community-built playgrounds, KaBOOM! had learned a thing or two about the process. Why not share this knowledge online with anyone who wants to build a community playground? KaBOOM! created a free website that helps you plan your project, communicate with your team, recruit local volunteers, and raise money. It also invited interested people to join a community of playmakers. As a result, thousands of playgrounds have been created by "self-organized" groups with minimal support from KaBOOM!

staff, including the playground built in memory of Cynthia Gentry's neighbors, discussed in Chapter Three. For those not ready to build their own playground, KaBOOM!'s play space finder invites volunteers to find, rate, or document a playspace in their own neighborhood, using a Google Maps mash-up.

In these ways, KaBOOM! is taking play—and volunteering—to new levels. An organization that does not think about a volunteer strategy not only loses the chance to build its social capital and the resources that it leads to, but it also leaves valuable tools on the table.

EDUCATORS

It's the rare education institution that doesn't need help for its weakest students or want to inspire and motivate students at every level. Therefore, educators should think about volunteers in two ways. Volunteers may tutor, mentor, translate, or otherwise improve the resources and climate of the school—a demand-side fix. And students themselves may volunteer, learning through service as discussed in Chapter Two, to help build the supply of volunteers. Remember, those people who serve as youths are much more likely to serve as adults.

Whether classroom teacher, principal, or superintendent, educators should start with their most important goals and think about how additional human resources could make a difference. For example, in 1995, Madison, Wisconsin, school superintendent Art Rainwater identified the racial disparities in his district as a significant problem to overcome. In 1995, African American children were seven times more likely than their white counterparts to test below the minimum reading performance level. Rainwater turned to local volunteer groups, including VISTA, RSVP, and the United Way, to mobilize more than six hundred community volunteers to work with classroom teachers to tutor three thousand K–5 students in twenty-four elementary schools and after-school programs. In a ten-year period, the program was instrumental in closing the racial achievement gap in reading.[7]

Like nonprofit organizations discussed earlier, schools may have a variety of needs that volunteers can meet. As outlined in Chapter Four, volunteers can

- Provide extra support in the classroom
- Build a learning culture and serve as positive role models

- Connect the school and the community, encouraging parental involvement and service learning
- Provide enriching programming during and after school
- Improve the physical environment in which children learn
- Offer low-income students the college-going supports that upper-income students typically enjoy

San Francisco School Volunteers, recently merged with the San Francisco Education Fund, developed a tool that can be used to determine a school's capacity to engage community volunteers. It assesses the school's system to welcome and place volunteers and to plan for volunteer involvement, recruitment, ongoing relationship, and ongoing support. To make sure that volunteers are providing what schools want—solving problems rather than making work for teachers—the organization meets with the principals over the summer to understand the school's needs. On the basis of these needs, the organization develops specific outreach for volunteers who can help, filling specific requests ranging from a person with photography skills to assist an art teacher to a Spanish speaker who can translate at parent night.[8]

In addition to the sources discussed in the section on nonprofit organizations, schools may have two ready-made cohorts of volunteers: parents and the students themselves. Engaging parents in the school in substantive ways, beyond fundraising and administrative tasks, pays another dividend: involved parents are an important ingredient in student success. Similarly, when students tutor other students both groups often make achievement gains.

Tying service to learning can also improve student outcomes, as it aids the community. Interested educators can find numerous resources, including service-learning curricula for a wide range of grades and subjects, online or through the Service-Learning Clearinghouse, National Youth Leadership Council, National Service-Learning Partnership, Children for Children, Youth Service America, and other organizations.

A growing number of school districts have implemented service-learning graduation requirements or otherwise obligate students to serve a specific number of hours. Districts that expect such requirements to have an impact on student learning should implement programming that supports students' ability to meet the required hours. In addition to offering service tied to specific curricular outcomes discussed earlier, such schools might form partnerships with local nonprofit organizations; join a national network such as Earth Force, The League, or the Youth Volunteer Corps of America; or provide "self-directed" service tools such as those described in the nonprofit section.

Students in higher education institutions also benefit from service-learning. It may enliven coursework, helping students learn through experience what may seem like abstract content if approached through traditional methods. It may also enable students to explore possible careers and enhance their skills. For example, Tufts University, with the leadership of its Jonathan M. Tisch College of Citizenship and Public Learning, has integrated service-learning into courses in virtually every department. At Tufts, engineering students have designed a wind turbine for a rural Ethiopian school, urban planning students work with homeless organizations, and entrepreneurial leadership students create business plans to achieve social missions. Universities and colleges that want to incorporate service-learning into their programs may find resources through Campus Compact, a national coalition of more than eleven hundred college and university presidents dedicated to promoting community service, civic engagement, and service-learning in higher education.

Tools for Volunteers: Technology

Technology presents seemingly unlimited opportunities to advance service in a wide variety of ways:

- *Matching volunteers to opportunities.* Numerous sites—including Craig's List, Idealist.org, HandsOnNetwork.org, the government-run Serve.gov, and uber site All for Good—allow organizations to post and individuals to search for volunteer opportunities.

- *Providing "how to" materials for "self-directed" service.* A growing practice has been the creation of "how to" materials that enable individuals to carry out a project on their own. Create The Good, sponsored by AARP, provides service-focused tool kits on everything from how to create a shredding event to guard against identity fraud to organizing a walking club. The site includes videos developed in partnership with Howcast, a site that provides how-to videos on a broad range of topics including demonstrations of good environmental practices.

- *Enabling online volunteering.* Online volunteering offers a rich array of opportunities, from telementoring to technical assistance. Wikipedia is a great example of an online volunteer opportunity—this user-generated encyclopedia employs fewer than twenty-five staff members but engages seventy-five thousand volunteers around the world to generate and edit its content. The UN offers online opportunities that enable anyone to help anywhere around the world. Some volunteer search engines, such as VolunteerMatch, include a virtual volunteering option.

- *Offering "microvolunteering" opportunities.* The Extraordinaries delivers service opportunities via mobile phone that take just a few minutes—when one is bored at work, a friend is late, or one is waiting for the train. Opportunities include translation, tagging or taking photos, transcription, fact checking, and citizen journalism to help museums, research institutions, advocacy groups, and others who can make use of these skills.

- *Disseminating curricula.* Teachers and group leaders can find curricula for educational service projects on websites such as Children for Children, the National Service-Learning Partnership, Youth Service America, and the National Youth Leadership Council.

- *Offering tools for lay people to help others.* With an online tool, volunteers can teach others using state-of-the-art methods. For example, Benetech, a nonprofit organization committed to creating technology to benefit society, worked with literacy experts to develop state-of-the-art software that volunteers, including parents, can use to help learning disabled students learn to read (see www.benetech.org/literacy/route66.shtml). Such tools could greatly expand opportunities to learn English, prepare for important tests such as the SAT, learn marketable skills, and otherwise advance the education of individuals who cannot access traditional classes.

- *Tracking outcomes.* Measuring engagement and impact is a challenge for most organizations. Zazengo provides a system, based on interactive widgets, that keeps track of each time a user takes action and aggregates group impact. It offers multiple ways to reengage the user, such as points, reward badges, and personal goal reminders. Piloted around the inauguration of President Obama, the Zazengo system was used to capture the accomplishments of two thousand people, many using a Facebook application. (See Social Edge, "Challenging Others to Give or Get Involved During Hard Times," http://www.socialedge.org/blogs/open-source-giving/archive/2009/02/23/challenging-others-to-give-or-get-involved-during-hard-times, accessed November 29, 2009.)

BUSINESS

Businesses have much to gain by deploying their employees as volunteers. Studies have long documented the link between corporate volunteer programs and employee recruitment and retention, a connection that is likely to grow as Gen Y enters the workforce—97 percent of Gen Y volunteers (born in the mid-1970s through the late 1990s) believe companies should provide opportunities for their employees to volunteer, according to a study by Deloitte.[9] In addition to attracting employees, volunteer programs can help them develop and refine their skills, improve teamwork, and improve the company's profile in the community. And, of course, corporate volunteers can help a cause the company cares about.

The consulting company Deloitte is a leader in corporate volunteering, not only by conducting research that expands knowledge about the topic but by engaging its own highly skilled employees to provide strategic, financial, and operations advice to its nonprofit partners. Deloitte has committed $50 million in pro bono time over three years, complemented by financial donations. For example, Deloitte has partnered with College Summit, a national nonprofit dedicated to seeing that all college-ready students, regardless of socioeconomic background, go to college (see Chapter Four). A team of Deloitte consultants worked to develop a "reporting warehouse"—a system that helps College Summit more efficiently measure and analyze which programs and methods are most effective in encouraging students to go to college. As a result, reports that previously took fifteen hours to complete now only take two-and-a-half hours, which allows College Summit employees to spend more time conducting the critical analysis that will ultimately get more low-income students into college.[10]

To expand or create an employee volunteer program, businesses should first identify their top goals for the effort from among the possibilities suggested earlier. The goals will dictate not only the type of service opportunity but which employees should be targeted, what partners are needed, and what support should be provided by the company. For example, if the goal is to build a tighter team, it will be important to find volunteer activities that enable team members to serve together in ways that require them to interact with one another. In contrast, if the goal is to help a specific set of employees hone their skills, it may be fine for them to serve independently but important that they have the chance to use the abilities they need to enhance. If the goal is to improve the company's community profile, look for opportunities that offer significant visibility—even the possibility of press coverage—or with influential local organizations.

Once a business has identified its goal, volunteer leaders should think about a cause and set of activities that fit. *Common Interest, Common Good* spells out in detail how a business can identify a cause to support. In short, it should look for causes that will resonate with employees and, if appropriate, customers. *Common Interest, Common Good* profiles partnerships between a cookware company and the cause of hunger and a family restaurant and a children's charity as well as other good fits. Many companies tie their volunteering to their corporate giving, which is often geared to business goals.[11]

Working with a nonprofit organization or school likely will make it easier for a company to manage its volunteers and have an impact. If your business is interested in promoting volunteering, find a local partner that shares your goal and offers good support for your efforts. Clues are whether staff resources are committed to supporting volunteers, the role that volunteers play in the organization's core programs, and the prospective partner's responsiveness to your early inquiries and subsequent project planning. Make sure that you and your partner talk about your goals and how you will measure success. Don't hesitate to communicate your needs—a good partner will want to make sure they are met, even if they aren't relevant to the cause at hand. And once the project is completed, be sure to talk about how it went, what could be improved, and when you might next engage together. *Common Interest, Common Good* provides a tested roadmap for business or social sector partners if you want to explore this topic further.[12]

Other ways that companies encourage volunteering include allowing time to volunteer, either on or off the clock, and offering employees help in finding volunteer opportunities. For example, more than three hundred thousand global employees and retirees of Bank of America are encouraged to volunteer through Bank of America Community Volunteers, led by leaders elected by their peers and local market leadership. Family and friends of employees are also encouraged to participate. Any associate who volunteers regularly with an organization for more than fifty hours during the year may request a $250 grant for that organization; the amount doubles for a hundred hours of service. In addition, Bank of America associates may take off two paid hours each week to volunteer at a nonprofit of their choice.

The company views its volunteer program not only as a valuable asset with benefits for the community and its employees, who gain skills development and team building through the volunteering, but as an opportunity for brand enhancement and long-term strategic business value. For example, as the company has expanded in recent years, volunteering has provided opportunities for employees to join together as a mobilizing force to help rebuild communities challenged in the economic downturn, leveraging their expertise in areas such as financial education. The company aligns its volunteer program with its philanthropy (more than $200 million donated annually) to create greater impact in the communities it serves.[13]

MEDIA AND ENTERTAINMENT

While any company can help by encouraging its employees to volunteer, businesses that speak to the public may play an important role by promoting service by their customers. For example, in 2009, the Disney Company, in partnership with the HandsOn Network, offered a free ticket to one of its theme parks for individuals who performed a day of service. The opportunity was featured in television advertisements and posted prominently on the Disney website. Whether through the form of encouragement on the back of a cereal box, discounts or incentives for individuals who volunteer, or integration of service messages into an advertising campaign, businesses can help build a climate that supports volunteers.

These messages can be even more effective when they come from those entities that inform the public and shape our culture. Media and entertainment companies have a unique role in unleashing the power of service: encouraging service as a norm, and helping people find their way to opportunities that make sense. It's no stretch to think that the forces that can start a trend, make a star, or launch a self-help movement could do the same for service. As one influential ad executive put it, "I volunteer every week but I don't talk about it." If "Where do you serve?" could become as common a conversation topic as "Where did you go to school?" or "Where do you work?" we might well see a dramatic increase in service.

Toward this end, the Entertainment Industry Foundation launched an unprecedented campaign in the fall of 2009 to mobilize the entire entertainment community to inspire a new era of service. The initiative "iParticipate" began with a week of network programming in which service was integrated into the plots of over sixty television shows and promoted through public service announcements (PSAs) following the shows. For example, the fictional staff of *Parks and Recreation* built a KaBOOM! playground and the characters on *Desperate Housewives* started a neighborhood watch. PSAs featuring Michelle Obama, Matthew McConaughy, Gwyneth Paltrow, and other celebrities directed viewers to the iParticipate website, where they could be matched with volunteer opportunities.

Any media organization can support an effort to make service a common part of American culture by highlighting service heroes and projects; helping people find opportunities by promoting matching sites and other volunteer centers; airing public service announcements; or encouraging its own employees, including those who are familiar to the public, to volunteer and talk about their experiences.

The most common reason people choose to volunteer is the simplest: "Because they were asked."[14] The media and entertainment industry can play an important role in making sure that every American hears that call.

PHILANTHROPY

Philanthropic organizations are a critical part of public problem-solving efforts, which makes them key to the demand-side equation. They can seed an innovation, set funding priorities, and provide resources to take a solution to scale. This influence can lift up specific strategies, even bring them to the attention of policymakers, significantly amplifying their impact. Most important, philanthropists can also be system builders, by funding those organizations that provide the infrastructure for service. Often, because there is a perception that engaging volunteers does not entail a monetary cost or that volunteers cannot have an impact on a problem, serious philanthropists overlook service as a strategy. That's unfortunate. Foundations and other organized donors can enlarge their impact by funding the organizations that provide systems that enable service in their own communities or at the state or national level. That was the recommendation of the Reimagining Service Task Force, which found that "[o]rganizations are eager to take advantage of the expertise and time of volunteers, but they often lack the management bandwidth and systems to appropriately manage this rich resource," and called on philanthropy and government to "prioritize investments that leverage citizen service."[15]

In fact, foundations have been critical in shaping the service field. The Ford Foundation, for example, funded *Youth and the Needs of the Nation*, the report of the Committee for the Study of National Service in 1979, which spurred interest in service in the 1980s. Other important grants by the Ford Foundation have included support for demonstration programs that proved the value of youth corps, grants to encourage community foundations to provide AmeriCorps matching funds, and seed funding for leading service organizations such as Innovations in Civic Participation, which has supported the invention of cutting-edge service programs, including the "Summer of Service" discussed in Chapter Two. In similar fashion, the WK Kellogg Foundation helped to grow the service-learning field dramatically by supporting leading organizations and sponsoring a national commission on service-learning. More recently, the Rockefeller Foundation made a major investment in the Cities of Service initiative in 2009 to enable mayors to help build an infrastructure for service in the wake of the Serve America signing. Many other foundations, too numerous to mention, have helped to build the nation's service infrastructure. Investments such as these are critical to the ability of the service field to engage volunteers and national service participants effectively.

Philanthropists can also use their influence with the nonprofit organizations that they fund by asking a routine question: "How will volunteers support this initiative?" Simply asking this question would cause organizations to think about the role of volunteers and might, in some cases, open minds and opportunities. Even better, funders could set aside a "volunteer premium"—an additional 10 percent of the grant amount to be used to involve volunteers. Given that 60 percent of nonprofits consider lack of funds to be a significant obstacle to providing volunteer management, according to a survey by Deloitte, such a dedication of resources could go a long way.

In addition to connecting grantees with volunteers, foundations can incorporate service into the strategies behind the initiatives they fund. For example, in its efforts to fight poverty in the Bay area, Tipping Point Community pairs its financial assistance to organizations with in-kind support to build the organizations' capacity. This support often comes in the form of skilled pro bono help from Tipping Point's corporate partners in areas such as technology, strategic planning, legal assistance, human resources, or real estate.[16]

The Case Foundation similarly recognized the value of volunteers in its PowerUP initiative, which sought to close the digital divide. PowerUP launched in 1999, a time when most Americans dialed-up the Internet through their phone lines, less than half of households were online, and adults were actually still teaching kids how to use the Internet.[17] Case married its $10 million cash contribution to support from other foundations, in-kind contributions from technology companies, and corporate volunteers to create community technology centers for youths. Obtaining the equipment, establishing AOL accounts for the youths, and setting up the centers was one thing. Staffing the centers was another. Housed in youth and community centers that often lacked tech-savvy workers, the centers required trained individuals who could help youths get online and use the programs that came with the computers. This challenge was quickly solved with the engagement of AmeriCorps*VISTA members specially trained to bring the centers to life.[18]

Service groups often lament the limited number of philanthropists that make volunteer and national service a program priority. But if service is a strategy to solve the problems we face as a nation, it can find a home in almost any foundation.

LOCALLY ELECTED OFFICIALS

Locally elected officials—mayors, county executives, and other leaders—face challenges every day that could be addressed, at least in part, with the help of volunteers. It's the rare local leader, however, who takes advantage of this resource or uses the bully pulpit to rally local citizens to serve. And even rarer the elected official who helps to build the systems necessary to make service happen.

New York Mayor Michael Bloomberg has done all three—and challenged other local leaders to do the same. The New York plan offers one blueprint for a robust local effort to make cities, towns, and counties hot spots for transformative service. The initiatives in NYC Service were the result of a sixty-day assessment and consultation process that engaged hundreds of service experts, nonprofit organizations, schools, colleges, private sector partners, and public agencies and surveyed fifteen hundred New Yorkers on volunteer participation and motivation.[19]

On the basis of this information, NYC Service initiatives connect volunteers with the city's greatest needs—strengthening neighborhoods and supporting neighbors in need. Additional efforts will target emerging or existing needs in education, the environment, health, and emergency preparedness. For example, neighborhood block watches, volunteers with the police department, and block beautification address safety, while a rooftop cooling program, volunteer-led exercise classes, and middle-school mentors focus on other needs.

In a survey, 17 percent of New Yorkers who do not volunteer said they did not know where to go to volunteer. So to make New York City the easiest city in which to serve, the plan calls for a state-of-the-art website; a volunteer hotline through the city's "311" referral system; a "Go Pass" to prescreen volunteers, taking the burden off of organizations to do background checks; and a civic corps to place VISTA and other AmeriCorps members with nonprofits.

Finally, NYC Service teaches young people the value of service in order to create a "sustained culture of service." Initiatives toward this end include requiring all schools to have a service plan as part of their Consolidated Plans. Through a partnership with Children for Children, up to a hundred AmeriCorps fellows will be deployed to provide training, technical assistance, data collection, and support to New York City educators to introduce or increase service in their schools. In addition, a thousand young New Yorkers participating in the Summer Youth Employment Program will be engaged in large-scale service projects that will have a measurable impact on the city's most pressing needs.

Finally, to oversee implementation of the nearly forty initiatives included in NYC Service, Mayor Bloomberg appointed the city's first chief service officer.

Any local leader could take these steps:

- Appoint a "service czar" to lead the effort.
- Assess the service infrastructure in the area. What organizations are using volunteers? Who is volunteering? What is happening in the schools? How do people find opportunities?
- Set priorities. What are the most important challenges facing the community that service can address? Part Two of this book can help you see what's possible.
- Find partners. What organizations can help manage volunteers?
- Build systems. Make sure there is an infrastructure to connect volunteers to opportunities. Local HandsOn Action Centers, AmeriCorps programs, and other organizations can help, as can online volunteer matching sites—if organizations are vigilant about posting opportunities.
- Then, issue a call to action.

Early American local leaders often turned to volunteers to solve challenges from fighting fires to lighting the streets in the days before electricity. Today's modern mayors can again make volunteering a vibrant part of their efforts to build strong communities. In addition to deploying valuable human resources to priority needs, these steps can build social capital, making cities places where people know one another, look out for one another, and engage together to create the society they want to see.

STATE POLICYMAKERS

Almost every governor appoints a state commission to lead volunteer efforts within the state and administer AmeriCorps funding. These commissions are led by a board appointed by the governor, often composed of prominent individuals enthusiastic about promoting service. Many commissions play a leadership role in their states that goes well beyond AmeriCorps—promoting volunteer service in all its forms, sponsoring service projects on Martin Luther King Day, 9/11, and other days of service, and encouraging service in other ways.

In 2008, California governor Arnold Schwarzenegger became the first governor to make the state commission leader, Karen Baker, a member of his cabinet. Wildfires and a San Francisco Bay oil spill in 2007 had put into stark view the disconnects between the service commission, known as CaliforniaVolunteers, and cabinet agencies charged with responding. Volunteers who came forward to help overwhelmed the agencies, and CaliforniaVolunteers was not brought in to organize them for several days.[20] "Buddhist monks were jumping over police tape to save waterfowl," recalls Baker. "The governor called them 'guerrilla volunteers.' He saw the passion they felt and he knew he had to put it to work. Maria Shriver had long championed giving the state's volunteers a more prominent voice in government. It was a perfect storm: a governor and first lady who valued service, an obviously demonstrable need, and a ready resource in our state's volunteers."

By sitting at the cabinet table, Baker helps other secretaries imagine how volunteers can meet specific needs. As the state's leaders discuss the state's challenges, Baker brings an often underutilized resource to the able—the people of California and the nonprofits at which they serve. As a result, new programs and cross-sector initiatives have launched, including the CalVet Corps, serving recently discharged veterans, and the Green Jobs Corps, combining job training, environmental stewardship and service. Serving on the cabinet means you are part of the discussions and can help shape the solutions, which is especially important in a state the size of California, according to Baker.[21]

The cabinet position makes it easier for service to be a part of the solution to emerging problems. However, as of 2009, only New York had followed suit. Most state policymakers, like their counterparts at other levels of government, neglect service as a way to address pressing needs. To change this, Serve Washington, Washington State's service commission, under the leadership of long-time executive director Bill Basl, took the approach of convening leaders from all sectors to discuss service as a strategy to address critical community needs and to guide in collaboration the future of the service movement. This summit drew over four hundred state leaders.[22]

Washington State has had a long history of deploying service as a strategy to address public problems. Former governor Gary Locke looked to members of AmeriCorps and VISTA to tutor, and to recruit and train volunteer reading tutors, to address the low reading performance in many elementary schools. They successfully raised reading levels by an average of one grade level. More recently, the Washington Commission created a Clean Energy Corps to install energy-generating and energy-saving devices in state parks and a veterans corps to engage wounded soldiers at Fort Louis in service that will support their recovery.

States play a lead role in setting educational policy, and most states receive Learn and Serve America funding through their educational agencies. In some cases, state education policy promotes or requires service-learning for students in public schools. Maryland, for example, has for many years required seventy-five hours of service-learning for all students as a graduation requirement. States could do more to support service through schools and connect it to priorities for the region.

States are often laboratories of innovation—informing other states and the federal government alike. The Corporation for National and Community Service with the Bureau of Labor Statistics tracks volunteering by state, and the American Association of State Service Commissions informs state commission staff and helps states learn from one another. Whichever state finds a breakthrough way for transformational service may lead the country to adopt new citizen-centered solutions.

FEDERAL POLICYMAKERS

Like their state and local counterparts, federal policymakers can do a lot to promote service, from using the bully pulpit to providing funding for service organizations. Only rarely, however, do federal policymakers make service an explicit part of their efforts to solve pressing problems—potentially one of the most powerful ways to increase volunteering and meet the challenges before us. If we are to solve the problems we face as a nation, it's time to take service seriously as a part of comprehensive strategies.

On the other hand, federal funding has played a large role in building systems for service. The Corporation for National and

Community Service administers a set of programs that channel human and financial resources to solve education, environment, public safety, and other human needs: AmeriCorps, which supports full- and part-time members who can earn education awards for their service; Learn and Serve America, which provides funding for service-learning in schools, community organizations, and higher education institutions; and Senior Corps, which includes the Foster Grandparent, Senior Companion, and RSVP programs. The Corporation recently received responsibility for programs authorized by the Edward M. Kennedy Serve America Act, which will grow AmeriCorps to address key issues and expand the Corporation's mission to include support for nonprofit organizations' capacity and innovation.

Other federal agencies support domestic civilian service in other ways. For example, the Department of Labor administers the Youth-Build program as part of its youth employment programs and the Park Service uses volunteers to perform a wide range of functions in national parks. These programs offer a model for integrating service strategies into state and federal efforts to address important issues.

Some presidents have on occasion incorporated service into major policy strategies. President Bill Clinton created the America Reads Challenge to support his goal to ensure that every child learn to read by third grade. Reading scores among young students had dropped significantly during the 1980s, and despite research demonstrating that reading to young children was the best way to increase reading skills, in 1991, just 35 percent of young children were read to at home every day. Clinton called on colleges, faith-based organizations, civic groups, AmeriCorps members, and other volunteers to read to children, ultimately reaching one million children. Reading scores increased, especially in the highest-poverty communities. From 1992 to 1996, reading scores of nine-year-olds in highest-poverty schools improved by nearly one grade level, reversing a downward trend. The Reading Excellence Act passed in 1998 incorporated these strategies, and by 1999, a majority of children ages three to five were read to daily.[23]

In a similar manner, the George W. Bush Administration looked to volunteers in the wake of 9/11 to make the nation better prepared for emergencies. Under the leadership of the Freedom Corps, directed by John Bridgeland, volunteers were positioned as a critical part of an effective emergency response infrastructure. The result was Citizen Corps, to encourage Americans to help prepare themselves and their communities, described in Chapter Six. In just a few years, communities across the country organized more than two thousand Citizen Corps Councils—local groups comprising first responders, volunteer organizations, hospitals, businesses, and other concerned citizens. These councils educate the public, organize volunteer opportunities, and share information so their best efforts can be replicated.[24]

Of course, both governors and presidents have other channels to promote service, beyond federal programs. Every recent president has made important speeches calling the nation to service, often during their State of the Union addresses. President George H. W. Bush's friends and supporters created the Points of Light Foundation, a private sector organization created to encourage everyone to "claim America's problems as your own; identify, enlarge, and multiply what is working; and discover, encourage, and develop leaders."[25] Bush also signed the National and Community Service Act of 1990, creating the Commission on National and Community Service, funding for service-learning, and the demonstration that led to AmeriCorps. President Bill Clinton promoted service in a variety of ways. In addition to creating the Corporation for National and Community Service and AmeriCorps, he frequently called on Americans to ask "three simple questions: What is right? What is wrong? And what are we going to do about it?"[26] President George W. Bush, in addition to creating Freedom Corps and Citizen Corps, launched "A Billion + Change" with the goal of generating $1 billion of skilled pro bono service to help nonprofits become more effective in meeting social and community needs. President Barack Obama may well take service to a new level, not simply by signing the Serve America Act but by inspiring All For Good and other partnerships and advancing social innovation in a variety of ways.

The true power of service to transform America lies in our ability to leverage the caring and commitment of its people to solve problems. Leaders in the White House and governors' mansions are critically important to this effort—challenging Americans to take action, making sure that opportunities are available, and supporting the systems that make it all possible.

POTENTIAL FOR TRANSFORMATION

Everyone and virtually every American institution can contribute meaningfully to the transformation of America through service. We can all help to build the supply of volunteers by mobilizing others or serving ourselves, creating demand for volunteers through well-thought-out strategies, or building the systems that connect volunteers to opportunities and offer the programming to support their effectiveness.

CHAPTER TEN

Conclusion

When President Clinton proposed the AmeriCorps legislation in March of 1993, he called national service "nothing less than the American way to change America." Indeed, over centuries of progress, Americans have worked together to solve problems, big and small. Even nearly two hundred years ago, Alexis de Tocqueville, sent by the French government to understand why representative democracy had succeeded in America while failing elsewhere, observed that association, the coming together of people for common purpose, was uniquely American.

But despite this tradition, we are far from reaching our potential. At times, the American way seems more connected to consumerism and a cult of celebrity than a culture of service. In fact, at the point in the past decade when Americans were most eager to act—after the 9/11 attacks—President Bush proposed wide-ranging government action but asked the American people to go about their daily lives. "Go down to Disney World in Florida," he told us. "Take your families and enjoy life the way we want it to be enjoyed." He later encouraged people to serve their own communities and created the Citizen Corps as a strategy to make the nation better prepared for emergencies. But the sense of shared sacrifice never emerged. When he made a similar call in 2006 in the face of an economic downturn, asking us to "go shopping more," pundits made much of the remark.

President Obama campaigned on a theme of change. His inaugural address evoked the many crises facing the nation and reminded us that our nation relies on "the kindness to take in a stranger when the levees break; the selflessness of workers who would rather cut their hours than see a friend lose their job." His charge, that "[w]hat is required of us now is a new era of responsibility—a recognition, on the part of every American, that we have duties to ourselves, our nation and the world," suggested that we might well need shared sacrifice to solve America's problems. As a first step, in his first hundred days in office, President Obama signed the Edward M. Kennedy Serve America Act, signaling a new era for service in America. He has continued the call to service in a myriad of ways, supporting new technology solutions, calling on the nonprofit world to engage Americans in a summer of service, and using the bully pulpit to call for more service-learning opportunities for students.

Whether the promise of the Serve America Act can be realized, however, depends on more than a president's pen or platform. The achievement of its potential to change America depends on Americans' willingness to step up against our biggest challenges. It depends on leaders whose responsibility it is to shape solutions to recognize the power of service as a strategy. And it depends on government and philanthropy to fund the systems and programs that can turn "the kindness of strangers" into a force for change.

In the short term, that means building on the strong base of organizations, both in and outside government, on the ground and virtual, that help people find service opportunities and prepare them to be effective. These organizations run the gamut from volunteer action centers to state service commissions to national AmeriCorps programs and nonprofits that create learning communities, offer training, and advocate for national service. These kinds of organizations often face challenges in finding funding—it's always easier to pay for a direct service program than to support the engine that drives it. But without these organizations, we risk losing both quality and quantity, and will find it hard to achieve the potential that service represents. In fact, it will be impossible even to reach the scale envisioned by the Serve America Act.

In the short term, it also means fully funding the new Act. This legislation will take AmeriCorps-style national service from 75,000 members to 250,000 members, expand the long-standing Corporation for National and Community Service programs, and invest in building the capacity of the nonprofit sector. It also envisions and authorizes a stronger connection between service and important issues facing the nation. However, if funding is not made available, these advances won't happen. It will amount to even less if service does not become a valued partner with those entities charged with solving problems.

And finally, in the short term, it means embracing innovation and investing in proven programs to take service to new levels. That requires more effective use of technology and letting go of traditional ways of doing things when they are less efficient. It also means scaling up what works—the models and organizations that offer the best returns on investment.

To realize the promise of the Act, then, requires several important shifts in mind-sets.

It will demand a shift on the part of advocates to think of service not as an end but as a means, to think of service as a strategy to solve problems, not the reason for being. This will open the door to new funding and new partners, and position service to gain far broader support.

It will demand a shift on the part of policymakers to move service from the nice to the necessary column. At the federal level, the entire budget of the Corporation for National and Community Service would be a rounding error at the Department of Defense, or even at Health and Human Services. Very little investment goes there because it is seen as innocuous or unimportant to solving the bigger problems of our country. But we can't solve those problems until service becomes a valued strategy, not just by the Corporation but by every department concerned with domestic challenges.

It will demand a shift on the part of leaders of nonprofit organizations and other service providers, including schools, to see volunteers and national service participants as important partners in achieving their missions, to get away from stereotypes and think about service more broadly as a source of skilled human resources, social capital, and credible communicators.

It will demand a shift by many service groups, nonprofits, and policymakers to be more outcome-oriented, to move beyond counting the number of volunteers and the hours they serve as their measure of accomplishment and start tracking whether volunteers moved the needle on a problem. And then it will demand that funders support those organizations that achieve the best results so they can grow even if it means that less effective organizations receive fewer resources.

It will demand a shift away from stereotypes about volunteers, and the blush of noblesse oblige that often colors their efforts, to believing in the words of Martin Luther King Jr. that "everyone can be great because everyone can serve"—and seeing how the act of serving others will benefit people traditionally thought of as clients, whether they are young; poor; immigrant; elderly; or struggling with physical, mental, or emotional challenges.

It will demand a shift from thinking that volunteers are free to understanding that the systems that make them effective cost something. It will also demand an appreciation that the federal money invested in an AmeriCorps member leverages the labor of someone who could probably command a higher salary elsewhere or, alternatively, a person who might otherwise draw public assistance.

Finally, it will demand a commitment to innovation by everyone, not to freeze in place any system once it's built but to innovate continuously for higher impact and efficiency. No one can see into the future, but a set of nimble organizations that can adapt to changing circumstances, adopt new technology, and engage new partners is essential to helping the entire field respond quickly to whatever comes next.

These shifts focus largely on the "demand" and "systems" parts of the service equation. I believe that if they are done right, the supply of volunteers will be there. This is indeed the rare case of "if we build it they will come." Virtually every study done to explore why people volunteer has included high on its list of answers "because someone asked me." If asked, people will serve.

Once these shifts occur, we will be in a very different place. Service will be an accepted part of the American story of change. Armed with that, service can go to the next level, and we can make substantial progress toward solving seemingly intractable challenges. Consider, for example, the impact of one million AmeriCorps members together with one hundred million volunteers. With this level of support we could

- Match every low-income family that includes preschoolers, or the child care and Head Start centers that serve them, with trained individuals who can help ready the children for school success so that no child starts kindergarten already behind peers

- Place a team of AmeriCorps members or trained volunteers in every "drop-out factory" middle school

- Make a summer service program a rite of passage for every eighth-grader

- Provide an AmeriCorps*VISTA volunteer to every community-based nonprofit working to alleviate poverty

- Train and equip teachers and tutors for one million adult English language learners

- Build or renovate a hundred thousand homes for low-income families
- Create or restore green spaces and community gardens in a thousand low-income neighborhoods
- Place a team of AmeriCorps members at every community health center
- Create a "Time Bank" run by AmeriCorps*VISTA members in a thousand low-income neighborhoods and rural areas
- Provide trained volunteers to assist one million frail elderly adults
- Expand youth corps slots preparing disadvantaged young people for "green jobs" to reach an additional 250,000 youths
- Teach all Americans how to halve their energy consumption
- Double the National Civilian Community Corps and other AmeriCorps programs that specialize in emergency response so they can respond anywhere disaster strikes
- Train Community Emergency Response Teams (CERTs) to make sure every community is prepared in the event of a small- or large-scale disaster

While this level of human engagement would necessitate a financial investment in service organizations and supplies, the benefits would far outweigh the costs. Looking at it the other way, without a serious investment in service, we are unlikely to see the kind of transformation America needs in order to thrive in the new millennium.

It's always been a false choice: Will we rely on government action to solve our problems, or can government step aside so volunteers and charitable organizations can take them on? We need both, and more important, we need government and the volunteer sector to work together for greatest impact. We can rise to this occasion. The American way to change America is, after all, to act together in common purpose.

Appendix: High-Impact Service Programs

TWENTY-FIVE ORGANIZED FOR IMPACT AND SCALE

Admission Possible

www.admissionpossible.org

Admission Possible identifies low-income high school students with the potential and motivation for college and provides them with four services: (1) ACT and SAT test preparation, (2) intensive guidance in preparing college applications, (3) help obtaining financial aid, and (4) guidance in transition to college.

Big Brothers Big Sisters

www.bbbs.org

Big Brothers Big Sisters helps children reach their potential through professionally supported, one-to-one relationships with mentors that have a measurable impact on youths.

Boys and Girls Clubs of America

www.bgca.org

The Boys and Girls Clubs of America inspire and enable young people to realize their full potential as productive, responsible, and caring citizens.

Citizen Schools

www.citizenschools.org

Citizen Schools partners with middle schools to expand the learning day for low-income children in fun, engaging ways that connect them to real-world skills and more caring adults from around the community.

City Year

www.cityyear.org

City Year unites young people of all backgrounds for a year of full-time service, giving them the skills and opportunities to change the world.

College Summit

www.collegesummit.org

College Summit partners with schools and districts to strengthen college-going culture and increase college enrollment rates, so that all students graduate career- and college-ready.

Communities in Schools

www.cisnet.org

Communities in Schools champions the connection of needed community resources with schools to help young people successfully learn, stay in school, and prepare for life.

EducationWorks

www.educationworks-online.org

EducationWorks enriches the lives of children, youth, and families by providing educational programs and services in communities confronting high rates of poverty and other barriers to educational achievement.

Equal Justice Works

www.equaljusticeworks.org

Equal Justice Works provides leadership to ensure a sustainable pipeline of talented and trained lawyers involved in public service.

Experience Corps

www.experiencecorps.org

Experience Corps partners with schools and local community organizations to create meaningful opportunities for adults over fifty-five to boost student performance.

Habitat for Humanity

www.habitat.org

Habitat for Humanity volunteers build or rehabilitate houses in partnership with homeowner families.

HandsOn Network

www.handsonnetwork.org

HandsOn Network inspires, equips, and mobilizes people to take action that changes the world.

HIPPY USA

www.hippyusa.org

HIPPY programs empower parents as primary educators of their children in the home and foster parent involvement in school and community life to maximize the chances of successful early school experiences.

Jumpstart

www.readfortherecord.org

To cultivate a child's social, emotional, and intellectual readiness, Jumpstart brings college students and community volunteers together with preschool children for year-long, individualized tutoring and mentoring.

KaBOOM!

www.kaboom.org

KaBOOM! creates playspaces through the participation and leadership of communities with the goal of a great place to play within walking distance of every child in America.

LIFT (formerly National Student Partnerships)

www.nspnet.org

LIFT enables college students to work side-by-side with low-income community members, first helping them address immediate needs, then providing comprehensive, long-term support designed to help families break the cycle of poverty.

LISC AmeriCorps

www.lisc.org

LISC AmeriCorps members serve with Local Initiatives Support Corporation (LISC) affiliates to help community residents transform distressed neighborhoods into healthy and sustainable communities of choice and opportunity—good places to work, do business, and raise children.

National Association of Community Health Centers (Community HealthCorps)

www.nachc.com

The Community HealthCorps promotes health care for America's underserved while developing tomorrow's health care workforce by placing AmeriCorps members at Community Health Centers.

Playworks (formerly Sports4Kids)

www.playworksusa.org

Playworks supports learning by providing safe, healthy, and inclusive play and physical activity to schools at recess and throughout the entire school day.

Project HEALTH

www.projecthealth.org

Project HEALTH mobilizes college student volunteers to connect low-income patients with the resources they need to be healthy and, in so doing, creates the next generation of leaders committed to tackling this country's greatest health challenges.

Reach Out and Read

www.reachoutandread.org

Reach Out and Read makes literacy promotion a standard part of pediatric primary care, so that children grow up with books and a love of reading.

Red Cross

www.redcross.org

The American Red Cross provides relief to victims of disaster and helps people prevent, prepare for, and respond to emergencies.

Share Our Strength

www.strength.org

Share Our Strength works hard toward the goal of making sure no kid in America grows up hungry by weaving together a net of community groups, activists, and food programs to catch children at risk of hunger and surround them with nutritious food where they live, learn, and play.

Teach For America

www.teachforamerica.org

Teach For America recruits outstanding recent college graduates from all backgrounds and career interests to commit to teach for two years in urban and rural public schools.

YouthBuild

www.youthbuild.org

YouthBuild unleashes the intelligence and positive energy of low-income youths to rebuild their communities and their lives.

TWENTY-FIVE MODELS WITH PROMISE

Adopt an Alleyway Youth Project

www.chinatowncommunitydevelopmentcenter.org

Chinatown CDC created the Adopt an Alleyway Youth Project as part of the neighborhood service and empowerment program in response to the lack of youth services targeted at the Chinatown community. The program promotes youth leadership and community involvement through youth-initiated and -led neighborhood service activities.

American Youthworks

www.americanyouthworks.org

American Youthworks is a comprehensive human investment organization that transforms young people into self-sufficient adults through education, job training, and community service.

Asian American LEAD (AALEAD)

www.aalead.org

AALEAD's overarching goal is to increase the opportunities and ability of low-income Asian American children to move out of poverty and become successful, self-sufficient adults.

Children's Defense Fund-Texas

www.cdftexas.org

CDF-Texas raises awareness about the condition of Texas children, connects children and families to programs and services that help meet their needs, and works with community partners statewide to formulate policy solutions and broad-based support for legislative action on behalf of children.

DC Volunteer Lawyers Project

www.dcvlp.org

The DC Volunteer Lawyers Project provides high-quality, free legal services to low-income District of Columbia residents in family law cases.

Earth Conservation Corps

www.ecc1.org

The Earth Conservation Corps is a nonprofit organization that engages the strong minds and muscles of Anacostia's youth in the restoration of the Anacostia River. As corpsmembers improve their own lives, they rebuild the environmental, social, and economic health of their communities.

Educate Tomorrow

www.educatetomorrow.org

Educate Tomorrow provides one-on-one educational mentors to children in foster care who are turning eighteen and "aging out" of the system.

Florida Breast Health Initiative

http://www.flbreasthealth.com/

The Florida Breast Health Initiative is an outreach organization dedicated to educating women about the importance of breast health and providing them with the resources to beat the disease.

Give an Hour

www.giveanhour.org

Give an Hour provides free mental health services to U.S. military personnel and families affected by the conflicts in Iraq and Afghanistan.

GRID Alternatives

www.gridalternatives.org

GRID Alternatives empowers communities in need by providing renewable energy and energy efficiency services, equipment, and training.

Growing Native

www.growingnative.org

Growing Native is a year-round volunteer project that collects hardwood seeds and plants trees to help restore and protect rivers and streams in the Potomac River watershed.

Harlem Children's Zone

www.hcz.org

Harlem Children's Zone offers education, social-service, and community-building programs to children and families in a one hundred–block area of Harlem.

IMPACT Silver Spring

www.impactsilverspring.org

IMPACT Silver Spring brings diverse people together to create a successful community for everyone by engaging new voices, developing leaders through training and support, building awareness in current leaders, and sparking collaboration and action to bring about positive change.

Manateens

www.volunteermanatee.org/manateens

The ManaTEEN Club engages youths in Manatee County, Florida, to address local needs through youth-designed projects.

The Mission Continues

www.missioncontinues.org

The Mission Continues awards fellowships to empower wounded and disabled veterans to serve in their communities.

Music National Service

www.musicnationalservice.org

Music National Service supports and expands the use of music to meet important civic and social goals. Its "musical Peace Corps," MusicianCorps, engages full-time fellows in a variety of settings.

National Indian Youth Leadership Project (NIYLP)

www.niylp.org

NIYLP nurtures the potential of Native youths to be contributors to a more positive world through adventure-based learning and service to family, community, and nature.

New York City Coalition Against Hunger

www.nyccah.org

The Coalition promotes food access for all New Yorkers by coordinating the activities of the emergency food providers in the city so that issues can be identified, prioritized, and addressed effectively.

Partners In Care

www.partnersincare.org

Partners In Care Maryland empowers older adults to remain independent in their own homes, using a time-exchange network that builds community by engaging people to help each other with the myriad tasks involved in everyday living.

Prison Entrepreneurship Program (PEP)

www.prisonentrepreneurship.org

PEP redirects prison inmates into legitimate enterprises, leveraging their proven entrepreneurial skill-sets by linking them with top business and academic talent through an MBA-level curriculum and mentor relationships.

Project SHINE

www.projectshine.org

Project SHINE is a national service-learning program that supports a broad and diverse group of college students in building relationships with elderly immigrants and refugees through language, literacy, and citizenship tutoring.

RelightUS

www.relightus.com

RelightUS informs and inspires people to protect the environment through the simple act of changing a light bulb.

Rhode Island Free Clinic

www.rifreeclinic.org

The Rhode Island Free Clinic provides free medical care to uninsured Rhode Islanders.

San Francisco Education Fund

www.sfedfund.org

San Francisco Education Fund engages school volunteers to improve student success in San Francisco public schools.

Western New York AmeriCorps

www.wnyamericorps.org

Western New York AmeriCorps creates opportunities for all individuals to serve, challenging citizens to turn their ideals into action and their passion into positive change.

TWENTY-NINE HIGH-IMPACT FIELD BUILDERS

Alliance for Community Trees

www.actrees.org

Alliance for Community Trees supports grassroots, citizen-based nonprofit organizations dedicated to urban and community tree planting, care, conservation, and education.

American Association of State Service Commissions (ASC)

www.asc-online.org

ASC is a peer network of governor-appointed state service commissioners and staff of service commissions.

America's Promise Alliance

www.americaspromise.org

With more than three hundred national partners, America's Promise Alliance is devoted to improving the lives of young people by ensuring they receive the "Five Promises" they need to graduate high school prepared for success.

AmeriCorps Alums

www.americorpsalums.org

AmeriCorps Alums connects, supports, and mobilizes AmeriCorps alumni to strengthen communities and the nation.

Campus Compact

www.compact.org

Campus Compact advances the public purposes of colleges and universities by deepening their ability to improve community life and to educate students for civic and social responsibility.

Center for American Progress

www.americanprogress.org

The Center for American Progress is a think tank dedicated to improving the lives of Americans through ideas and action.

Children for Children

www.childrenforchildren.org

Children for Children mobilizes the energy, ingenuity, and compassion of young people, beginning at an early age, to discover their power and potential to solve real-world problems through volunteer opportunities and service-learning programs that instill a lifelong commitment to service.

Civic Enterprises

www.civicenterprises.org

Civic Enterprises is a public policy firm that helps corporations, nonprofits, foundations, universities, and governments develop and spearhead innovative public policies to strengthen our communities and country.

Civic Ventures

www.civicventures.org

Through an inventive program portfolio, original research, strategic alliances, and the power of people's own life stories, Civic Ventures demonstrates the value of experience in solving serious social problems, from education to the environment and health care to homelessness.

The Corps Network

www.corpsnetwork.org

Corps are versatile, cost-effective programs that allow young people to accomplish important conservation, community restoration, and human service projects, while also developing employment and citizenship skills.

Create The Good

www.createthegood.org

Create The Good is a website where good people get connected to opportunities to create good, in whatever way works for them.

Earth Force

www.earthforce.org

Earth Force trains and supports educators who engage young people in hands-on, real-world opportunities to practice civic skills, acquire and understand environmental knowledge, and develop the skills and motivation to become life-long leaders in addressing environmental issues.

Generations United

www.gu.org

Generations United improves the lives of children, youths, and older people through intergenerational collaboration, public policies, and programs for the enduring benefit for all.

Green For All

www.greenforall.org

Green For All collaborates with the business, government, labor, and grassroots communities to create and implement programs that increase quality jobs and opportunities in green industry while holding the most vulnerable people at the center of its agenda.

Innovations in Civic Participation (ICP)

www.icicp.org

ICP supports the development of innovative high-quality youth civic engagement policies and programs both in the United States and around the world.

National Service-Learning Partnership

www.service-learningpartnership.org

The Partnership strengthens the impact of service-learning on young people's learning and development, especially their academic and civic preparation.

National Youth Leadership Council

www.nylc.org

The National Youth Leadership Council creates a more just, sustainable, and peaceful world with young people, their schools, and their communities through service-learning.

Public Allies

www.publicallies.org

Public Allies advances new leadership to strengthen communities, nonprofits, and civic participation.

RespectAbility

www.ncoa.org

The National Council on Aging's RespectAbility initiative seeks to help nonprofit organizations make more effective use of older Americans in their community-based efforts.

Rural School and Community Trust

www.ruraledu.org

The Rural School and Community Trust helps rural schools and communities get better together by involving young people in learning linked to their communities and a variety of other ways.

ServeNext

www.servenext.org

ServeNext expands voluntary service opportunities as a strategy to address our most pressing social challenges and strengthen our democracy.

ServiceNation

www.servicenation.org

ServiceNation is a campaign to inspire a new era of voluntary citizen service in America.

Taproot Foundation

www.taprootfoundation.org

The Taproot Foundation strengthens nonprofits by engaging business professionals in service.

Time Banks USA

www.timebanks.org

Time Banks enable neighbors to earn an hour of help for each hour of volunteer service they provide.

Tipping Point Community

www.tippoint.org

Tipping Point Community screens nonprofits rigorously to find the most effective groups connecting Bay Area individuals and families to the services and opportunities needed to break the cycle of poverty and achieve economic self-sufficiency.

Voices for National Service

www.voicesforservice.org

Voices for National Service seeks to ensure the growth and development of national service programs and works to educate the American public and our nation's leaders about the power and impact of national service.

William J. Clinton Foundation

www.clintonfoundation.org

The Clinton Foundation strengthens the capacity of people in the United States and throughout the world to meet the challenges of global interdependence.

Youth Service America

www.ysa.org

Youth Service America improves communities by increasing the number and diversity of young people ages five through twenty-five serving in important roles.

Youth Volunteer Corps of America

www.yvca.org

Youth Volunteer Corps of America creates and increases volunteer opportunities to enrich America's youths, address community needs, and develop a lifetime commitment to service.

SIXTEEN HIGH-IMPACT PUBLIC PROGRAMS

AmeriCorps

www.americorps.gov

AmeriCorps members perform full-time or substantial part-time service to meet educational, public safety, environmental, and other human needs and may earn Segal AmeriCorps Education Awards.

AmeriCorps*NCCC (National Civilian Community Corps)

www.americorps.gov/about/programs/nccc

AmeriCorps*NCCC is a full-time, team-based residential program for men and women age eighteen through twenty-four that strengthens communities and develops leaders.

CaliforniaVolunteers

www.californiavolunteers.org

CaliforniaVolunteers is the state office charged with managing programs and initiatives to increase the number and impact of Californians involved with service and volunteering.

Citizen Corps

www.citizencorps.gov

Citizen Corps harnesses the power of every individual through education, training, and volunteer service to make communities safer, stronger, and better prepared to respond to the threats of terrorism, crime, public health issues, and disasters of all kinds.

Foster Grandparents

www.seniorcorps.gov/about/programs/fg

Foster Grandparents are individuals age fifty-five and over who thrive on direct interaction with children and believe they can make a difference in their lives.

Learn and Serve America

www.learnandserve.gov

Learn and Serve America provides direct and indirect support to K–12 schools, community groups, and higher education institutions to facilitate service-learning projects.

The National Park Service

www.nps.gov

Since 1916, the American people have entrusted the National Park Service with the care of their national parks. With the help of volunteers and park partners, the Park Service safeguards nearly four hundred places and shares their stories with more than 275 million visitors every year.

NYC Service

www.nycservice.org

NYC Service oversees more than forty innovative initiatives that aim to make New York City the easiest place in the world to volunteer, target volunteers to address the city's greatest needs, and promote service as a core part of what it means to be a citizen.

Peace Corps

www.peacecorps.gov

Peace Corps volunteers travel overseas to make real differences in the lives of people.

Presidio Trust

www.presidio.org

The Presidio Trust preserves and enhances the Presidio as an enduring resource for the American public. The Trust's work encompasses the natural areas, wildlife, and native habitats of the park, as well as the historic structures and designed landscapes that make the park a National Historic Landmark District.

RSVP

www.seniorcorps.gov/about/programs/rsvp

RSVP offers adults who are age fifty-five and older a full range of volunteer opportunities with thousands of local and national organizations.

Senior Companions

www.seniorcorps.gov/about/programs/sc

By becoming a companion to a frail person, Senior Companions, who are age fifty-five and over, help people stay in their own homes.

Serve Washington

www.ofm.wa.gov/servewa

Serve Washington expands the ethic of service throughout Washington State by inviting citizens of all ages and backgrounds to contribute their time and talents to strengthen and promote service and volunteerism as strategies for building healthy communities.

VISTA (Volunteers in Service to America)

www.americorps.gov/about/programs/vista

VISTA members commit to serve full time for a year at a nonprofit organization or local government agency, working to fight illiteracy, improve health services, create businesses, strengthen community groups, and much more.

Volunteer Florida

www.volunteerflorida.org

Volunteer Florida, the governor's commission on service, strengthens Florida's communities through volunteerism and service.

Youthbuild

http://www.doleta.gov/youth_services/youthbuild.cfm

The Federal Department of Labor provides funding to support Youthbuild programs, highly successful alternative education programs that assist youths who are often significantly behind in basic skills with obtaining a high school diploma or GED credential.

Notes

Preface

1. W. Marshall, *Citizenship and National Service: A Blueprint for Civic Enterprise* (Washington, DC: Democratic Leadership Council, 1988).
2. G. H. W. Bush, *Address Accepting the Presidential Nomination at the Republican National Convention in New Orleans,* August 18, 1988.
3. Other members of the Commission on National and Community Service included former Congressmen Pete McCloskey (R-CA), who was its first chair, and Tom Ehrlich, former president of Indiana University, who succeeded McCloskey as chair. Reatha Clark King, head of the General Mills Foundation, was a vice chair with the author and Alan Khazei. Other members included Joyce Black; Father William Byron; former Senator Daniel Evans (R-WA); Maria Ferrier; Frances Hesselbein, former head of the Girl Scouts; Les Lenkowski; Jack MacAllister, the CEO of America West Airlines; Wayne Meisel; Digger Phelps, former Notre Dame Basketball Coach; Johnnie Smith; Glen White; Gayle Wilson, the First Lady of California; Robert Woodson; and Karen Young. The Commission hired Catherine Milton as executive director.
4. Commission on National and Community Service, *What You Can Do for Your Country,* Report of the Commission on National and Community Service, January 1993 (Washington, DC: U.S. Government Printing Office, 1993).
5. Steven Waldman provides an excellent account of the efforts to pass AmeriCorps in his book *The Bill: How Legislation Really Becomes Law, A Case Study of the National Service Bill* (New York: Penguin Books, 1995).
6. A detailed account of the effort to "Save AmeriCorps" can be found in S. Sagawa and D. Jospin, *The Charismatic Organization: Eight Ways to Grow a Nonprofit that Builds Buzz, Delights Donors, and Energizes Employees* (San Francisco: Jossey-Bass, 2008).

7. S. Sagawa, *Serving America: A National Service Agenda for the Next Decade* (Washington, DC: Center for American Progress, 2007).

8. ServeNext was founded by Zach Maurin and Aaron Marquez.

9. ServiceNation was convened by five leaders in the service field: Alan Khazei, co-founder of City Year and CEO of Be the Change; Michael Brown, co-founder and CEO of City Year; AnnMaura Connolly, leader of Voices for National Service; John Bridgeland, CEO of Civic Enterprises; and Michelle Nunn, then CEO of the HandsOn Network, which subsequently merged with the Points of Light Foundation.

10. President Barack Obama, *Address to A Joint Session of Congress*, February 24, 2009.

Chapter 1: Introduction

1. Corporation for National and Community Service, *Volunteering in America: Research Highlights* (Washington, DC: CNCS, 2009).

2. Corporation for National and Community Service, Office of Research and Policy Development, *Still Serving: Measuring the Eight-Year Impact of Ameri-Corps on Alumni* (Washington, DC: CNCS, 2008), p. 36.

3. Corporation for National and Community Service, *What Do We Know About Volunteering in America?* (Washington, DC: CNCS, 2007); Corporation for National and Community Service, Office of Research and Policy Development, *AmeriCorps: Changing Lives, Changing America: A Report on AmeriCorps' Impact on Members and Nonprofit Organizations* (Washington, DC: CNCS, 2007).

Part I: Changing Lives

1. S. Waldman, *The Bill: How Legislation Really Becomes Law, A Case Study of the National Service Bill* (New York: Penguin Books, 1995), p. 20.

Chapter 2: Powering Life Transitions

1. Fresno County Economic Opportunities Commission, "Getting a Grip on Life," http://www.fresnoeoc.org/news.html, accessed November 25, 2009; The Corps Network, "Arthur Jacuinde, Fresno Local Conservation Corps, 2009 Corpsmember of the Year Awardee," http://www.corpsnetwork.org/index.php?option=com_content&view=article&id=124:forum09arthur&catid=34:about, accessed November 25, 2009.

2. Interview with Doris Thomas, May 22, 2009.

3. W. Damon, *The Path to Purpose: Helping Our Children Find Their Calling in Life* (New York: Free Press, 2008), p. 50.

4. Ibid., p. 33.

5. Ibid., pp. 28–29, 41.

6. Bradley Center for Philanthropy and Civic Renewal, Hudson Institution, Transcript, *Preventing Failure to Launch: Is Service a Path to Purpose?* Washington, DC, May 15, 2008, p. 21.

7. Parker's name has been changed to protect his identity.

8. S. Sagawa, *Summer of Service: A New American Rite of Passage?* (Washington, DC: Innovations in Civic Participation), p. 8.

9. R. Balfanz and N. Legters, "The Graduation Crisis We Know and What Can be Done About It," *Education Week,* July 12, 2006.

10. Guttmacher Institute, "Facts on American Teens' Sexual and Reproductive Health," September 2009, http://www.guttmacher.org/pubs/fb_ATSRH .html; L. Johnston, P. O'Malley, J. Bachman, and J. Schulenberg, *Monitoring the Future: Results on Adolescent Drug Use: Overview of Key Findings, 2008* (Bethesda, MD: National Institutes of Health, 2008).

11. D. Kirby, *No Easy Answers: Research Findings on Programs to Reduce Teen Pregnancy* (Washington, DC: The National Campaign to Prevent Teen Pregnancy, 1997).

12. J. Kielsmeier, *Growing to Greatness: The State of Service-Learning Project* (Saint Paul, MN: National Youth Leadership Council, 2006), p. 35.

13. See www.americaspromise.org.

14. Damon, *The Path to Purpose,* p. 38.

15. Interview with Mary Barahona, September 18, 2009.

16. Example found at Chicago Public Schools, Service Learning, 2002, http://servicelearning.cps.k12.il.us/Successful.html.

17. Adapted from National Youth Leadership Council, "Improving Reading with Peer Tutoring," 2009, http://www.nylc.org/pages-resourcecenter-projectexamples-Improving_Reading_with_Peer_Tutoring?emoid=20:429 &null=1250031093234.

18. Example found at National Youth Leadership Council, "Quilt-Makers Project," 2009, http://www.nylc.org/pages-resourcecenter-project examples-Quilt_Makers_Project?emoid=20:412&si=1&null= 1250031186250.

19. Example provided by the Rural School and Community Trust. "Voices from the Fisheries," http://www.ruraledu.org/articles.php?id=2250, accessed December 9, 2009.

20. Example found at Campus Compact, "Spanish—Service-Learning," http://www.compact.org/syllabi/foreign-language/spanish-service-learning/3847, accessed November 25, 2009.

21. Extensive research links service-learning to a wide range of academic and other outcomes. For example, a large-scale Michigan study found service-learning to be positively correlated with test scores on the standardized test results for fifth-grade students; a Philadelphia study found similar results for sixth-graders. The National Research Council's summary of research on high school engagement found that active participation by students is important for learning, and identifies service-learning as one of the most effective strategies. Various studies confirm the linkage between high-quality service-learning and student engagement. Studies show that students who engaged in service-learning had higher attendance rates than those of control-group peers. Studies link attendance to key educational outcomes, including achievement and diploma attainment. An evaluation of service-learning programs in California found that middle and high school students who engaged in quality service-learning programs showed increases in personal and social responsibility and communication. Several studies have found that service-learning decreases disciplinary referrals and reduces behaviors that lead to pregnancy or arrest. See Corporation for National and Community Service, "The Impact of Service-Learning: A Review of Current Research," January 2007, http://www.learnandserve.gov/pdf/07_0224_issuebrief_servicelearning.pdf. Studies also show that high-quality opportunities for young people to contribute increase their sense of mattering and efficacy, moral and civic identity, and meaningful connections with adults and peers. See Benson and others, "Measuring Youth Contribution Indicators: A Conceptual Framework," in J. Kielsmeier, S. Root, B. Lyngstad, and C. Pernu (eds.), *Growing to Greatness, 2009: The State of Service-Learning* (St. Paul, MN: National Youth Leadership Council, 2009), p. 8.

22. K. Spring, R. Grimm Jr., and N. Dietz, *Community Service and Service Learning in America's Schools, 2008* (Saint Paul, MN: National Youth Leadership Council, 2009); J. Kielsmeier, M. Neal, N. Schultz, and T. Leeper, *Growing to Greatness, 2008: The State of Service-Learning* (St. Paul, MN: National Youth Leadership Council, 2008), p. 14.

23. K. Spring, N. Dietz, and R. Grimm Jr., *Youth Helping America: Leveling the Path to Participation: Volunteering and Civil Engagement Among Youth from Disadvantaged Circumstances* (Washington, DC: Corporation for National

and Community Service, March 2007); Kielsmeier, Root, Lyngstad, and Pernu, *Growing to Greatness, 2009,* p. 23.

24. National Indian Youth Leadership Project, "Walking in Beauty: A Program for Young Women," 2008, http://www.niylp.org/projects/walking-in-beauty.htm.

25. YouthBuild USA, "Stories of Transformation," http://www.youthbuild.org/site/c.htIRI3PIKoG/b.1281091/k.770D/Stories_of_Transformation/apps/nl/newsletter2.asp, accessed November 25, 2009.

26. YouthBuild USA, "Demographics and Outcomes," 2008, http://www.youthbuild.org/site/c.htIRI3PIKoG/b.1287531/k.6BF6/Demographics_and_Outcomes.htm.

27. Ibid.; A. Hahn, T. Leavitt, A. Horvitt, and J. Davis, *Life After Youthbuild: 900 Youthbuild Graduates Reflect on Their Lives, Dreams, and Experiences* (Somerville, MA: YouthBuild USA, 2004).

28. K. Dunham, J. Henderson-Frakes, H. Lewis-Charp, S. Soukamneuth, and A. Wiegand, comp. 2006, *Evaluation of the YouthBuild Youth Offender Grants* (Oakland, CA: Social Policy Research Associates, December 21, 2006); A. Leslie, *Youthful Offender Project: Year 1* (Somerville, MA: YouthBuild USA, August 2007); The Corps Network, "Civic Justice Corps," 2009, http://www.corpsnetwork.org/index.php?option=com_content&view=article&id=59&Itemid=77.

29. Corporation for National and Community Service, Office of Research and Policy, *Still Serving: Measuring the Eight-Year Impact of AmeriCorps on Alumni* (Washington, DC: CNCS, 2008), p. 38.

30. P. Shapiro (ed.), *A History of National Service in America* (College Park, MD: Center for Political Leadership and Participation, University of Maryland at College Park, 1994).

31. Ibid., p. 28.

32. Ibid.

33. James F. Justin Civilian Conservation Corps Museum, http://www.geocities.com/famjustin/ccchis.html, accessed November 25, 2009.

34. A. McDuffie, "75th Anniversary of New Deal's CCC," May 24, 2008, http://fredericksburg.com/News/FLS/2008/052008/05242008/381347/printer_friendly.

35. L. Anglin, "Biography of Leonard Anglin," http://www.justinmuseum.com/oralbio/anglinbio.html, accessed November 25, 2009.

36. J. Jastrzab, J. Blomquist, J. Masker, and L. Orr. *Youth Corps: Promising Strategies for Young People and Their Communities,* Studies in

Workforce Development and Income Security No. 1–97 (Cambridge, MA: Abt Associates Inc., 1997).

37. The Corps Network, "Service and Conservation Corps," 2009, http://www .corpsnetwork.org/index.php?option=com_content&view=article&id= 84&Itemid=64.

38. M. Boteach, J. Moses, and S. Sagawa, *National Service and Youth Unemployment: Strategies for Job Creation Amid Economic Recovery* (Washington, DC: Center for American Progress, November 16, 2009), p. 3; additional data provided by YouthBuild USA, email from Dorothy Stoneman to Shirley Sagawa, October 30, 2009.

39. YouthBuild U.S.A., "Hall of Achievement," http://www.youthbuild.org/site/ apps/nlnet/content2.aspx?c=htIRI3PIKoG&b=1497083&ct=2088097, accessed November 25, 2009.

40. Submitted by AnnMaura Connolly, City Year, ServiceNation database. Used with permission.

41. Bureau of Labor Statistics, http://stats.bls.gov/web/cpseed8.pdf, accessed November 25, 2009.

42. Corporation for National and Community Service, Office of Research and Policy Development, *AmeriCorps: Changing Lives, Changing America* (Washington, DC: CNCS, 2007), pp. 2, 5; The Conference Board, Partnership for 21st Century Skills, Corporate Voices for Working Families, and Society for Human Resource Development, *Are they Really Ready to Work?* 2006, p. 9, http://www.21stcenturyskills.org/documents/FINAL_REPORT_PDF09- 29-06.pdf.

43. D. Stauffer, *"Pay" from Volunteer Service Can Include Career Gains* (Cambridge, MA: Harvard Business Publishing, 1998).

44. Points of Light Foundation, *Using Employee Volunteering to Benefit HR Departments* (Washington, DC: POLF, 2006).

45. Markitects and Women's Way, *Power Skills: How Volunteerism Shapes Professional Success* (Wayne, PA: Markitects and Women's Way, 2006).

46. Deloitte, *2005 Volunteer Impact Survey*, 2008.

47. Corporation for National and Community Service, *Still Serving*.

48. T. Tierney, *The Nonprofit Sector's Leadership Deficit* (Boston: The Bridgespan Group, 2006); The Bridgespan Group, *Finding Leaders for Nonprofits* (Boston: The Bridgespan Group, 2009); Boteach, Moses, and Sagawa, *National Service and Youth Unemployment*, p. 4.

49. Information provided by Jyni Koschak, Volunteers of America, Minnesota, to the ServiceNation database. Used with permission.

50. J. Bridgeland, R. Putnam, and H. Wofford, *More to Give: Tapping the Talents of Today's Baby Boomer, Silent, and Greatest Generations* (Washington, DC: AARP, 2008), p. 9.

51. J. Barron and others, "Potential for Intensive Volunteering to Promote the Health of Older Adults in Fair Health," *Journal of Urban Health* 86(54), July 2009.

52. R. Grimm Jr., K. Spring, and N. Dietz, *The Health Benefits of Volunteering: A Review of Recent Research* (Washington, DC: Corporation for National and Community Service, 2007).

53. A. Herzog, M. Franks, H. Markus, and D. Holmberg, "Activities and Well-Being in Older Age: Effects of Self-Concept and Educational Attainment," *Psychology and Aging,* 13(2), 2008, pp. 179–185; E. Greenfield and N. Marks, "Formal Volunteering as a Protective Factor for Older Adults' Psychological Well-Being," *The Journals of Gerontology,* Series B, 59(5), 2004, S258–S264; R. Harlow and N. Cantor, "Still Participating After All These Years: A Study of Life Task Participation in Later Life," *Journal of Personality and Social Psychology,* 71(6), 1996, pp. 1235–1249, cited in R. Grimm Jr., K. Spring, and N. Dietz, *The Health Benefits of Volunteering.*

54. M. Freedman, *Encore: Finding Work That Matters in the Second Half of Life* (New York: Public Affairs, 2007), p. 23.

55. Ibid., p. 119.

56. National Council on Aging, "First-Ever Grants to Engage Adults 55+ to Increase Nonprofit Capacity," June 6, 2007, http://www.ncoa.org/content.cfm?sectionID=65&detail=1972.

57. M. Turk, *Blood, Sweat and Tears: An Oral History of the American Red Cross* (Robbinsville, NJ: E Street Press, 2006), pp. 105–114.

58. A. Luks and P. Payne, *The Healing Power of Doing Good* (Lincoln, NE: iUniverse.com, 2001), p. 13.

59. Ibid., p. 16.

60. Ibid., p. 17.

61. Ibid., p. 37.

62. J. Murray, S. Bellringer, and A. Easter, *Report of Evaluation of Capital Volunteering 4th Interim Report Outcomes at 12 Months* (London: Institute of Psychiatry, May 2008).

63. Information provided by Christopher Marvin, The Mission Continues, to the ServiceNation database. Used with permission.

Chapter 3: Strengthening Civic Engagement

1. "Playmaker of the Month: Cynthia Gentry," http://kaboom.org/help_save_play/playmaker_network/playmaker_month/cynthia_gentry, accessed December 15, 2009; Play Atlanta, http://playatlanta.ning.com/, accessed December 15, 2009; information provided by Darell Hammond to the ServiceNation database; additional interview with Darell Hammond, June 20, 2009.

2. Corporation for National and Community Service, Office of Research and Policy Development, *What Do We Know About Volunteering in America? Executive Summary of Recent Research* (Washington, DC: CNCS, 2007), p. 1.

3. S. Nunn, "Forward" [*sic*], in W. Marshall, *Citizenship and National Service: A Blueprint for Civic Enterprise* (Washington, DC: Democratic Leadership Council, 1988).

4. Marshall, *Citizenship and National Service.*

5. People for the American Way, *Democracy's Next Generation: A Study of Youth and Teachers* (Washington, DC: People for the American Way, 1989), pp. 13, 20.

6. B. Clinton, "National and Community Service Trust Act of 1993," South Lawn at the White House, Washington, DC, September 21, 1993.

7. J. McCain, "Putting the 'National' in National Service," *Washington Monthly,* October 2001, http://www.washingtonmonthly.com/features/2001/0110.mccain.html.

8. B. Obama, *A New Era of Service,* address at the University of Colorado, Colorado Springs, July 2, 2008; B. Obama, *Remarks by the President at the Signing of the Edward M. Kennedy Serve America Act,* The SEED School, Washington, DC, April 21, 2009.

9. American Jewish Committee, *Imagining America: Making National Service a National Priority* (New York: American Jewish Committee, 2007), p. 3.

10. R. Stengel, "A Time to Serve," *Time,* September 8, 2009, http://www.time.com.

11. R. Emanuel and B. Reed, *The Plan: Big Ideas for America* (New York: Public Affairs, 2006), pp. 61, 64.

12. Public Allies, "Our Results," 2007, http://www.publicallies.org/site/c.liKUL3PNLvF/b.2887847/k.AB6A/Our_Results.htm; Corporation for National and Community Service, Office of Research and Policy Development, *Still Serving: Measuring the Eight-Year Impact of AmeriCorps on Alumni* (Washington, DC: CNCS, 2008).

13. S. H. Billig and D. Jesse, *Evaluation of Partnerships in Character Education* (Denver: RMC Research Corporation, 2005).

14. A. Furco, "Is Service-Learning Really Better Than Community Service? A Study of High School Service Program Outcomes," in A. Furco and S. Billig, *Service-Learning: The Essence of the Pedagogy* (Greenwich, CT: Information Age Publishing, 2002), pp. 23–50; P. Scales, B. Byth, and J. Kielsmeier, "The Effects of Service-Learning on Middle School Students' Social Responsibility and Academic Success," *Journal of Early Adolescence*

20(3), August, pp. 331–358, cited in S. Billig, "Support for K–12 Service-Learning Practice: A Brief Review of the Research, *Educational Horizons,* Summer 2002, p. 184.

15. RMC Research Corporation, "Character Education and Service Learning (Expanded)," September 2006, available at Learn and Serve America's National Service-Learning Clearinghouse, http://www.servicelearning .org/instant_info/fact_sheets/k-12_facts/char_ed/expanded.php#, accessed November 25, 2009.

16. Corporation for National and Community Service, Office of Research and Policy Development, *Reaching Our Goals, An Overview of Research in Support of the Strategic Initiatives* (Washington, DC: CNCS, 2009), p. 14; Corporation for National and Community Service, *Still Serving.*

17. R. Stengel, "A Time to Serve."

18. R. Putnam, *Bowling Alone: The Collapse and Revival of American Community* (New York: Simon & Schuster, 2000).

19. R. Putnam, "*E Pluribus Unum*: Diversity and Community in the Twenty-First Century, The 2006 Johan Skytte Prize Lecture," *Scandinavian Political Studies,* 30(2), 2007, pp. 137–174.

20. L. Anderson, K. Laguarda, and L. Fabiano, *The City Year Alumni Studies* (Washington, DC: Policy Studies Associates, 2007).

21. Project Shine, "Our Impact," www.projectshine.org/about/impact, accessed November 25, 2009; SF State News, "Students Help Immigrants in Citizenship Quest," November 13, 2008, http://www.sfsu.edu/~news /2008/fall/25.html.

22. See, for example, M. Vadum, "Democrats Kill Provision in AmeriCorps Bill that Would Keep Funds from ACORN," *American Spectator,* March 30, 2009, http://spectator.org/blog/2009/03/30/democrats-kill-provision-in-am; see also B. Fritz, "Esprit D'AmeriCorps: How the Right Learned to Love Clinton's Pet Program," *American Prospect,* February 11, 2002, http://www.prospect.org/cs/articles?article=esprit_damericorps; Memorandum from Doug Hilton to Frank Trinity, March 2009.

23. R. Stengel, "A Time to Serve."

24. C. Gibson, *Citizens at the Center: A New Approach to Civic Engagement* (Washington, DC: The Case Foundation, 2006), p. 1.

25. S. Keeter, C. Zukin, M. Andolina, and K. Jenkins, *The Civic and Political Health of the Nation: A Generational Portrait* (College Park, MD: CIRCLE, 2002), p. 33; M. Lopez and others, *2006 Civic and Political Health of the Nation* (College Park, MD: CIRCLE, 2006).

26. Corporation for National and Community Service, *Still Serving,* p. 19.

27. Project for Public Spaces, "Chinatown Alleyway Tours," http://www.pps.org/tcb/chinatown_sf.htm, accessed November 25, 2009.

28. Innovations in Civic Participation, *Service to Civics* (Berkeley, CA: The Grantmaker Forum on Community and National Service, October 2003), pp. 6–7.

29. LISC Bay Area, "Youth Weigh In on the Central Subway," 2009, http://www.bayareanext.org/index.php?option=com_content&view=article&id=52:chinatown-youth-weigh-in-on-the-central-subway&catid=35:graphic-design&Itemid=75#.

30. J. Kahne and J. Westheimer, "Teaching Democracy: What Schools Need to Do," *Phi Delta Kappan,* 85(1), September 2003.

Chapter 4: Advancing Education

1. Site visit and interview with Myung Lee, May 11, 2009.

2. Child Trends DataBank, "Early School Readiness," http://www.childtrendsdatabank.org/indicators/7EarlySchoolReadiness.cfm, accessed November 25, 2009.

3. Head Start Bureau, *Head Start Volunteer Policies* (Washington, DC: U.S. Department of Health and Human Services, 1989).

4. C. Bafile, "Jumpstart Charges Kids Up for Learning!" *Education World,* 2001, http://www.education-world.com/a_curr/curr343.shtml#.

5. National Association for Child Care Resource and Referral Agencies, "Your Child Care Provider," Child Central Express, February 2007, http://highqualitychildcare.org/naccrra/notice-description.tcl?newsletter_id=5740324.

6. Child Care Services Association, *2006–2007 Annual Report* (Chapel Hill, NC: CCSA, 2008), p. 10.

7. K. Young, K. Davis, C. Schoen, and S. Parker, "Listening to Parents: A National Survey of Parents with Young Children," *Archives of Pediatric Adolescent Medicine,* 152, 1998, pp. 255–262. See also, "Why Is Reading Aloud to Young Children So Important?" http://www.reachoutandread.org/impact/importance.aspx, accessed December 8, 2009.

8. Reach Out and Read, "20 Million Kids' Books Distributed, 25% of U.S. Children in Poverty Getting Books, 50,000 Doctors Trained: Three Key Milestones for Reach Out and Read," *PR Newswire,* April 29, 2009; "History of Reach Out and Read, Milestones and Achievements in the History of Reach Out and Read," April 2009, http://www.reachoutandread.org/about/history.aspx, accessed December 9, 2009.

9. Colorado Child and Parent Foundation, "Linking HIPPY and National Service," www.coloradoparentandchildfoundation.org/hippydocs/ AmeriCorps-History%20and%20HIPPY.doc, accessed November 25, 2009; HIPPY USA, "The HIPPY Model," October 2009, http://www.hippyusa .org/site/view/135854_TheHIPPYModel.pml; HIPPY USA, *HIPPY Research Summary* (Little Rock: AR, HIPPY USA, March 2009).

10. Email from Jim Balfanz to Shirley Sagawa, November 2, 2009.

11. A. Ripley, "Rhee Tackles Classroom Challenge," *Time,* Nov. 26, 2008. Unpublished transcript, *City Year National Leadership Summit,* Washington, DC, June 9, 2009, p. 36.

12. Ibid., pp. 37–38.

13. Ibid., p. 39.

14. Ibid.

15. Alliance for Excellent Education, "Dropout Factories," http://www.all4ed .org/about_the_crisis/schools/dropout, accessed November 25, 2009.

16. K. Carey, *The Real Value of Teachers: If Good Teachers Matter, Why Don't We Like It?* (Washington, DC: Education Trust, 2004).

17. Interview with Wendy Kopp, June 10, 2009.

18. D. Gitomer, *Teaching Quality in a Changing Policy Landscape: Improvements in the Teacher Pool* (Princeton, NJ: Education Testing Service, 2007).

19. Z. Xu, J. Hannaway, and C. Taylor, *Making a Difference? The Effect of Teach For America on Student Performance in High School* (Washington, DC: Urban Institute and CALDER, 2009); P. Decker, D. Mayer, and S. Glazerman, *The Effects of Teach For America on Students: Findings from a National Study* (Princeton, NJ: Mathematica Policy Research, 2004); "*Teach For America* 2007 National Principal Survey," Policy Studies Associates, July 2007; Harvard Graduate School of Education, "Study Finds Teach For America Teachers Stay in the Classroom Past Initial Commitment," May 21, 2008, http://www.gse.harvard.edu/news_events/features/2008/05/21_project.php.

20. Teach For America, *Alumni Social Impact Report, 2009,* http://www .teachforamerica.org/mission/documents/2009_ASIR_Final.pdf, accessed December 10, 2009.

21. N. Morrow-Howell and others, *Evaluation of Experience Corps: Student Reading Outcomes* (St. Louis: Center for Social Development, Washington University, 2009); Experience Corps, "Hopkins Research Documents Positive Impact of Experience Corps," http://www.experiencecorps .org/publications/jhu_summary.cfm, accessed November 25, 2009.

22. Experience Corps, "Hopkins Research Documents."

23. Interview with Willem Vroegh by Tamara Chao, 2007; statistics provided by Playworks, email from Jill Vialet to Shirley Sagawa, September 30, 2009.

24. A. Henderson, *The Evidence Continues to Grow: Parent Involvement Improves Student Achievement. An Annotated Bibliography. National Committee for Citizens in Education Special Report* (Columbia, MD: National Committee for Citizens in Education, 1987).

25. San Francisco School Volunteers, "Interpretation Volunteers," http://www.sfedfund.org/programs/volunteers_individuals_ways_interpretation.php, accessed November 25, 2009.

26. EducationWorks, "Summary of Accomplishments," http://www.educationworks-online.org/Evaluation-Impact.htm, accessed November 25, 2009.

27. J. Vile, E. Arcaira, and E. Resner, *Progress Toward High School Graduation: Citizen Schools' Youth Outcomes in Boston* (Boston: Policy Studies Associates, July 2009).

28. M. Filardo, *Good Buildings, Better Schools: An Economic Stimulus Opportunity with Long-Term Benefits* (Washington, DC: Economic Policy Institute, 2008).

29. "Hands On Schools: Buffalo Academy of Science Charter School," online video, June 12, 2009, *YouTube,* http://www.youtube.com/watch?v=uFONiZu0LfA.

30. P. Kalkowski, "Peer and Cross-Age Tutoring," *School Improvement Research Series* (Portland, OR: NWREL, 1995).

31. Commission on the Future of Higher Education, *A Test of Leadership: Charting the Future of U.S. Higher Education* (Washington, DC: U.S. Department of Education, 2006), p. 9. See also S. Sagawa and J. B. Schramm, *High Schools as Launch Pads: How College-Going Culture Improves Graduation Rates in Low-Income High Schools* (Washington, DC: College Summit, 2008).

32. College Summit, "Our Outcomes," http://www.collegesummit.org/aboutus/results_and_metrics/our_outcomes, accessed November 25, 2009.

33. Information provided by J. B. Schramm, College Summit. Email from J. B. Schramm to Shirley Sagawa, October 17, 2009.

Chapter 5: Improving Health and Well-Being

1. B. Lefkowitz, *Community Health Centers: A Movement and the People Who Made It Happen* (New Brunswick, NJ: Rutgers University Press, 2007), pp. 29–49; D. Dutton, T. Preston, and N. Pfund, *Worse Than the Disease: The Pitfalls of Medical Progress* (Cambridge, U.K.: Cambridge University Press, 1992), pp. 370–371.

2. National Association of Community Health Centers, *The Community HealthCorps: Promoting Health Care for America's Underserved, Developing Tomorrow's Health Care Leaders* (Washington, DC: NACHC, 2005–2006).

3. *The Uninsured, A Primer: Key Facts About Americans Without Health Insurance* (Menlo Park, CA: Kaiser Family Foundation, 2009); National Association of Community Health Centers and The Robert Graham Center, *Access Denied: A Look at America's Medically Disenfranchised* (Washington, DC: National Association of Community Health Centers, 2007), p. 3.

4. J. Hadley, *Sicker and Poorer: The Consequences of Being Uninsured* (Washington, DC: Kaiser Commission on Medicaid and the Uninsured, 2003).

5. M. King, *Community Health Interventions: Prevention's Role in Reducing Racial and Ethnic Health Disparities* (Washington, DC: Center for American Progress, 2007), p. 4.

6. America's Promise Alliance, "All Kids Covered," 2009, http://www .americaspromise.org/Our-Work/Action-Strategies/All-Kids-Covered .aspx.

7. Corporation for National and Community Service, *VISTA: Overcoming Poverty, Building Capacity* (Washington, DC: CNCS, date), pp. 63–65; Rhode Island Free Clinic, "Reaching Out with Comprehensive Care to the Uninsured," http://www.rifreeclinic.org, accessed November 27, 2009.

8. K. King-Jackson, "Connecting Uninsured Children to Health Coverage Webinar Recording," America's Promise, June 11, 2009, http://www .americaspromise.org/News-and-Events/News-and-Features/APB-2009-23/Childrens-Healthcare-Webinar.aspx, accessed December 10, 2009; email from Kelli King-Jackson to Shirley Sagawa, November 24, 2009.

9. Share Our Strength, "Facts on Childhood Hunger," http://www.strength .org/childhood_hunger/hunger_facts, accessed November 27, 2009.

10. Share Our Strength, "Operation Frontline: Courses That Make a Difference," http://www.strength.org/operation_frontline/courses, accessed November 27, 2009; see also S. Swindle, S. Baker, and G. Auld, "Operation Frontline: Assessment of Longer-Term Curriculum Effectiveness, Evaluation Strategies, and Follow-Up Methods," *Journal of Nutrition Education and Behavior,* July 2007.

11. Mayo Clinic Staff, "Exercise: 7 Benefits of Regular Physical Activity," Mayo-Clinic.com, July 25, 2009, http://www.mayoclinic.com/health/exercise /HQ01676.

12. K. Ginsburg, "The Importance of Play in Promoting Healthy Child Development and Maintaining Strong Parent-Child Bonds," Clinical Report, American Academy of Pediatrics, 2007, http://www.aap.org/ pressroom/playFINAL.pdf, accessed December 10, 2009.

13. KaBOOM!, "Our Story," http://kaboom.org/about_kaboom/our_story, accessed November 27, 2009.

14. L. Landro, "Alone Together: Cancer Patients and Survivors Find Treatment—and Support—Online: It Can Make All the Difference," *The Oncologist* 4(1), 1999, pp. 59–63.

15. University of Wisconsin-Madison News, "Study: Online Health Support Groups Have Emotional Impact," March 26, 2006, http://www.news.wisc.edu/12344.

16. Give an Hour, *The Wounds of War Are Not Always Easy to See* (Bethesda, MD: Give an Hour, 2009).

17. Partners In Care video, http://www.partnersincare.org/Watch_the_Video.php, accessed November 27, 2009.

18. Partners In Care, "Time Banking Explained," http://www.partnersincare.org/Time_Banking_Explained.php, accessed November 27, 2009.

19. Partners In Care, "Building Community with Time Exchange," http://www.partnersincare.org/Home_Page.php, accessed November 27, 2009.

20. S. Dentzer, "Service Credit Banking," in S. Isaacs and J. Nickman (eds.), *To Improve Health and Health Care, Vol. 5: The Robert Wood Johnson Foundation Anthology* (San Francisco: Jossey-Bass, 2003), citing J. Feder, J. Howard, and W. Scanlon, "Helping Oneself by Helping Others: Evaluation of a Service Credit Banking Demonstration," *Journal of Aging and Social Policy,* 4(3-4), 1992, pp. 111–138.

21. Robert Wood Johnson Foundation, *Service Credit Banking Project Site Summaries* (Baltimore: University of Maryland, 1990).

22. Time Dollar Institute, *Angels and Health: Time Dollars and Health Care* (Washington, DC: Time Banks USA, 1999).

23. Metlife MMI and NAHB, *55+ Housing: Builders, Buyers, and Beyond* (Westport, CT: Metlife Mature Market Institute, 2009); Joint Center for Housing Studies, Harvard University, *Housing America's Seniors* (Cambridge, MA: Joint Center for Housing Studies, Harvard University, 2000); U.S. Department of Health and Human Services, "National Clearinghouse for Long-Term Care Information," October 22, 2008, http://www.longtermcare.gov/LTC/Main_Site/Understanding_Long_Term_Care/Basics/Basics.aspx.

24. Institute for Health and Aging, *Chronic Care in America: A 21st Century Challenge* (Princeton, NJ: Robert Wood Johnson Foundation, 1996).

25. Consumeraffairs.com, "Nursing Home Cost Hits $70,000 per Year," October 4, 2004, http://www.consumeraffairs.com/news04/nursing_home_costs.html#ixzz0TAZob6QJ.

26. Right at Home, "The Hidden Costs of Caregiving," August 2006, http://www.poststat.net/rightathome/pub.59/issue.367/#; National Alliance for

Caregiving and AARP, *Caregiving in the U.S.*, (Washington, DC: NAC and AARP, 2004).

27. Corporation for National and Community Service, *The Role and Value of Senior Companions in Their Communities* (Washington, DC: CNCS, 2001).

28. Corporation for National and Community Service, "Providing Telephone Reassurance for Senior Community Members," June 24, 2002, http://www.nationalserviceresources.org/node/17401.

29. Interview with Adraine LaRoza, May 27, 2009; Volunteer Manatee, "The Manateen Club," 2007, http://www.volunteermanatee.org/manateens.html.

Chapter 6: Helping People and Communities in Distress

1. Interview with Frankie Blackburn, September 9, 2009; "POV41: Region, Division and Type of Residence—Poverty Status for All People, Family Members and Unrelated Individuals by Family Structure: 2008," Current Population Survey, http://www.census.gov/hhes/www/cpstables/032009/pov/new41_100_01.htm , accessed December 10, 2009.

2. N. Peirce, "Outreach to Immigrants: A Suburb's Exiting New Way," *Washington Post*, citiwire.net, May 14, 2009.

3. F. Blackburn, "First Neighbors Exchange in Gaithersburg—March 26th at Mercy Seat Chapel," weblog entry, Neighbors Campaign, March 30, 2009.

4. "POV41."

5. E. Press, "The New Suburban Poverty," *The Nation*, April 13, 2007; S. Alfano, "Suburban Poverty Rising in U.S.," CBS News, Dec. 7, 2006; "POV41."

6. Information provided by LIFT. Email from Colleen Flynn to Shirley Sagawa, October 2, 2009. Used with permission.

7. Save the Children, *America's Forgotten Children: A Report to the Nation* (Westport, CT: Save the Children, 2002).

8. Letter from Joel Berg, New York City Coalition Against Hunger, to Nicola Goren, Corporation for National and Community Service, May 19, 2009.

9. Interview with Sandy Dang, April 13, 2009.

10. M. McHugh, J. Gelatt, and M. Fix, *Adult English Language Instruction in the United States: Determining Need and Investing Wisely* (Washington, DC: Migration Policy Institute, 2007).

11. Corporation for National and Community Service, *VISTA: Overcoming Poverty, Building Capacity* (Washington, DC: CNCS), pp. 31–32.

12. National Low Income Housing Coalition, *America's Neighbors: The Affordable Housing Crisis and the People It Affects* (Washington, DC: NLIHC, 2004), www.nlihc.org.

13. National Law Center on Homelessness and Poverty, "Homelessness & Poverty in America: Overview," 2008, http://www.nlchp.org/hapia.cfm.

14. Information provided by Habitat for Humanity, n.d. Used with permission.

15. Habitat for Humanity, www.habitat.org, accessed November 27, 2009.

16. Story Copyright ©Alliance for Community Trees. Provided by Jared Liu, Action for Community Trees, to the ServiceNation database. Used with permission.

17. The William J. Clinton Foundation, "Entrepreneurship," http://www .clintonfoundation.org/what-we-do/clinton-economic-opportunity-initiative/our-approach/entrepreneurship#, accessed November 27, 2009.

18. The William J. Clinton Foundation, "Our Approach," http://www .clintonfoundation.org/what-we-do/clinton-economic-opportunity-initiative/our-approach, accessed November 27, 2009.

19. Prison Entrepreneurship Program, "What We Do," http://www .prisonentrepreneurship.org/what/problem.aspx, accessed November 27, 2009.

20. Prison Entrepreneurship Program, "Who We Are," http://www .prisonentrepreneurship.org/who/story.aspx, accessed November 27, 2009; Prison Entrepreneurship Program, "Our Impact," http://www .prisonentrepreneurship.org/what/impact.aspx, accessed November 27, 2009.

21. Local Initiatives Support Corporation, *Fifteen Years of Building the Next Generation of Community Leaders* (New York: LISC, 2008).

22. L. Kirchoff, "Rebuilding After Katrina to Take Monumental Effort," *USA Today*, October 5, 2005; Cholene Espinoza, *Through the Eye of the Storm*, "Hurricane Katrina Facts and Hurricane Katrina Information," 2006, http://www.throughtheeyeofthestorm.com/KatrinaFacts.htm; S. Debus and S. Irazola, *Delivering Legal Aid After Katrina: The Equal Justice Works Ameri-Corps Legal Fellowship and Summer Corps Programs* (Washington, DC: Urban Institute, 2009), p. 1.

23. Corporation for National and Community Service, *National Service Responds: The Power of Help and Hope After Katrina* (Washington, DC: CNCS, 2006), p. 7; HurricaneKatrinaRelief.com, "Hurricane Katrina Relief," August 29, 2009, http://hurricanekatrinarelief.com.

24. M. Turk, *Blood, Sweat and Tears: An Oral History of the American Red Cross* (Robbinsville, NJ: E Street Press, 2006), p. 160.

25. Corporation for National and Community Service, *National Service Responds*, p. 7.

26. Interview with Kellie Bentz, May 19, 2009.

27. FEMA, "Declared Disasters by Year or State, November 24, 2009, http://www.fema.gov/news/disaster_totals_annual.fema.

28. Turk, *Blood, Sweat and Tears,* p. 91.

29. Ibid., p. 160.

30. Ibid., p. 161.

31. Ibid., p. 165.

32. Ibid., p. 168.

33. Corporation for National and Community Service, *National Service Responds,* p. 22.

34. Ibid., p. 15.

35. Information provided by Equal Justice Works. Email from Cole McMahon to Shirley Sagawa, October 2, 2009.

36. Ibid.

37. Debus and Irazola, *Delivering Legal Aid After Katrina.*

38. S. Litvin, "Crystal Utley," *Jackson Free Press,* Aug. 22, 2007; Corporation for National and Community Service, *2007 Spirit of Service Awards* (Washington, DC: CNSC, September 16, 2007), p. 7.

39. N. Wallace, "Legal Wrangling Nonprofit Law Center Is Helping Displaced Gulf Coast Residents Navigate the Recovery Maze," *Chronicle on Philanthropy,* Aug. 23, 2007.

40. Interview with Wendy Spencer, May 20, 2009.

41. Interview with John Bridgeland, May 19, 2009.

42. Port Richmond Community Emergency Response Team, "History of CERT," http://www.sicert.org/History%20of%20C.E.R.T.htm, accessed November 27, 2009.

43. Interview with John Bridgeland, May 19, 2009.

44. Interview with Wendy Spencer, May 20, 2009.

45. Ibid.

46. Interview with Adraine LaRoza, May 27, 2009.

47. Interview with Wendy Spencer, May 20, 2009.

Chapter 7: Protecting the Environment

1. Interview with Sara Levinson, May 11, 2009; RelightUS, "Change a Light Bulb, Change the World," www.relightus.com, accessed November 27, 2009; E. White, "Relight and Save," Scholastic, April 9, 2009, http://www2 .scholastic.com/browse/article.jsp?id=3751698. The RelightUS estimates are based on three hours per day per bulb usage in the United States.

2. ClimateCrisis, "What Is Global Warming?" http://www.climatecrisis.net/ climate-change.php, accessed November 27, 2009.

3. SmartBrief, "JWT Survey Reveals Four of Five U.S. Teens Share Concern for the Environment," PR Newswire, March 19, 2007, http://www.smartbrief .com/news/iab/industryPR-detail.jsp?id=58C823A3-E2A0-4F1B-AC9E-5CFA602C8A83, accessed December 11, 2009.

4. E-mail from Margarita Dangel to Shirley Sagawa, August 4, 2009; Earth Force, *Earth Force 2007–08 Program Evaluation* (Denver: Earth Force, n.d.).

5. Create The Good AARP, "Operation Energy Save," http://www .createthegood.org/operation-energy-save, accessed November 27, 2009.

6. J. Roberts, "Douglass High Students 'Green the Block'," *Memphis Commercial Appeal*, September 12, 2009.

7. GRID Alternatives, *Empowering Communities, One Rooftop at a Time* (Oakland, CA: GRID Alternatives, n.d.), http://www.gridalternatives.org/files/ GRID_Alternatives.pdf, accessed December 11, 2009.

8. E. Ritch, "Solar Industry's Rapid Growth Leaves Shortage in Work Force," *Silicon Valley/San Jose Business Journal*, May 16, 2008.

9. "Casa Verde Buildings," http://www.americanyouthworks.org/casa %20verde.htm, accessed December 11, 2009; "Spotlight on Casa Verde Builders," *YouthBuild Bulletin*, Fall 2005, pp. 13–14.

10. Wikipedia, "Manzanita," http://en.wikipedia.org/wiki/Manzanita, accessed November 27, 2009.

11. Wild Equity Institute, "About the GGNP Endangered Species Big Year," 2009, http://wildequity.org/sections/2.

12. K. Sullivan, "Going Native at the Presidio: Volunteers Log Thousands of Hours Collecting and Propagating Plants," *San Francisco Chronicle*, Aug. 28, 2002, http://www.sfgate.com/cgi-bin/article.cgi?f=/chronicle/ archive/2002/08/28/BA170864.DTL. Email from Joshua Steinberger to Shirley Sagawa, October 26, 2009.

13. U.S. Fish & Wildlife Service, "Why Save Endangered Species?" 2005, http://www.fws.gov/endangered/pdfs/Why_Save_End_Species_July_ 2005.pdf.

14. Grinning Planet, "Water Pollution Facts," July 26, 2005, http://www .grinningplanet.com/2005/07-26/water-pollution-facts-article.htm.

15. C. Freudenrich, "How Landfills Work," http://www.howstuffworks.com/ landfill.htm, accessed November 27, 2009.

16. Zero Waste America, "Landfills: Hazardous to the Environment," http: //www.zerowasteamerica.org/Landfills.htm, accessed November 27, 2009; S. Evans, "Landfill Problems and Global Warming Effects," Articlesbase, December 5, 2008, http://www.articlesbase.com/technology-articles/ landfill-problems-and-global-warming-effects-672693.html#.

17. Information found at www.growingnative.org, accessed December 11, 2009.
18. Information found at www.freecycle.org, accessed December 11, 2009.
19. Wikipedia, "Manzanita," http://en.wikipedia.org/wiki/Manzanita.
20. National Resources Defense Council, May 8, 2002, "Cleaning up the Anacostia River," http://www.nrdc.org/water/pollution/fanacost.asp.
21. Ibid.
22. Earth Conservation Corps, "About Us," http://www.ecc1.org/ht/d/ OrganizationDetails/i/19703/aboutus/Y/pid/19774, accessed November 27, 2009.

Chapter 8: Inspiring and Sustaining Innovative Solutions

1. Interview with Geoffrey Canada, May 11, 2009.
2. Urban Institute, National Center for Charitable Statistics, email from Tom Pollak to Shirley Sagawa, September 24, 2009.
3. W. Foster and G. Fine, "How Nonprofits Get Really Big," *Stanford Social Innovation Review,* Spring 2007.
4. Interview with Kirsten Lodal, October 1, 2009.
5. Interview with Kiff Gallagher, October 1, 2009.
6. Information provided by Admission Possible, email from Tracy Kirtley to Shirley Sagawa, October 7, 2009; *Admission Possible Evaluation Results* (St. Paul, MN: Wilder Research, 2006).
7. Interview with Virginia Emmons, February 24, 2009.
8. Teach For America, *Alumni Social Impact Report, 2008,* http://www .givewell.net/files/Round2Apps/Cause4/Teach%20For%20America/B/ Alumni%20survey.pdf, accessed December 11, 2009; http://www.usnews .com/articles/education/high-schools/2008/12/04/best-high-schools-gold-medal-list.html, accessed Dec. 8, 2009.

Chapter 9: What You Can Do

1. Interview with Jenny Brody, October 1, 2009.
2. Urban Institute, National Center for Charitable Statistics, email from Tom Pollak to Shirley Sagawa, September 24, 2009.
3. A. Blackwood, K. Wing, and T. Pollak, *The Nonprofit Sector in Brief* (Washington, DC: Urban Institute, 2008), p. 2.
4. S. Sagawa and D. Jospin, *The Charismatic Organization: Eight Ways to Grow a Nonprofit that Builds Buzz, Delights Donors, and Energizes Employees* (San Francisco: Jossey-Bass, 2008).

5. L. Crutchfield and H. McLeod, *Forces for Good: The Six Practices of High-Impact Nonprofits* (San Francisco: Jossey Bass, 2007).

6. S. Sagawa and E. Segal, *Common Interest, Common Good: Creating Value Through Business and Social Sector Partnerships* (Cambridge, MA: Harvard Business School Press, 1999).

7. Corporation for National and Community Service, *VISTA: Overcoming Poverty, Building Capacity* (Washington, DC: CNCS, 2009), p. 76.

8. Interview with Lisa Spinali, October 23, 2009.

9. J. Yuva, "Corporations Should Know 'Y,'" *Inside Supply Management*, July 2007, pp. 20–23.

10. Deloitte Pro Bono Action Tank, "Deloitte and College Summit," http://www.probonoactiontank.org/case-studies/deloitte-and-college-summit, accessed November 27, 2009.

11. Sagawa and Segal, *Common Interest, Common Good.*

12. Ibid.

13. Email from Ernesto Anguilla to Shirley Sagawa, December 11, 2009.

14. Corporation for National and Community Service, *Pathways to Service: Learning from the Potential Volunteer's Perspective* (research brief) (Washington, DC: CNCS, 2009), p. 3.

15. *Reimagining Service: Converting Good Intentions into Greater Impact*, http://www.reimaginingservice.org/Shared/FullReport.pdf, p. 4, accessed December 12, 2009.

16. Tipping Point Community, *Tipping Point: The Basics*, http://www.tippoint.org/storage/tippingpoint/documents/2009%20tipping%20point%20press%20kit.pdf, accessed December 11, 2009.

17. M. Smith, "Closing the Digital Divide: West Coast to West Bank," The Case Foundation, Dec. 22, 2008, http://www.casefoundation.org/blog/closing-digital-divide-west-coast-west-bank.

18. A. Layne, "Another Brick in the Bridge," *Fast Company*, December 19, 2007.

19. M. Bloomberg, *NYC Service: A Blueprint to Increase Civic Engagement* (New York: New York City Government, 2009).

20. D. Bulwa, "New State Cabinet Post Devoted to Volunteers," *San Francisco Chronicle*, February 27, 2008.

21. Interview with Karen Baker, October 10, 2009.

22. Serve Washington, "Washington State Service Summit," http://www.ofm.wa.gov/servewa/about/initiatives.asp, accessed November 27, 2009.

23. U.S. Department of Education, "Raising Student Achievement," citing National Assessment of Educational Progress and other data, http://www.ed.gov/inits/record/1chap.html, accessed November 27, 2009.

24. Citizen Corps, "Citizen Corps Councils," http://www.citizencorps.gov/councils, accessed November 29, 2009.

25. The President's Advisory Committee on The Points of Light Initiative Foundation, *Report to the President*, December 1989, p. 31.

26. *Remarks by the President and Vice President at the AmeriCorps Swearing In*, September 12, 1994, http://www.ibiblio.org/pub/archives/whitehouse-papers/1994/Sep/1994-09-12-President-and-VP-at-AmeriCorps-Swearing-In.

Index

THE CHARISMATIC ORGANIZATION

8 Ways to Grow a Nonprofit That Builds Buzz, Delights Donors, and Energizes Employees

Shirley Sagawa | Deborah Jospin
Foreword by Johnathan M. Tish

ISBN: 978-0-470-19546-8 | US $34.95 | CAN $37.95

"...an authoritative blueprint for using social capital to transform good intentions into concrete results." —**Former President BILL CLINTON**

Certain patterns are evident among successful nonprofits. In the same way charismatic individuals attract followers, dynamic organizations draw dedicated donors and committed champions. These groups don't depend on charismatic leaders—rather, they strengthen their core and build strong networks of support within and around themselves. In *The Charismatic Organization*, renowned experts Shirley Sagawa and Deborah Jospin show nonprofits of all types how to restructure their organizations, internally and externally, to become more charismatic, and more effective.

The authors offer a framework that allows organizations to go beyond quick fixes and fundraising strategies to a broader paradigm that encompasses community and organization building. What if every person involved with an organization was fully engaged and shared a common goal? What if the efforts of a relatively small ring of staff and board members were amplified by everyone touched by the organization, including current and former volunteers, staff, board members, clients, constituents, funders and supporters? That, the authors show, is the way a charismatic organization operates. The book provides numerous examples of how successful organizations have made this shift, as well as action steps that all organizations can take to perform better. Too many nonprofits today are unable to operate at their full potential because they are stuck in ineffective "business as usual" paradigms. *The Charismatic Organization* offers a guide to reframing nonprofit work so that organizations can expand their resource base and sphere of influence to further their missions and achieve greater impact.

JB JOSSEY-BASS™
An Imprint of WILEY
Now you know.